A History of Early
Christian Literature

THE UNIVERSITY OF CHICAGO PRESS
CHICAGO, ILLINOIS

*

THE BAKER & TAYLOR COMPANY
NEW YORK

THE CAMBRIDGE UNIVERSITY PRESS
LONDON

A History of Early Christian Literature

By

EDGAR J. GOODSPEED

THE UNIVERSITY OF CHICAGO PRESS
CHICAGO · ILLINOIS

TO
PRESIDENT ROBERT GORDON SPROUL
AND MY COLLEAGUES IN THE UNIVERSITY
OF CALIFORNIA AT LOS ANGELES

PREFACE

TO MANY the New Testament appears an island of religious literature in an ancient sea. That it is the beginning of a new continent of literature escapes them. Yet the New Testament was the source of a whole range of literary movements that in a few generations gave Christianity a literature that in sheer bulk and vigor dominated the ancient scene.

The New Testament was really the bursting-forth of a great spring of religious expression that flowed on copiously far and wide for five hundred years. This literature sprang not only out of Christian life and experience but also directly out of the New Testament. Its first literary models and patterns were found in the sermons, letters, revelations, gospels, and acts of the New Testament. There was something about the Christian experience that drove men to record it in books, to express it, defend it, and explain it. This is an aspect of early Christianity too often forgotten.

Much of this literature has perished, although the discoveries and studies of the last sixty years have recovered some long-lost pieces of striking interest. But not a few of these lost writings can be pictured and in part recovered from mentions of them and quotations from them in later writers, particularly from Eusebius.

That remarkable young man came to Caesarea in Palestine about A.D. 280 to study with Pamphilus in the library the latter had assembled there about the library of Origen. Eusebius not only catalogued these books, he read them; and to good purpose, for when in A.D. 326 he published his *Church History*, it covered much of the history of Christian literature as well as of Christian life. That is why he is so constantly referred to in these pages. Eusebius was so devoted to Pamphilus, his friend and teacher, that he adopted him as his father and ever after called himself the son of Pamphilus. It was in his *Life of Pamphilus*, now lost, that he included the catalogue of his library. Ah, Eusebius! Immortal cataloguer, who read and summarized the books he catalogued!

Half a century or more later, Jerome flourished. He wrote in Latin, and he still influences the religious and learned worlds through his version of the Bible, the Latin Vulgate. He wrote a short dictionary of Christian biography which he called "On Illustrious Men" (*De viris illustribus*). He sometimes leans heavily on Eusebius for his information, but his book has some independent value, too, and will be frequently referred to in this and every book on early Christian literature.

And then there is Photius, most extraordinary of them all; that Byzantine officer who, while master of the horse, suddenly emerged as the logical man for patriarch of Constantinople. He was not even in holy orders and had to go through a series of rapid clerical ordinations and promotions to achieve in a single week the transformation from soldier to prelate. This was a thing Roman ecclesiasticism could not tolerate, and it gave lasting offense to the Church of Rome.

And yet what we know as the *Library* of Photius, his *Bibliotheca*, is one of our chief helps in the recovery of early Christian literature. For it seems that, when he and his brother Tarasius were stationed at different places in the empire, Photius sent Tarasius summaries of a whole library of ancient works as he read them. They formed, in fact, a kind of medieval book club. And these book reviews by Photius, made, it would seem, for his faraway brother's enlightenment, still play a notable part in the study of these same books, too many of which have disappeared altogether since Photius wrote them up, about A.D. 890.

With these and other lesser aids from the fourth century onward, we can do much to fill the gaps in our early Christian library. And certainly the development of Christian thought and life can never be understood from the New Testament alone. Early Christian literature is an indispensable aid for its understanding. The rise of the rites, creeds, doctrines, clergy, and liturgy is reflected here, in that heroic age when Christianity moved through persecution and conflict to become the religion of the empire.

The field of study assigned to me during almost forty years of service at Chicago was Biblical and Patristic Greek, and most of the positions taken in these pages were worked out with groups of graduate students of early Christian literature there, in the course of those years. But new discoveries in recent years have surprisingly supplemented our patristic resources and encouraged us to anticipate still greater reinforcements in the years to come. It is with this in mind that I have added a chapter on the works of early Christian literature that are still conspicuously missing and to be looked for.

I am once more indebted to my brother, Charles T. B. Goodspeed, of the profession of Tertullian and Minucius Felix, who has generously assisted me with the proofs of this book.

This book has been written primarily for continuous reading; but to facilitate casual consultation also, dates have been purposely repeated with each mention of the names of ancient writers with whom the casual reader can hardly be expected to be familiar.

EDGAR J. GOODSPEED

BEL-AIR, LOS ANGELES
October 23, 1941

TABLE OF CONTENTS

CHAPTER I

EARLY CHRISTIAN LITERATURE

Christianity began as a spiritual movement. Its founder wrote nothing. He sought to change men's

Primitive Christianity Not Literary

hearts. He struck at the sources of attitude and action. His early followers continued this course. They were further committed to it by their expectation of his early return in messianic triumph to judge the world. They had no thought of producing a literature; indeed, the Jewish world in which they lived was altogether averse to literary composition, being absorbed, in the first half of the first century, in the contemplation of its Hebrew heritage, which it held sacred and almost worshiped.

Palestinian aversion to original written composition in Hebrew in the first half of the first century is glaringly revealed by two facts. First, the Jews were making a Hebrew commentary on the Jewish Law, but they would not permit this to be written; to write it would seem to put it on a level with That Which Was Written—the Scripture itself. So it was memorized and recited. It is repeatedly referred to in the Sermon on the Mount, where this interpretation of the Law is contrasted with Jesus' teaching. More than a century was to elapse before this Mishnah, as it was called, was committed to writing.

And, second, the Jews in that half-century were engaged in translating their sacred scriptures from Hebrew into Aramaic, the vernacular language which
everybody used and understood. But this, too, must
not be written down; it must be committed to memory,
and when about A.D. 50 Gamaliel I came across a
written copy of the Aramaic translation of Job, he
promptly destroyed it, for to write down such versions
seemed to put them on a level with that which was
written—the Hebrew scripture itself. And, here
again, it was years before these translations—the
Targum—were committed to writing.

Everything, in short, was at first unfavorable to
the production of a Christian literature: the Jewish
environment of the first believers and the basic attitudes of the Christians themselves—their emphasis
upon the inner life, the spirit, not the letter; and their
messianic expectation.

It is improbable that primitive Palestinian Christianity produced any written records of Jesus' life or
The Oral   teaching of even the most meager propor-
Gospel   tions. But, true to their Jewish habits,
              they do seem to have produced an oral
gospel, comprising an account, in their vernacular
Aramaic, of his doings and sayings. It would have
been altogether natural for them to do this; the Jews
were handing down by a similar oral tradition, but in
Hebrew, the sayings of their great rabbis, and these
now form part of the Mishnah—the *Pirke Aboth*, or
"Chapters of the Fathers." The evangelists often
speak of Jesus as a rabbi, and it would be natural to

preserve the memory of his life and teaching in this way.

Such an oral gospel was evidently known to Paul, who quotes it as something handed down to him, or, as we say, tradition (I Cor. 11:23; 15:3). Luke uses it once at least in the Acts: "Remembering the words of the Lord Jesus" (Acts 20:35). His contemporary, Clement of Rome, in his *Letter to the Corinthians*, seems clearly to be quoting it: "Remember the words of the Lord Jesus" (13:1; 46:7). Polycarp of Smyrna, twenty years later, in his *Letter to the Philippians*, quotes Jesus with the words, "Remembering what the Lord said" (2:3). Not only does the manner of quotation in all these instances suggest memorized material but the items quoted cannot be found in these forms in any written gospel. It is reasonable to suppose that they were derived from the traditional oral gospel.

But have we any actual mention of such a work—if anything so nebulous can be called a "work"—on the part of any early Christian writer? Yes, what Papias (*ca*. A.D. 140) says of Matthew composing the "Sayings" in the Aramaic language, and each one translating them as best he could, sounds like an attempt to describe just such a work. If early Christians learned it by heart, in Aramaic, and then carried the Christian message into the Greek world, they would naturally have to translate this oral gospel into Greek for the use of their converts, each one doing it as well as he could. This process of oral transmission is probably referred to in Luke's opening sentence, "Just as the original eye-witnesses who became teachers of the message have handed it down to us" (1:2).

While this elusive primitive gospel must have had a great influence on Christian preaching, and through it indirectly upon the gospels that were later written, we cannot recover it, or even describe it, in any detail. It contained some characteristic pieces of Jesus' teaching, with accounts of the Last Supper, the Crucifixion, and the Resurrection experiences. We might expect relics of it to survive in Luke or in Matthew; but, if so, they cannot be identified.

It is true, the written gospels, when they appeared, sprang up under its shadow, and not so much to reproduce it as to supplement it. The earliest written gospels seem to have assumed its existence. And from the point of view of the story of Christian literature, this lost oral gospel is chiefly significant as conclusive evidence that the primitive Christians had no thought at all of creating a literature. Their whole concern was for the inner life of the spirit, through which they came into communion with God. A full generation was to pass before Christians thought of writing gospels, and then they were to arise in Greek, not Aramaic, and in circles far removed from Jewish Palestine.

With the letters of Paul and the earliest gospels a new and extraordinary force began to find written *Letters and* expression—a force destined powerfully *Gospels* to affect the spiritual life of mankind. From small and obscure beginnings—mere personal letters long left unpublished—this literary phase of Christianity gradually gathered strength, until it became a great tide not only potent in itself but also influencing other literatures not definitely Christian.

Its beginnings were in the Greek world, and for a century Greek was its sole vehicle; then it spread to Latin and Syriac and, in the third century, to Coptic, though at first Syriac and Coptic attempted no more than translations of works originally written in Greek. It was in Greek and then in Latin that it was at first creative.

This voluminous literature breaks conveniently for us at the Council of Nicaea in 325, for the actions there taken so colored the literature that fol-

Organiza-tion of the Literature

lowed that it can hardly be mistaken; every page of it bears their stamp. An even more practical terminus is afforded by the *Church History* of Eusebius, published in A.D. 326, for that book is in no small degree a history of early Christian literature as well as of the march of events, and Eusebius gives us information on not a few books which he had examined but are now lost. It is safe to say that no book is more in the hands of the student of early Christian literature than the *Church History* of Eusebius, long available in English in the admirably translated and annotated edition of President A. C. McGiffert, Sr.,[1] and more recently in the translations of Lawlor and Oulton (1927–28) and of Lake and Oulton (1926–32).[2]

[1] Arthur C. McGiffert, *Eusebius* ("Select Library of Nicene and Post-Nicene Fathers of the Christian Church: Second Series," Vol. I [New York, 1890]).

[2] H. J. Lawlor and J. E. L. Oulton, *Eusebius: The Ecclesiastical History and the Martyrs of Palestine* (2 vols.; London, 1927–28); Kirsopp Lake and J. E. L. Oulton, *Eusebius: The Ecclesiastical History, with an English Translation* ("Loeb Library" [2 vols.; London and New York, 1926, 1932]).

The literature of these first three Christian centuries breaks again conveniently with Irenaeus, who between A.D. 181 and 189 wrote his principal work, the *Refutation of Gnosticism*. He begins a new period in Christian literature because with him the new standard type of Christianity of the Catholic church begins to appear, in contradistinction from the sects.

What has come down to us from Christian writers before Irenaeus can be thought of as grouped in four volumes of moderate size: the New Testament, the Apostolic Fathers, the pre-Catholic apologists, and the uncanonical gospels, acts, and apocalypses, though such a collection as this last for just this period has never been actually produced in print.

But these four groups of books are not to be thought of as separate or successive. The Apostolic Fathers overlap the books of the New Testament in date, and some of the apologies are earlier than the latest books of the New Testament. Uncanonical gospels, acts, and apocalypses are scattered over the years from A.D. 100 on, so that some of them are as old as the later books of the New Testament. Moreover, these books are sometimes closely related in occasion and date with New Testament books; *I Clement* is a sidepiece to I Peter, emanating from the same church at the same time and under the same impulse. The Gospel of John is in part, at least, a reaction against the Docetic heresy, like the *Letters of Ignatius*. The letters to Timothy and to Titus contradict some of Marcion's positions and oppose asceticism and the allowing of women to teach, the very things the *Acts of Paul* advocated, probably in A.D. 160–70.

To a considerable extent this earliest Christian literature before Irenaeus reproduced literary types already developed and standardized in books that we find in the New Testament—letters, apocalypses, gospels, and acts. These were most of them anonymous or pseudonymous and formed the somewhat popular background against which arose the more conscious products of Christian authors who wrote under their own names.

The order in which these writings can best be arranged and approached presents a difficult problem,
Order of Treatment which has been variously dealt with, not to say solved. The earlier literature can be grouped according to type as letters, revelations, gospels, and acts, with the individual works arranged chronologically within the several groups. But when the more conscious literary movement begins, with the apologists and the writers against the sects, the scene is constantly changing from West to East and back again, and soon in the West we have Latin writers at work simultaneously with Greek and presently taking over the Western literary field from them. The arrangement by types of literature—apologies, antiheretical works, commentaries, etc.—is helpful, but those diligent writers who worked in three or four such types would under such a treatment have to be taken up over and over again. So it seems preferable to present the work of each of these many-sided individuals as a unit in relation to his

times and problems, which is admittedly the best way
to describe the writings of men like Irenaeus, Clement,
Tertullian, Hippolytus, and Origen.

The literary disposition that began to pervade
Greek Christianity in the earlier years of the second
Literary Expansion century swelled to a flood in the last third
of the century and reached proportions
that amaze the modern reader. The volume, variety, and vigor of this literature must be
realized if we are to understand what manner of faith
it was that was beginning to turn the Greco-Roman
world upside down, for not the least of the elements
of its strength was the intellectual attack it was making upon paganism.

We have been too much inclined to pass by all this
literature and go directly to the New Testament, as
though it existed apart from the contemporary and
later Christian literature. And it is true that it was
in the books of the New Testament and in the earliest
collections of them—of the letters of Paul and of the
Four Gospels—that the letter and gospel types were
first set powerfully before the early church, while the
Revelation and the Acts offered patterns for the apocalypses and acts that were to come. But the development of Christian thought did not stop with the writing of the New Testament, and though none of these
later writers achieved the insight of Paul, the first of
its authors, they have something of value to con-
tribute to our understanding of historical Christianity, the development of Christian doctrine, and the
extraordinary movement, so largely literary, that in a

century and a half after its formation made the New
Testament the religious authority of that ancient
world.

It was the conviction of the early church that the
acceptance of the attitude of faith released new powers
in the human spirit, and never was this truer than in
these first centuries when in the defense and advocacy
of Christianity men like Irenaeus, Tertullian, and
Origen stood forth to fight the literary battle for the
new faith. It was an age of writers, publishers,
books, and readers, to a degree that may well surprise
the modern reader and give him a new idea of the intelligence and reading interest of Christian circles in
the second and third centuries.

Many Christian books not included in the New
Testament are really older than some of those that
found a place in it, and they throw light upon the
situations that called these latter forth. In origin
these books are closely interwoven. But the story of
the New Testament books has been often told and
must not be repeated here. The reader is referred instead to the leading introductions to the New Testament and to my *An Introduction to the New Testament*,
which points out the remarkable way in which particular New Testament books tie in with other Christian writings. In the present study it will be enough
to mention these genetic relations, without undertaking to repeat what has already been said in print about
New Testament origins.

CHAPTER II

LETTERS

The earliest form of Christian writing was naturally the letter—the personal communication from man to *Paul's* man or man to group of men, such as *Letters* first-century Greeks and Romans, and doubtless Jews as well, constantly wrote. In the hands of Paul this simplest form of composition had developed into a powerful instrument of religious instruction, and the collection and publication of his letters soon after A.D. 90 had standardized it as a Christian literary type. This is the background of all the other early Christian letters; particularly of what we know as the *Letter of Clement*.

Toward the end of the first century, about A.D. 95, something like a revolt broke out among the Christians at Corinth against the officers of the *Clement of* church, the presbyters or elders, as they *Rome* were called. This disturbance became so notorious that news of it reached Rome and distressed the church there. The Roman church accordingly sent a long letter to the Corinthians, urging them to harmonize their differences and to show their church officers the respect due them. The letter does not name its writer. It is written simply in the name of "the church of God that sojourns in Rome to the church of God that sojourns in Corinth," but it was very early

10

recognized as the work of Clement, the head of the Roman church from A.D. 88 to 97. Ancient writers, from Dionysius of Corinth (*ca.* A.D. 170) down, agree in ascribing the letter to Clement; Eusebius himself does so in his *Church History* (iii. 16; iv. 23. 11). Dionysius wrote to Soter, bishop of Rome between 166 and 174, that it was the custom of the Corinthian church to read Clement's letter from time to time in its meetings. So religiously useful did the letter prove that it passed into some early New Testaments, like the Codex Alexandrinus, of the fifth century, and into a Syriac manuscript of the New Testament in the Harclean version, written in the twelfth century, with the *Letter of Clement*[1] immediately following the general letters, to which it was evidently believed to belong.

To the modern student the position of presbyter or elder first comes into prominence in the Acts, written about A.D. 90 or soon after. The Corinthians had from the beginning made much of spiritual endowments (I Cor., chaps. 12–14), and it is easy to see how the new regard for church officers might have had difficulty in gaining support in that church. Clement, however, speaks as though the office was of long standing and the Corinthian disloyalty to it was an innovation. He rebukes them sharply for their attitude and dwells upon the bad effects discord always produces. He urges them to follow the example of the great figures of Scripture; he is remarkably familiar with the Greek version of the Jewish Bible and quotes it copiously. He reminds them of the humility of

---

[1] Followed by the so-called *II Clement*.

Christ and points to the harmony of the natural world. He tells the story of the phoenix, which he may have thought was referred to in Ps. 92:12, where the Greek word *phoenix*, meaning "palm tree," might be taken to mean the bird whose story was told in Herodotus (ii. 73) and in Pliny the Elder (*Natural History* x. 2). After a long admonition to lead a godly life, Clement returns to the Corinthian situation (chap. 44), points out that the officers of the church have taken over its leadership from the apostles, and urges them to love, forgiveness, humility, and reconciliation. After a prayer (59:3—61:3) he closes with a summary of the letter.

It may seem strange that the Roman church should take it upon itself to direct the church at Corinth, but a number of recent events in Christian history had prepared the way for such a step. The collection and publication of the letters of Paul, soon after A.D. 90, had, as we have seen, had the effect of standardizing the letter type of Christian instruction and of showing its extraordinary possibilities. Hebrews had called upon the Roman church, in view of its noble behavior in Nero's persecution (10:32–36) and by reason of its age, to take the lead in teaching other churches (5:12), and the Revelation, with all its heroic faith in persecution, had inculcated a vengeful attitude toward the persecuting emperor and empire. The Roman church, looking about for some church that needed instruction, saw that the churches of Asia needed to be reminded to love their enemies and respect the emperor and wrote I Peter to convey this corrective. As the

Revelation had claimed the authority of a Christian prophet, writing in the name of Jesus himself, the Roman church wrote in the name of the chief of the apostles, as it could do, the ancients thought, since it was the custodian of his tomb and so of his memory and his teaching.

In writing to the Corinthians, however, it needed no such aids for its message and wrote simply as the church of God that sojourned in Rome. The curious left-handed apology with which it begins is explained if the church was stirred to write by the stinging challenge of Hebrews, now generally regarded as written to the Roman church: "Because of the sudden and successive misfortunes and disasters that have overtaken us," Clement begins, "we think that we have been too slow to pay attention to the matters under dispute among you, beloved." If the duty of the Roman church in such cases had been recently brought to its attention by Hebrews, we can understand this apology, which is not really meant for the Corinthians but rather for the Romans themselves.

The influence of Hebrews on the *Letter of Clement* is very marked. It is just here that we first find Hebrews reflected in Christian literature; for Clement is largely interspersed, as Lightfoot said, with thoughts and expressions from Hebrews.[2]

The acquaintance of Clement with the collected letters of Paul is also clear; he is the first Christian writer to quote one of Paul's letters expressly: "Take

[2] J. B. Lightfoot, *The Apostolic Fathers* (5 vols.; 2d ed., London and New York, 1889, 1890), I, 95.

up the letter of the blessed Paul, the apostle; what did he first write you, at the beginning of the gospel preaching?'' chapter 47 begins, and goes on with an unmistakable reference to I Cor. 1:10–12. Not only I and II Corinthians but Romans and Ephesians are clearly reflected in Clement.

This knowledge of the collected letters of Paul on the part of Clement enables us to push the earliest possible date down fifteen years later than A.D. 75, suggested by Lake as the *terminus a quo*. No one as early as that can be shown to have known Paul's collected letters, and after that date the authors of Matthew and Luke-Acts (A.D. 80–90), writing probably in Antioch and Ephesus, respectively, were still unacquainted with them. The familiar use of the Pauline letter collection by Clement is an important element in dating his letter.

The resemblances of the *Letter of Clement* to I Peter are generally taken to show his use of that letter but are probably due to the fact that both letters emanated from the church at Rome at about the same time and probably under the same impulse. I Peter's curious reference to Peter as a "fellow elder" (5:1)—a strange designation for the chief of the apostles—becomes clear when we recognize that I Peter and *I Clement* are companion letters to the Christians of the East, *I Clement* to those of Greece, and I Peter to those of Asia Minor, and that the position of the elder was precisely the point at issue in Corinth, which *I Clement* was meant to correct. To picture Peter as a fellow-elder would enhance the prestige of that office among the churches of Asia Minor.

Clement cannot be said to show acquaintance with any written gospel; his quotations of Jesus' words in chapters 13 and 46 seem more naturally explained as derived from the oral gospel; they are, in fact, in both chapters introduced with the words "remembering" or "Remember the words of the Lord Jesus," the usual way of introducing a quotation from the oral gospel, as in Acts 20:35: "Remember the words of the Lord Jesus."[3]

Lightfoot in his great commentary on the epistles of Clement, which Harnack called the finest commentary we have on any Church Father, says that Clement's characteristics are comprehensiveness, order, and moderation. The *Letter* is certainly a fine example of first-century Christian teaching and almost won a place in the New Testament. It was accepted as Scripture by Clement of Alexandria, writing between A.D. 190 and 210. The so-called *II Clement* became attached to it, and the two stand after the Revelation in the Alexandrian manuscript of the Greek Bible, as we have seen. They are mentioned as part of the New Testament in the *Apostolic Canons*, a Syrian work of about A.D. 400, and stand between the Catholic letters and those of Paul in the Harclean Syriac New Testament manuscript already noted. Abu'l Barakat (†1363), in his account of Christian Arabic literature, speaks of the two letters of Clement as belonging to

---

[3] Cf. Polycarp *To the Philippians* 2:3.

the New Testament. But on the Greek side, the *Stichometry of Nicephorus*, a list of books of scripture giving the size of each in lines of Homeric length (*ca.* A.D. 850), lists them among the rejected books, its "apocrypha." But, in or out of the New Testament, *I Clement* is a noble monument of Christian attitudes in Rome toward the end of the first century.

Yet for all its ancient renown, for it was one of the best-known books of early Christian literature, until *Modern Discoveries* 1875 *I Clement* was known to the modern world only through a single defective Greek manuscript—the fifth-century Codex Alexandrinus, from which a leaf was lost just before the end of the letter. As no versions were known to exist, no one knew how much or how little was really gone, until, in 1873, Bryennius discovered in Constantinople a complete Greek text of it in a manuscript dated A.D. 1056. This text he published in 1875. One Syriac, one Latin, and two Coptic manuscripts of it have since been found, one of these last a papyrus leaf-book of the fourth century.

Clement himself was spoken of in the *Shepherd* of Hermas, about A.D. 100 (*Vis.* ii. 4. 3); and his letter is mentioned or quoted by Dionysius of Corinth, about 170 (*Church History* iv. 23. 11); by Hegesippus, in his *Memoirs* now lost, about 180 (*Church History* iv. 22. 1); by Irenaeus, 181–89 (*Refutation* iii. 3. 3); by Clement of Alexandria several times, but without naming Clement; by Origen (*On First Principles* ii. 3. 6, etc.); and by Eusebius (*Church History* iv. 22. 1, etc.). While its almost complete disappearance in medieval Greek manuscripts shows its decline in prestige, its translation into Latin, Syriac, and Coptic shows its wide currency in the early period, and the fact that *II Clement* does not accompany it in the Latin and Coptic versions shows at how early a date these translations must have been made.

It was the Codex Alexandrinus that first made the *Letter of Clement* known in Europe, and when Cyril

The Apostolic Fathers Lucar, patriarch of Constantinople, sent that manuscript to the king of England in 1628, one of the first acts of the royal librarian, Patrick Young, was to edit and publish the *Letters of Clement* in 1633. The subsequent publication of the *Letter of Barnabas*, the *Letter of Polycarp*, and the Ignatian letters made it possible for Cotelier in 1672 to publish the *Works of the Holy Fathers Who Flourished in Apostolic Times (temporibis Apostolicis)*; and, when Ittig in 1699 carried on that task, he called his collection a library of Apostolic Fathers (*Bibliotheca Patrum Apostolicorum*). In the principal collections of "Apostolic Fathers" to this day (Lightfoot; Gebhardt, Harnack, and Zahn; Lake) Clement has usually had the place of honor, at first probably because he was identified with the Clement mentioned in Phil. 4:3, but more recently because his letter is so clearly the earliest writing outside of the New Testament that we possess.[4]

---

[4] In the Paris edition, *Les Pères apostoliques* (1907–12), and in Bihlmeyer's revision (1924———) of Funk's *Die apostolischen Vaeter* (1901, 1906), the *Didache* and *Barnabas* precede *I Clement*, as being supposedly of earlier date; but the grounds for such early datings of these two works are insufficient.

Early in the second century a Christian prisoner was being taken through western Asia Minor by a guard of *Ignatius of Antioch* ten Roman soldiers, on his way to Rome, where he was to be executed. He was the bishop of Antioch, in Syria, and his name was Ignatius. News of his coming had preceded him, and when at Laodicea his guards took the north fork of the road, that led through Philadelphia to Smyrna, Christian messengers hurried along the south fork, through Tralles and Magnesia, to Ephesus, to tell the brethren that he had gone the other way and that they must go to Smyrna if they hoped to see him. A number of them did so, and when, very soon after, his guards took him on to Troas, one of these brethren went with him to that port. A little later his party touched at Philippi, on their westward way. That is the last we see of Ignatius. But at Smyrna and Troas he managed to write seven letters which, though they are of no great length, are of extraordinary interest.

Ignatius flashes into the field of Christian literature like a bird out of the night and, after a few days, flashes out again into the obscurity from which he had come. Though he was the bishop of Antioch, it is only when he enters the circle of the churches of Asia that he does any writing significant enough to have been preserved. We know of no writings of his from his years at Antioch, and of none after he left Troas for Rome; and it is probable that his one sudden burst of literary activity at Smyrna and Troas was stimulated by the Christian leaders of Asia—Polycarp of Smyrna and Onesimus of Ephesus.

We can hardly suppose that his brutal guards—"ten leopards," he calls them—did anything to facilitate his letter-writing in the way of providing him with writing materials or forwarding his letters. But an Ephesian deacon named Burrhus, who came to Smyrna with his bishop Onesimus and three others from Ephesus to see and cheer him, seems to have assisted him and then, at his request, to have gone on with him as far as Troas and helped with his letter-writing there. In fact, he was probably his amanuensis. Ignatius says that the Ephesians and Smyrnaeans had been instrumental in getting him this assistance.

Where the west-bound roads diverged at Laodicea, Ignatius' guards had chosen the northern route that led through Philadelphia to Smyrna, instead of the southerly one that ran through Tralles and Magnesia to Ephesus. But the churches at Tralles, Magnesia, and Ephesus, as we have seen, were informed of the route he was following, and ten representatives of these churches were able to join the brethren of Smyrna in making him welcome when he reached the coast.

While he was at Smyrna, Ignatius recognized this expression of Christian sympathy by writing a letter to each of these churches. He also addressed one to the Christians of Rome, preparing them for his coming and urging that nothing be done to prevent his martyrdom, to which he had now fully made up his mind. This attitude of Ignatius can be understood if we remember the terrible prospect of a cruel death to which he must have been striving to adjust himself through these weeks of travel.

His guards took him on from Ephesus to Troas, and there he wrote three more letters: one to the church at Smyrna, where he had been so kindly treated; one to that at Philadelphia, with which he had had a hurried contact on his way to Smyrna; and one to Polycarp, the bishop of Smyrna, who had evidently done all that could be done for him during his stay in that city. The persecution at Antioch is now over, and Ignatius wishes the Asian churches to write letters of encouragement to his old flock, especially as he cannot rally them himself. He is being hurried on to Neapolis, and even with the aid of Burrhus cannot write to all the churches through which he will pass on his way to Rome, but he asks Polycarp to do this for him, so that this triumphal progress of his may continue all the way to the city of his martyrdom.

We catch one more glimpse of him at Philippi, where he met the church. Then he disappears from our ken, for the later book on the *Martyrdom of Ignatius* has little historical worth. We can only suppose that he was thrown to the lions in the Coliseum; Eusebius places the date in A.D. 107–8, but modern learning inclines to a somewhat later time, about A.D. 110–17.

Second-century Christianity was clouded over by a succession of schismatic movements: Docetism, Marcionism, Gnosticism, and Montanism. The first, Docetism, is reflected and opposed in the letters of Ignatius and the letters and Gospel of John. The seven Ignatian letters are, in fact, deeply concerned over the progress of the Docetic movement among the churches of Asia. Ignatius is the first Christian writer to describe the Docetic position—that Christ's suffering was not real but only a "semblance" (*dokein*), so that he only seemed to suffer. Over against these views, Ignatius insists that his sufferings were real (*Tral.*, chaps. 9 and 10), and he bitterly retorts that the holders of such views are themselves but "semblance!"

Against the danger that Docetism might divide the churches, Ignatius urges unity upon believers, and he finds the surest guaranty of this in a uniform church organization, with bishop, elders (presbyters), and deacons. "Do nothing without the bishop" is his remedy (*Philad.*, chap. 7). Christians must be in harmony with their bishop, and, since the bishop has the mind of Christ, they will find themselves in harmony with Christ. Ignatius is strongly ecclesiastical in his views; men must belong to the church and obey the bishop and presbyters. He is the first clear representative of the threefold ministry—bishop, presbyters, and deacons—though it was not until fully half a century later that this organization became standard Christian usage.

The style of Ignatius is far from that of an experienced writer, and he seems to have written nothing worth preserving before or after the few days he spent at Smyrna and Troas. But the circle of Ephesus, including the northwest quarter of Asia, was the literary center of Christianity at the time, and it must have been this that led Ignatius to take up the pen. It would seem that the Asian leaders, probably Onesimus and Polycarp, dreading further inroads of Docetism in the region, urged upon Ignatius the duty of attacking it. His immediate position, as a Christian confessor, a man already condemned to death for his faith and on the way to execution, would give his words great weight, and whatever he wrote they could circulate as widely as they pleased.

Ignatius himself speaks in his letters of the aid the brethren of Ephesus and Smyrna had given him in writing and sending his letters, and, of course, without such local aid how could a prisoner like him have either written or sent them? The Ephesians and Smyrnaeans had sent Burrhus of Ephesus (*Eph.* 2:1) with Ignatius to Troas to write or carry his letters (*Philad.* 11:2; *Smyrn.* 12:1). Ignatius directs Polycarp to write to the churches in the cities he is likely to pass through on the rest of his journey to Rome. And a few weeks later we find Polycarp sending a collection of his letters to the church at Philippi. Probably Ignatius was stirred to write by the great Asian leaders, Onesimus and Polycarp; they provided him with an amanuensis who could also carry his letters written in Troas to the Philadelphians, the Smyrnaeans, and Polycarp, and they made it their business, after he was gone, to collect and circulate his letters. The whole Ignatian correspondence, therefore, appears as an item in the literary activity going on in Ephesus and the neighboring churches, which found expression about this time in the Gospel and Letters of John, and a few years later in the collection and promotion of the Fourfold Gospel, the greatest piece of publishing enterprise in the whole history of Christianity. The evident inexperience of Ignatius as a writer, his inactivity in writing except for this brief visit to Asia, the danger Christian leaders in Asia saw in Docetism, the express statements of Ignatius himself, and the subsequent collection and circulation of his letters among other churches than those he had addressed fit well with the view that he was stirred to write and helped with his letters by men like Polycarp and Onesimus. The concern that was felt in their circle at this very time about the menace of Docetism was one of the factors that produced the Gospel and Letters of John. And out of this Asian circle had come, some twenty years before, the Book of Revelation and, in all probability, the first collection of the letters of Paul. Nowhere else among Christians, toward the end of the first and in the early years of the second century, was there such active interest in using literary techniques for the promotion of Christianity.

The free interchange of letters among the churches of Asia, Macedonia, and Syria that is implied or reflected in the letters of Ignatius and Polycarp shows in what close touch these churches, and probably the other leading churches of Italy and Greece, already were. Paul's letters to the churches had led the way in this, and the letter collection that begins the Revelation, together with Hebrews, I Peter, and *I Clement* had continued it. These churches of East and West were in frequent communication by letter, and these letters sometimes rose to the stature of permanent contributions to the growing treasures of what was to be Christian literature.

The letter of Polycarp to the Philippians is an immediate sequel to the letters of Ignatius. Ignatius had

Polycarp of Smyrna

been taken by his guards from Troas to Neapolis and thence, it appears, to Philippi, where the Philippian Christian leaders had visited him (Pol. *Phil.* 9:1). After his departure they had written to Polycarp, asking him to send their letter with his to Antioch, for Ignatius had requested them to write to the Christians of his diocese. They had also asked Polycarp to send them whatever letters of Ignatius he could, and this he now does, writing them on his own account a kind of covering letter. He urges them to be harmonious, steadfast, and faithful but says nothing about the threefold ministry of which Ignatius made so much; in writing he simply groups himself with his presbyters: "Polycarp and the elders with him." Not only in polity but in doctrine and use of Christian literature he stands apart from Ignatius. Ignatius is the first writer to show acquaintance with Matthew, and he knows the Pauline letters, but Polycarp knows the Pauline letters, the Acts, Hebrews, and I Peter and uses Christian literature much more frequently than Ignatius does. But he lacks the rugged vigor and the very unconventional metaphors that make Ignatius interesting and sometimes perplexing. Polycarp evidently wrote his letter within a few weeks of the departure of Ignatius for Rome, for he has no news of his fate and asks the Philippians if they have any.

Harrison has recently argued that chapters 13 and 14 of Polycarp's letter form the covering letter which accompanied the Ignatian collection when Polycarp sent it to the Philippians about A.D. 115; while chapters 1–12 constitute another letter, written in a time of crisis in the Philippian church, about A.D. 135, when, as he thinks, Marcion's views in an early stage were appearing in the church at Philippi, perhaps brought there by Marcion himself. But this seems to exaggerate the crisis atmosphere in the letter and loses sight of the important fact that, while Polycarp is familiar with the Pauline corpus (in the ten-letter form), he shows no acquaintance with the Fourfold Gospel, a thing incredible in a Christian leader in Asia after A.D. 120.[5] Yet Harrison's view was at least tentatively approved by both Burkitt and Streeter.[6]

[5] The widespread influence of the Fourfold Gospel in A.D. 120–60 is evidenced by Papias, II Peter, the *Gospel of Peter*, the *Epistle of the Apostles*, the works of Justin, and the new British Museum gospel fragment, which is dated not later than A.D. 150. This particular manuscript can hardly be supposed to be the original manuscript of this new gospel which, it is reasonable to suppose, had been in existence a dozen or fifteen years before this copy of it was made, or perhaps since 135. Its author probably did not see the Fourfold Gospel until it had been in circulation a few years; and, even if the idea of blending its four narratives into one at once occurred to him, it would take him some little time to do this and get his work into circulation. This would carry us back perhaps ten or a dozen years further, to A.D. 120–25 (cf. Goodspeed, *The Formation of the New Testament*, chap. iv; *New Chapters in New Testament Study*, pp. 39–48; *Christianity Goes to Press*, p. 66). Dr. Lloyd V. Moore's searching and illuminating study of this subject still awaits publication ("The Use of Gospel Material in Pre-Catholic Christian Literature" [Doctor's dissertation; Chicago, 1929]).

[6] P. N. Harrison, *Polycarp's Two Epistles to the Philippians* (Cambridge, 1936).

This brings up the matter of the forms in which the Ignatian letters have come down to us. Eusebius speaks of seven letters (*Church History* iii. 36): *Ephesians, Magnesians, Trallians,* and *Romans,* written from Smyrna, and *Philadelphians, Smyrnaeans,* and *Polycarp,* written from Troas. In the manuscripts of Ignatius, however, the letters begin with *Smyrnaeans* and *Polycarp,* continuing: *Ephesians, Magnesians, Philadelphians, Trallians;* these being followed by a string of spurious letters which cannot be earlier than the latter part of the fourth century, among which *Romans* appears following a late and unhistorical account of the *Martyrdom of Ignatius,* to which it has evidently given rise. The order in which the genuine letters thus appear—*Smyrnaeans, Polycarp, Ephesians, Magnesians, Philadelphians, Trallians, ... Romans*—recalls Polycarp's words to the Philippians as to what he was sending them: "We send you, as you asked, the letters of Ignatius which were sent to us by him [that would be *Smyrnaeans* and *Polycarp*] and such others as we had in our possession" (that is, those to other churches of which Burrhus would have retained copies). This is probably the original order in which Polycarp circulated the collection, much as the Pauline letter collection had been put in circulation perhaps twenty-five years earlier. That Polycarp has that collection in the back of his mind is shown when he says to the Philippians, "Neither am I nor is any other like me able to follow the wisdom of the blessed and glori-

Forms of the Ignatian Letters

ous Paul, who . . . . when he was absent wrote letters
to you" (3:2). The collection he is now sending them
cannot compare with that of the Pauline letters; yet
he also speaks (9:1) of the endurance the Philippians
had seen with their own eyes "not only in the blessed
Ignatius and Zosimus and Rufus . . . . but in Paul
himself and in the other apostles" (9:1), thus suggesting that Ignatius, like Paul, is a martyr and so deserves a hearing.

Both Ignatius and Polycarp were well aware of the
great value the collected letters of Paul had possessed
for the churches; they speak of it (*Eph*. 12:2; Pol.
Phil. 11:3) very much as though they had had that
great collection of the martyred Paul in mind in creating this new collection by the soon-to-be-martyred
Ignatius. At the same time Ignatius is unnecessarily
solicitous to subordinate himself to Paul ("I do not
order you, as did Peter and Paul" [*Rom*. 4:3]). It is
Ignatius' remark to the Ephesians that Paul "in every
letter reminds (*mnemoneuei*) of you" that points to
Ephesus as the place where Paul's letters had been collected and published.

It seems clear that Polycarp, who now becomes active in circulating the collected letters of Ignatius, had
had a part in stimulating Ignatius to write them. Nor
is it necessary to suppose that he has now painfully to
send around among the Asian churches and gather
them up again for the purpose. He tells the Philippians that he is sending them "the letters of Ignatius
which were sent to us by him, and such others as

we had in our possession." How does Polycarp happen to have any others besides Ignatius' letters to himself and to his church at Smyrna? He has already made a collection, it appears, before the Philippians ask him for it; indeed, Ignatius has told them to ask, for he understands what Polycarp has in mind. It seems clear that Burrhus, the deacon of Ephesus, who had accompanied Ignatius from Smyrna to Troas, had kept copies of the letters he wrote for him, for the use of his principals, Polycarp and Onesimus, and that Ignatius was aware of this and agreeable to it.

It is reasonable, then, to suppose that the letter to the Romans was among the letters Polycarp had in his possession and sent copies of to the Philippians.

Two other forms of the Ignatian letters illustrate their popularity in ancient times. For they were not only generally accompanied by from six to ten spurious letters ascribed to Ignatius and written in his name, probably late in the fourth century, but they were themselves each of them interpolated and expanded, as Greek and Latin texts show. On the other hand, three of them—*Polycarp*, *Ephesians*, and *Romans*—are found in Syriac much abbreviated.

The letters of Ignatius were, therefore, known in the early church in at least four different forms:

1. The seven genuine letters, known to Eusebius in A.D. 326

2. These seven letters, accompanied by ten spurious ones[7]

---

[7] In the Latin text which contains the seven genuine letters in the translation made or directed by Robert Grosseteste, bishop of Lincoln (*ca.* 1250), the contents are: *Smyrnaeans, Polycarp, Ephesians, Magnesians, Philadel-*

3. The seven letters individually expanded and interpolated and accompanied by several spurious letters

4. In Syriac three letters—*Polycarp, Ephesians, Romans*—compressed, on no particular principle, to a little more than half their original length

Polycarp's *Letter to the Philippians* was not usually copied with the Ignatian letters; indeed, no complete Greek text of it is known, and while a group of Greek manuscripts preserve almost nine chapters of it, and Eusebius in his *Church History* (iii. 36. 14, 15) supplies the thirteenth, for the other four chapters we are dependent upon the Latin version. The study of the *Letter* would be greatly helped if a manuscript containing the complete Greek text could somewhere be found.

Some forty years later, in A.D. 155 or 156, Polycarp suffered martyrdom in Smyrna, at the age of eighty-six. An account of this, substantially historical, was embodied in a letter from the church of Smyrna to that at Philomelium, a town in Phrygia not far from Pisidian Antioch. It is the earliest example that has come down to us of that type of literature—the "martyrdom"—which was to become so abundant. It will be more fully discussed in its chronological position in the development of Christian letter literature.

------

phians, Trallians, Mary of Cassobola to Ignatius, Ignatius to Mary of Cassobola, Tarsians, Antiochenes, Hero, the *Martyrdom* (numbered the twelfth letter), and *Romans* (numbered the thirteenth). Then follows the correspondence of Ignatius with John the Evangelist and with St. Mary (four letters). The longer Greek form has a *Letter to the Philippians* also but usually contains only thirteen letters.

The view Christians were to take of the Jewish scriptures was a serious problem for the early church *The Letter of* for almost a century and a half. What *Barnabas* were Christians to think of the Jewish Law? How were they to regard the utterances of the prophets? The Letter to the Romans and the Gospel of Matthew had grappled with these questions, and Marcion and Justin in the middle of the second century took opposite views upon them. But about A.D. 130 a Christian teacher, probably in Alexandria, offered a compromise. The Jewish scriptures were true, not literally, as the Jews believed, but allegorically. When Genesis declared that Abraham circumcised 318 males of his household (14:14; 17:23), it meant to predict Jesus on the cross, for the Greek figures for 18 are iota eta (IH), the first two letters of Jesus' name, and the Greek figure for 300 is tau, or T, which might be taken as representing the cross. The allegorizing teacher who offered this interpretation was very proud of it. "No one has learned a truer lesson from me," he goes on, "but I know that you deserve it" (9:8, 9).

The food laws of Leviticus are also allegorized. They only mean that we are not to be like swine, wild beasts, or birds of prey. The six days of creation are the six thousand years the earth is to last before the Messiah's return, "for a day with him means a thousand years." So interpreted, the author finds the Jewish scriptures full of religious meaning and of predictions fulfilled in Christ.

One of these touches seems to date the book, for the

writer speaks of the temple as having been destroyed
and being rebuilt by those who had destroyed it, and
he goes on, "It is happening. For because of the war it
was destroyed by the enemy; now even the servants of
the enemy will build it up again themselves" (16:4).
This points to the heathen rebuilding of the temple of
Jupiter on the temple site in Jerusalem, on the eve of
the Bar-Cochba War of A.D. 132–35, and would date
the *Letter* about A.D. 130–31, when Hadrian ordered
the building of the new city.

The *Letter of Barnabas* begins not in the usual Greek
letter fashion but in the informal epistolary style used
in family letters and addresses its readers as "sons and
daughters." Its atmosphere changes suddenly at the
end of chapter 17: "So much for this. Now let us pass
to another lesson and teaching." (The words are
Gnosis and Didache.) What follows is a bald statement of Christian ethics, as the Way of Light over
against the Way of Darkness. It is cast in fifty-one curt
commands of the "Thou shalt" and "Thou shalt not"
order, twenty-three of them positive and twenty-eight
negative (chap. 19). A brief description of the Way of
the Black One follows, and a general exhortation concludes the book.

No one can miss the sharp cleavage at the end of
chapter 17. The idle if ingenious fancies of the allegorical interpreter give place to the stern, blunt
commandments of the Christian lawgiver, with only
the crudest of transitions between. It is evident that
two short Christian tracts have been put together.
And this impression becomes a conviction when we

find that each part has been found by itself in a Latin version. The Latin translation of *Barnabas* extends only through chapter 17, which is properly finished off with a doxology. The remaining portion has also been found in a Latin version (published by Schlecht in 1899), which is entitled *The Teaching of the Apostles* (*De doctrina Apostolorum*) and contains almost every line of *Barnabas* chapters 18–20 but arranged in quite another order.

This curious little tract, in its original Greek form, was evidently used also by the writer of the *Didache*, or *Teaching of the Apostles*, discovered by Bryennius in a Constantinople manuscript in 1873; but the name seems originally to have belonged to this ancient leaflet which, in spite of its crudity and unattractiveness, was destined to be taken up into a whole series of Christian writings, beginning with *Barnabas* and the *Didache*. It has usually been dismissed as a Jewish work, the "Two Ways," but historians of Jewish literature have not accepted it; the Latin text of it found by Schlecht bears the Christian title *De doctrina Apostolorum;* and unmistakable Christian touches here and there mark the tract from beginning to end. In fact, it is clear that this little leaflet on Christian morals is the original *Didache* or *Teaching of the Apostles*, and when it was expanded into the *Didache* discovered by Bryennius it carried its original name with it.

Literary study often analyzes an ancient writing into its component sources on the basis of the internal evidence, the glaring joints in the structure, and the fact that one part may be totally different in style and interest from the other. Very rarely, however, is this judgment confirmed by the actual discovery of the two parts existing as separate independent units in other manuscripts. Yet for *Barnabas* this has actually happened. We cannot doubt that sometime very early in the second century a little manual of Christian behavior was composed, probably at Antioch, and called the *Teaching of the Apostles*. A generation later, perhaps in the neighborhood of Alexandria, the *Letter of Barnabas* was written. And then, a few years after, it was expanded by the addition to it of the substance of the *Teaching of the Apostles*. About the same time *The Teaching*, under its own name, was itself expanded by the addition of some rules for church life into the *Teaching of the Apostles* as Bryennius published it from the Constantinople manuscript in 1883 and as we know it today. But this little tract was originally not Jewish but Christian and was not called the "Two Ways" but the *Teaching of the Apostles*.

The *Letter of Barnabas* was thus probably written about A.D. 130, on the eve of the Bar-Cochba War, and a few years later, perhaps 150–75, was enlarged by the addition of the *Teaching of the Apostles* in its primitive form.

Not only are these Latin manuscripts of parts of *Barnabas* of singular interest but the Greek manuscripts of it have an interesting history. A century ago it was known in Greek only in a group of eight manuscripts, all copied directly or indirectly from an earlier manuscript from which several leaves had been lost, so that the text skipped from Polycarp *To the Philip-*

pians 9:2 toward the end of one sentence to the
Letter of Barnabas 5:7 in the middle of another. But
in 1859, when Tischendorf found the Codex Sinaiticus
at St. Catherine's on Mount Sinai, he saw at once that
it contained the complete Greek text of *Barnabas*, and,
fearing that the manuscript might be taken away from
him the next morning, he sat up all night to copy that
long-desired text. A few years later, in 1873, Bryennius made his famous discovery of the Constantinople
manuscript, from which he published first (1875) the
full Greek text of *I* and *II Clement*, and then (1883) the
long-lost *Didache*. It also contained the full Greek
text of *Barnabas*, and its readings Bryennius supplied
for Hilgenfeld's edition of 1877. Von Gebhardt also
found a partial Latin text of what he supposed were
the opening lines of the *Didache* but have proved to be
the beginning of the Latin leaflet, the *Doctrina*, already
discussed.

The influence of the *Letter of Barnabas* was very considerable, and it was long held in high regard. It
seems to be quoted in *Didache* 16:2 (= *Bar.* 4:9).
Clement of Alexandria, toward the end of the second
century, accepted it as Scripture and commented upon
it in his lost *Outlines*. He spoke of Barnabas as an
"apostle," but so, of course, did Acts (14:14). Origen,
too, included it among his disputed books, which he
himself accepted as Scripture. The Sinaitic manuscript includes it in the New Testament, putting it
after the Revelation and before Hermas. Jerome speaks
of it as read among the apocryphal writings (*On Illustrious Men* 6). The *Clermont List*, representing Egyp-

tian usage about A.D. 300, has it at the end of the Catholic or general letters, between Jude and the Revelation of John. Eusebius classes it as disputed and rejected (*Church History* iii. 25. 4). The *List of the Sixty Canonical Books* mentions it among the rejected books, the apocrypha; and the *Stichometry of Nicephorus* (*ca.* A.D. 850) puts it with the disputed books—the *Revelation of John*, the *Revelation of Peter*, and the *Gospel of the Hebrews*—not among the rejected ones.

About the middle of the second century a Greek Christian of Asia, probably in the vicinity of Ephesus,

The Epistle of the Apostles wrote in the name of the apostles a letter to all the churches, gathering up out of the Four Gospels, the Acts, and other sources what he considered of most value and interest in the way of Christian history and tradition, ethics and expectation. He meant it as a kind of summary, for the whole world, from all the apostles, of Christian beliefs and hopes. Perhaps he felt that the growing number of Christian books must confuse simple minds, and so he tried to bring it all into one small book, about the length of I Corinthians. The idea of writing in the name of all the apostles was taken up in the *Teaching of the Lord through the Twelve Apostles*, early in the second century, and, toward the end of it, in the *Gospel of the Twelve Apostles*.

No mention of the *Epistle of the Apostles* has been found in any early Christian writer,[8] and the book

---

[8] The fifth-century Christian poet Commodian seems to reflect chap. 11 in the words "Vestigium umbra non facit" ("A phantom does not make a footprint").

itself was entirely unknown until Carl Schmidt reported the discovery of a part of it in Coptic in 1895. A Latin fragment of it—a single leaf from the fifth century—came to light in 1908. Meantime in 1907 a work in Ethiopic called *The Testament of Our Lord in Galilee* had been reported and described, and this was recognized by M. R. James as including a version of the *Epistle of the Apostles;* it was published in 1913 and preserves the work in full. From these three sources—Coptic, Latin, and Ethiopic—Schmidt in 1919 published the text. But no part of it has yet been found in Greek, the original language of the book.

The writer of the *Epistle of the Apostles* names its authors as John, Thomas, Peter, Andrew, James, Philip, Bartholomew, Matthew, Nathanael, Judas the Zealot, and Cephas; although John 1:42 explains that Cephas, so often mentioned in Paul, really means Peter. Nathanael is, of course, never mentioned in the gospel lists of apostles. The book begins with a warning against the "false apostles" Simon (meaning Simon Magus) and Cerinthus, the latter the earliest of the schismatic leaders (*ca.* A.D. 100). It records the creation by God the Father and his incarnation in God the Son. A summary of Jesus' miracles is given, followed by his crucifixion, burial, and resurrection. He rejoins the apostles, apparently in Galilee, and tells them of his experiences in the other world. He promises to release Peter from prison and instructs them to observe the Lord's Supper. They ask when he is to return,

and he answers that it will be when a hundred and
fifty years are past (so the Ethiopic; the Coptic has
"When the hundred and twentieth part is fulfilled,"
evidently counting not from Jesus' birth but from his
death). He teaches the apostles and answers their
questions, promising them resurrection, and declaring
that he will go with them as they preach. He predicts
the conversion, work, and martyrdom of Paul and describes the signs of the end. He justifies the condemnation of the wicked but encourages the apostles
to pray for sinners and commissions them as "fathers,
servants, and masters." He explains the parable of
the bridesmaids, giving each one the name of some
virtue or faculty. The wise ones were Faith, Love,
Grace, Peace, and Hope; the foolish were Knowledge,
Understanding, Obedience, Patience, and Compassion.
(This suggests the names given the twelve virgins in
the *Shepherd* of Hermas, *Parable* 9:15.) After further
moral instruction and the prediction of schismatic
teaching, a cloud carries him away.

The writer's historical weakness is obvious; he can
assemble only eleven apostles, though he counts both
Cephas and Peter and includes Nathanael (of John
1:45–49). He describes Jesus as crucified by Pontius
Pilate and Archelaus, although the latter disappeared
from history in A.D. 6; Antipas is, of course, meant.

He draws heavily upon the Four Gospels and the
Acts and uses the Revelation of John, the *Revelation of
Peter*, I Peter, and probably Ignatius (*Eph.* 7:2), the

Letter of Barnabas, and the *Shepherd* of Hermas.[9] He tells the famous story of Jesus and his alphabet teacher (chap. 4), which appears in the *Gospel of Thomas* and is quoted in Irenaeus (*Ref.* i. 20. 1), but we cannot be sure he derived the story from that gospel; he may have gotten it from tradition. He describes Jesus as quoting extensively from the Psalms (Pss. 3 [in full], 13, 49).

There are gropings toward a creed, as when the writer in chapter 3 proclaims his doctrine of God the Father and God the Son and in chapter 5 explains the five loaves as the symbol of our faith in "the Father, the Lord Almighty, and in Jesus Christ our Redeemer, in the Holy Spirit the Comforter, in the holy church, and in the forgiveness of sins." This was just the time when the Roman church (A.D. 140–50) was first shaping its baptismal confession, which we know as the Apostles' Creed.

The fixing of the second coming "when a hundred and fifty years are past" points to a date between A.D. 140 and 150, and some touches sound as though Marcion were a contemporary of the writer; he flourished at just that time. (Justin Martyr, in *Apology* xlvi. 1, speaks of Jesus as having been born one hundred and fifty years before he writes.) On the whole, the *Epistle* was probably written between A.D. 140 and 160.[10]

[9] There may even be a reflection of the Short Conclusion of Mark in sending the apostles out to preach "from the east to the west" (chap. 30).

[10] Staehlin regards as probable the view advanced by H. J. Cladder (in the *Theologische Revue,* Vol. XVIII [1919]) that the date announced for the second coming in chap. 17 was the nine hundredth anniversary of the founding of Rome, or A.D. 147. But Schmidt inclines to a date about 160.

Early Christianity was constantly liable to persecution, and one Christian leader after another met his death by martyrdom. The first of these to be fully recorded in a narrative and circulated among the churches was that of Polycarp, the famous bishop of Smyrna, who seems to have been active in circulating the letters of Ignatius and whose *Letter to the Philippians* has already been discussed. It was written about A.D. 110–17, and Polycarp continued to be a Christian leader in Asia for forty or fifty years thereafter. It is natural to suppose he was one of those energetic men who assembled the Four Gospels and put them into circulation between A.D. 115 and 120, an act destined to have the most far-reaching consequences.

The Martyrdom of Polycarp

In 154 Polycarp visited Rome to confer with the Roman bishop Anicetus about the day on which the institution of the Lord's Supper should be celebrated. Polycarp and the Christians of Asia observed it on the fourteenth of the month Nisan, no matter on what day of the week it fell; but the Roman church celebrated the death of Christ on Friday and his resurrection "on the Sunday following the first full moon after the vernal equinox."[11] This was the "quartodeciman controversy" that was soon to divide Christianity. Polycarp and Anicetus could not agree about it, but they partook of the communion together and parted amicably. Very soon after his return to Smyrna, however,

[11] Arthur C. McGiffert, *Eusebius* ("Select Library of Nicene and Post-Nicene Fathers of the Christian Church: Second Series," Vol. I [New York, 1890]), p. 241, n. 1.

Polycarp was arrested, condemned to death, and suffered martyrdom, being bound to the stake, stabbed, and burned. This occurred on February 22, A.D. 156.[12]

Polycarp was eighty-six years of age and had been bishop of Smyrna for at least forty years. He was greatly respected and beloved by Christians everywhere, and an account of his last days and death was very soon written in the form of a letter from the church at Smyrna to that at Philomelium, two hundred miles to the east. It tells, for the most part with much restraint, of the arrest, examination, and execution of Polycarp. And with it begins a new form of Christian literature which became immensely popular —the "acts of martyrdom"—revived in modern times with such effect in Foxe's *Book of Martyrs* (1563). Such narratives played an important part in early Christian history in keeping Christians steadfast in persecutions, as members of the noble army of martyrs. The acts of martyrdom also played a very large part in such works as the *Golden Legend*, written in 1275 by Jacobus de Voragine, the archbishop of Genoa, translated into English and printed by Caxton in 1483, and in such great collections as the *Acta Sanctorum*, which contains sixty-nine volumes in both the Antwerp (1643–1910) and the Brussels (1845–1926) editions.

Further light is thrown upon the life of Polycarp by the accounts of Irenaeus, who when he was a boy in Asia had seen Polycarp and heard him, as he relates in

[12] Eusebius says in the *Chronicon* that Polycarp suffered martyrdom in A.D. 166–67. Harnack dates it on February 23, 155.

his letter to his friend Florinus, fortunately preserved in Eusebius *Church History* v. 20. 4–8. Irenaeus tells us more about Polycarp in his *Refutation of Gnosticism* iii. 3. 4, where he records Polycarp's appointment by the apostles as bishop in Asia, his journey to Rome to see Anicetus, and his famous encounter with Marcion. Marcion said to him, "Do you know me?" "I know you for the firstborn of Satan," was Polycarp's sharp reply. Eusebius seems to have learned what he knew about Polycarp from Ignatius' *Letter to Polycarp*, Polycarp's *Letter to the Philippians*, the *Martyrdom of Polycarp*, and what Irenaeus had to say about him.

Eusebius copied most of the *Martyrdom of Polycarp* into the pages of his *Church History* iv. 15. There are at least five Greek manuscripts of the *Martyrdom*. They end with a scribal note of unusual interest, for it states that the text was copied from the papers of Irenaeus by Gaius, who lived with him. Gaius' manuscript was copied by one Socrates, in Corinth, and his again by Pionius, possibly the martyr of that name who suffered in the Decian persecution (A.D. 250). This last scribe declares that Polycarp in a vision showed him where to find the outworn manuscript written by Socrates. All our manuscripts go back to this copy of Pionius, but the text represented in Eusebius omits some of the few miraculous touches it contains. The *Martyrdom* is, on the whole, a moving and convincing account of a tragic and heroic story, too often repeated in the second and third centuries, and it marks the beginning of the great literature of martyrology.

The position of Christians in the ancient world was extremely precarious; they might at any time be re-

The Letter of the Gallican Churches

ported to the authorities, who would then have no choice but to proceed against them, as followers of an unauthorized religion. Any offense given to the rabble of a city by the Christians there might cause an outbreak of legal procedure against the church, and this is what occurred in the Gallican cities of Lyons and Vienne in A.D. 177 as the reign of Marcus Aurelius was drawing to its close. The pitiful and yet heroic story of those who suffered martyrdom in these places was soon afterward told in a letter from the "servants of God who sojourn in Vienne and Lyons, in Gaul, to the brethren throughout Asia and Phrygia." This letter ranks next to the *Martyrdom of Polycarp* as among the earliest acts of martyrdom. But it has disappeared, and for our knowledge of it we are dependent upon the copious extracts from it which Eusebius fortunately copied into the fifth book of his *Church History* (1–4).

The letter records the attack of the mob upon the brethren, the intervention of the city authorities, of course against the Christians—the defense offered by one of them, Vettius Epagathus, the examination of the others, the defection of some and the steadfastness of others. Their slaves were examined and, in fear of torture, confessed that the Christians were guilty of the crimes usually charged against them—infanticide, cannibalism, and incest. Some of the brethren displayed conspicuous courage—Sanctus, a deacon of

Vienne, Maturus, Attalus, and Blandina, a slave, whose mistress was also undergoing torture. Pothinus, the bishop of Lyons, a man over ninety, was so maltreated that he died in prison. The final sufferings of Maturus, Sanctus, Attalus, Blandina, Alexander, a physician, and a boy named Ponticus are narrated in some detail—how they were flogged, thrown to wild beasts, hung from stakes, and roasted on an iron chair.

The little letter, as far as can be judged from the portions Eusebius preserves, stands out as one of the classics of the martyrological literature. Eusebius included it in his collection of acts of martyrdom, but that work has disappeared.[13]

The third century witnessed a marked rivalry among leading Christian centers as to their apostolic founders; Rome took pride in the names *The Abgar* of Peter and Paul, Ephesus rejoiced in the *Letters* memory of John or Luke, and Alexandria, probably quite groundlessly, claimed the name of Mark. But the quaintest and boldest of such claims was that of the Syrian church of Edessa, which went straight back to Jesus himself. Syriac Christianity documented this great claim by two letters, believed to have been exchanged between Jesus and Abgar the Black, king of Edessa in A.D. 13–50. Abgar wrote to Jesus as follows:

Abgar, ruler of Edessa, to Jesus the excellent Savior, who has appeared in the country of Jerusalem, greeting. I have

---

[13] An energetic effort to undermine the authenticity of the *Letter* and to prove it a forgery of the third century, from the time of Aurelian, was made by James W. Thompson (*American Journal of Theology*, XVI [1912], 358 ff.; XVII [1913], 249 ff.) but seems to rest on insufficient grounds.

heard the reports of you and of your cures as performed by you without medicines or herbs. For it is said that you make the blind see and the lame walk, that you cleanse lepers and cast out foul spirits and demons, and that you heal those afflicted with lingering disease, and raise the dead. After having heard all these things about you, I have concluded that one of two things must be true; either you are God, and having come down from heaven you do these things, or else you who do these things are the son of God. I have therefore written to you to ask you to take the trouble to come to me and heal the disease I have. For I have heard that the Jews are murmuring against you and are plotting to injure you. But I have a very small yet noble city, which is large enough for us both.

To this charming letter, Jesus is said to have replied:

Blessed are you who have believed in me without having seen me. For it is written of me, that those who have seen me will not believe in me, and those who have not seen me will believe and be saved. But in regard to what you have written me, that I should come to you, it is necessary for me to fulfil all things here for which I was sent, and after I have fulfilled them thus to be taken up again to him that sent me. But after I have been taken up I will send to you one of my disciples to heal your disease and give life to you and yours.

Syriac Christianity did not begin until Tatian, about A.D. 172, and did not reach the stage of ecclesiastical consciousness implied in these letters until the middle of the third century, when they were probably written. Eusebius found them in the archives of Edessa and translated them from Syriac into Greek (*Church History* i. 13). They were early embellished with the story that Abgar's messenger painted a portrait of Jesus and took it back to Edessa. The fuller form of the correspondence, the *Teaching of Addai*, passed into Armenian and Greek. The original story became widely known in the West through Eusebius' account of it, especially in Rufinus' Latin version of this. Jesus' letter has been found in a cave inscription at Edessa, and both letters in an inscription at Philippi. The Gelasian Decree stigmatized them as apocrypha.

CHAPTER III

REVELATIONS

In later Judaism a favorite type of religious instruction had emerged in the apocalypse, which made use

Jewish
Apocalyptic
of grotesque symbols to interpret the
present and forecast the future. The
books of Daniel and Enoch were notable
examples. Before the end of the first century, one
early Christian writer made use of this style in the
Revelation of John. This special kind of apocalyptic
writing revived among Christians in the second century, when the Jewish collection of apocalypses
known to us as II Esdras was laid hold of and given a
Christian preface and then, after the middle of the
third century, was given a Christian conclusion, and
thus adopted into Christian literature.

But, in general, Jewish apocalyptic was not congenial to Greek Christianity, which instinctively
found its own paths to apocalyptic expression of
various kinds. Indeed, the first book of this more
Greek kind followed almost immediately upon the
publication of the Revelation of John and dealt not so
much with the guilt and doom of empires as with the
sense of sin and the need of repentance in the human
heart. The Revelation of John was, of course, already
well known in Rome in the last years of the first century, as I Peter clearly shows, and no doubt had the

general effect of leading Christian prophets to write down and publish their oracles; but its specific influence upon them was singularly slight.[1]

The continued influence of Hebrews upon the Roman church is reflected in the *Shepherd* of Hermas, written *The Shepherd of Hermas* in the last years of the first century, A.D. 95–100. Hermas was a Christian prophet in Rome, who understood Hebrews to teach that there could be no repentance for serious sins committed after baptism. The real meaning of Hebrews was that if anyone renounced his faith, and became an apostate, he could never regain it and re-enter the church. Hermas records his interviews with the angel of repentance, who appeared to him in the guise of a shepherd and taught him that there might be one repentance for sin after baptism, but only one. It is from the prominence of the shepherd in the work that it takes its name.

Hermas was or had been a slave in Rome. His work, which was probably a gradual growth, begins with five *Visions*, in which repentance is emphasized. In the third the church appears to him as a woman and shows him a great tower being built, which also symbolizes the church. In the fourth he is shown a hideous dragon, which foreshadows persecution. In the fifth, which is entitled an apocalypse and formed the introduction to the *Commands* and *Parables* that make up the bulk of the book, the Shepherd appears.

[1] Recent editors of the *Shepherd* of Hermas report only one line reminiscent of the Revelation—*Vis.* iv. 2. 1—while the Revelation, less than half the length of the *Shepherd*, is credited with at least seventy reminiscences of Daniel alone.

The Shepherd gives Hermas a new series of twelve commandments, diffuse in style and quite unlike the Ten Commandments of the Mosaic Law. In general, they explain how the repentant Christian should live. They are followed by ten Parables, which deal with the operations of repentance and its theological bearings. It is characteristic of the free spirit of the early Christian prophets that Hermas is not deterred by the Jewish Ten Commandments from offering twelve more or by the parables of Jesus from hazarding ten of his own. Indeed, he shows much less influence of Paul and the early gospels and even of the Greek Old Testament than we might expect. The Revelation of John is full of reflections of the Old Testament, but this second of Christian apocalypses shows very few indeed.

Hermas is described by the Muratorian writer (*ca.* A.D. 200) as having been the brother of Pius, the bishop of Rome, and as having written during his episcopate, A.D. 140–55. But recent study has shown that the *Shepherd* was written long before; in fact, at the very end of the first century, or very early in the second.

The second Vision states that it was the business of Clement to send copies of the Visions to other churches and these first visions may go back to the last part of his leadership, or episcopate, which covered the years 88–97. Hermas certainly expected them to be widely circulated among the churches, and his book did have a great vogue in the second century. It found its way into more than one early form of the New Testament and, translated into Latin, even influenced Dante, whose guides Beatrice and Vergil evidently reflect Rhoda and the Shepherd, who revealed divine truth to Hermas.

While Hermas has come down to us in Ethiopic and in two Latin versions, no complete Greek form of it has come to light. It stood at the end of the New Testament in the Sinaitic manuscript (fourth century), but the last three-fourths of it are lost from that codex. The Athos manuscript of it (fifteenth century), part of which is now at Leipzig, preserves about nine-tenths of the Greek but in an inaccurate and badly written text. The Michigan papyrus (third century) contains almost a fourth of the Greek text but does not include the part missing in the Athos manuscript. More than a dozen smaller pieces, on parchment or papyrus, have come to light, some of them covering parts missing from these more considerable manuscripts. These numerous fragments from Egypt reflect its wide popularity there, already evidenced by its acceptance as Scripture by Clement of Alexandria, Origen, and the scribe of the Sinaitic manuscript. But Tertullian, at Carthage, though he at first accepted it, later repudiated and condemned it. Irenaeus accepted it as Scripture; Eusebius classed it among the rejected writings, and Athanasius excluded it from the New Testament but recommended it for private reading by new converts.

The *Shepherd* is the second Christian apocalypse, but, unlike the Revelation of John, it owes little or nothing to the old Jewish apocalyptic; it is not even pseudonymous; in fact, it possesses a naïve freshness and originality that along with its evident sincerity gave it its early influence, which reached not only to Egypt and Abyssinia but in later centuries, through the sect of the Manichees, as far east as Chinese Turkestan.

The book manifestly gathers up the prophetic utterances composed by Hermas over a series of years. The Michigan papyrus throws new light upon the literary development of his work, for when complete this manuscript evidently began with what we know as Vision 5 (which is called an "apocalypse" in the manuscripts) and contained the twelve Commandments and the ten Parables.

At least three stages can be traced in the growth of Hermas' work. He first published Visions 1–4, of which he was told to give one copy to Clement, for churches elsewhere, and one to Grapte, for the widows and orphans, while he was himself to read it with the elders to the local church. A few years later he completed the *Shepherd* proper, beginning with a short "apocalypse" (which we know as Vision 5) and including the twelve Commandments and the ten Parables. This is the form preserved in the third-century Michigan papyrus. Finally, the earlier work was prefixed to this, and in this longest form Hermas appeared in the later Greek manuscripts (Sinai, Athos) and in the versions. There may have been even more stages in its publication (Parables 9 and 10 sound like later additions by Hermas), but this much is now certain. The whole makes a work much longer than any single book in the New Testament.

It has been suggested that Hermas got his idea of a shepherd as a revealer of truth from the *Poimandres*, or *Shepherd of Men*, written perhaps toward the end of the first Christian century—the most ancient of the Greek theosophical tracts ascribed to Hermes Trismegistus, meaning Thoth, the Egyptian god of wisdom. It is more likely, however, that if Hermas knew anything about that Hermetic teaching, it was through hearing it talked about. He was not a great reader, even of the books Christians most prized; but he would hear of shepherds, in the religious sense, just from going to church, where the Psalms ("The Lord is my Shepherd") and the prophets would have familiarized him with the idea of which he makes so much. The Epistle to the Hebrews, so well known to the Roman church in his day, spoke of Christ as the great shepherd of the sheep. The Roman church itself, in I Peter (2:25) had recently described Christ as "the shepherd and guardian of your souls." And while Hermas identifies his shepherd not with Christ but with the angel of repentance, Christian ministers were already spoken of as shepherds (Eph. 4:11). Moreover, Hermas is far from being interested in theosophical speculations about the divine wisdom and intelligence. His concern is practical—with his own sins and weaknesses and with those of his wife and children and of his brethren in the Roman church.

The mention of Clement as still active in the church carries the first stage of the work back to A.D. 95 or 96, while the statement of the Elkesaite Alcibiades that a new repentance was proclaimed in the Roman church

in the third year of Trajan[2] strongly suggests that the
second work, the *Shepherd* proper, came out in A.D.
100. It might well be described as proclaiming a new
repentance.

The statement of the Muratorian writer that Hermas was the brother of Pius, bishop of Rome in A.D.
140–55, is on every account difficult to accept. Hermas seems from his opening words to have been exposed as an infant and picked up and reared for the
slave market. It is hard to see how any brother of
such a foundling could be identified, though it is not
absolutely impossible. Certainly he did not write the
Shepherd at as late a date as A.D. 140–55, as the Muratorian says.

With this work of Hermas the Roman church
rounded out its literary contribution to first-century
Christianity—the Gospel of Mark, I Peter, I Clement,
and the *Shepherd*, a varied group of writings; a gospel,
a church letter, a general letter to a whole province,
and a revelation. No wonder Ignatius ten or fifteen
years later can write to the Roman church, "You have
taught others."[3]

Direct divine revelation, or apocalyptic, was an
idea familiar to the early church from the Hebrew
prophets Ezekiel and Zechariah and from
Jewish apocalypses like Daniel and Enoch.
The Gospel of Mark, about A.D. 70, contained a striking apocalyptic passage
(chap. 13), but the Revelation of John, about A.D. 93,
was the first Christian apocalypse and was much in-

*The Reve-
lation of
Peter*

2 Hippolytus *Ref.* 9:13 (Eng. 9:8).   3 Ignatius *Rom.* 3:1.

debted to Daniel. The *Shepherd* of Hermas also took the form of a revelation, though it was little influenced by Jewish literature.

Sometime between A.D. 125 and 150 a Greek Christian wrote an apocalypse in the name of Peter. He is the first to introduce pagan ideas of heaven and hell into Christian literature. The Orphic and Pythagorean religions had much to say about the punishments to be inflicted in the other world upon sinful men and women, and these hideous pictures this Christian writer lays hold of to warn men of the awful personal dangers of sin. Daniel and John had been concerned with the ultimate triumph of the Kingdom of God, but the *Revelation of Peter* is devoted to the precise punishments to be expected after death by individuals who commit certain sins. While he has something to say of the rewards of the faithful, he is principally a preacher of hell-fire, a subject on which the teachers of Orphic and Pythagorean religion had had so much to say; indeed, we meet it as early as the *Odyssey* of Homer, where, in Book 11, Odysseus visits the underworld and sees the punishments endured by Sisyphus and Tantalus. Perhaps the writer had belonged to one of these older Greek religions before he became a Christian.

The *Revelation* runs somewhat as follows: Peter relates how, as Jesus sat upon the Mount of Olives, Peter and the other disciples asked him about the signs that would precede his coming and the end of the world. Jesus answers his questions, for the most part in language taken from the Four Gospels. There is

also some use of the Revelation of John, which must
have suggested the writing of the *Revelation of Peter*.
The day of judgment and the triumphal coming of
Christ are described. The wicked will be punished in
ways corresponding to their particular sins. Demons,
led by Ezrael and Tartaruchus, will torment them
with serpents, worms, and vultures, on fiery wheels
and in rivers of fire. Then follows a briefer description of the perfumed garden, full of beautiful trees and
blessed fruits, where the redeemed will be found.

Short as it is, the *Revelation of Peter* is full of reflections of earlier Christian and Jewish writings. The
Ezra Apocalypse in II Esdras (5:33–35), written probably about A.D. 100, is clearly reflected, but an even
better *terminus a quo* is afforded by the writer's use of
the Fourfold Gospel, which appeared toward A.D. 120.
The book cannot therefore be earlier than A.D. 125.[4]

On the other hand, it is evidently used in the recently discovered *Epistle of the Apostles* (chap. 16), where
the coming of the Messiah is described in language so
much like that in the *Revelation of Peter*. The *Epistle* is
probably to be dated between A.D. 140 and 160. The
Revelation of Peter is also reflected in II Peter, a work of
about the same date as the *Epistle of the Apostles*. It is
also used in the *Acts of Paul*, especially in III Corinthians (*ca.* A.D. 160–70). These literary facts fix the
date of the *Revelation of Peter* in the quarter-century
between A.D. 125 and 150.

The *Revelation of Peter* is first mentioned in the Mura-

---

[4] Weinel's argument, in Hennecke, *Neutestamentliche Apokryphen*, p. 317,
that the false Christ mentioned is Bar-Cochba, and hence the *terminus
a quo* is pushed down to A.D. 135, is not convincing.

torian fragment, a Roman list of books that may be
read in church, from about the end of the second century, where it stands after the Revelation of John,
with the warning that "some of our people will not
have it read in church." Clement of Alexandria, about
the same time, accepted it as the work of Peter:
"Peter says in the *Revelation*" (*Prophetic Extracts* 41:2;
48:1). Early in the third century it is quoted or para-
phrased at some length in the *Acts of Thomas* (chaps.
55–57). It stands at the end of the *Clermont List*, representing Egyptian usage about A.D. 300, which closes
with the Revelation of John, the Acts of the Apostles,
the *Shepherd*, the *Acts of Paul*, and the *Revelation of
Peter*. Methodius, of Olympus in Lycia, who died in
311, makes use of it, and Eusebius (A.D. 326) reckons it
among the rejected writings (*Church History* iii. 25. 4).
Macarius of Magnesia, early in the fifth century,
mentions it and puts its words into the mouth of his
heathen adversary. Sozomen, in the fifth century,
says it was read every year on Good Friday in some
churches of Palestine (*Church History* vii. 19). In the
Stichometry of Nicephorus (*ca.* A.D. 850) it follows the
Revelation of John among the disputed books. It is
mentioned again by name in an old Latin sermon of
uncertain date on the ten bridesmaids. Its influence
continued down the centuries, strongly affecting
Dante, in the *Divine Comedy*, with its accounts of
heaven and hell (A.D. 1300). Gustave Doré's fearful
pictures illustrating Dante owe much indirectly to
the *Revelation of Peter*, and there is a far-off echo of the
high esteem at first enjoyed by this little book in the

fact that it finally found refuge in the closing section of the Ethiopic New Testament.

While the *Revelation of Peter* is mentioned by this long series of early Christian writers, the book had long since disappeared when in 1886 a part of it was discovered in a small parchment manuscript in a tomb near Akhmim, in Upper Egypt, together with a considerable fragment of the *Gospel of Peter*, in a hand not later than the fifth century. The old stichometrical lists gave the length of the *Revelation of Peter* as from 270 (in the *Clermont List* of A.D. 300) to 300 lines (in the Nicephorus list, A.D. 850), so that this discovery put in our hands almost one-half of the little document, which must have been about four-fifths the length of Galatians.

The contents of this fragment were later recognized in the so-called *Books of Clement*[5] which form an appendix to the New Testament in Ethiopic manuscripts of it, and it was found that the whole of the *Revelation of Peter* was actually imbedded in the Ethiopic text but that in the Greek fragment found at Akhmim the descriptions of heaven and hell had been transposed; it gives the picture of the saved first and then that of the lost; while the Ethiopic has them in the reverse order. A comparison of the Ethiopic with the Greek suggests that the Greek fragment is from a condensed form of the book.

We also get some light on what the little book contained from some quotations from it in Clement of

---

[5] The *Books of Clement*, extant also in Arabic, contain a series of revelations supposed to have been communicated to Clement by Peter.

Alexandria (*Prophetic Extracts*), from the *Sibylline Oracles*, late second or early third century (2:190–338), from Methodius of Olympus, in the third century (*Symposium* 2:6), and from Macarius of Magnesia, about A.D. 400 (*Apocritica* 4:6, 7). There is also a small parchment leaf in the Bodleian Library, containing twenty-six short lines of the Greek text, and a double leaf from the same codex, probably of the fourth century, in the Rainer Collection in Vienna. The discovery of the complete Greek text of this early apocalypse would be a great boon to the study of early Christian literature.

The Sibyl of Cumae or elsewhere was a Greek source of revelation, mentioned, though with disapproval,

The Sibyl-line Oracles as early as Heraclitus of Ephesus (500 B.C.). Early writers knew of but one, but gradually a number came to be recognized, and shrewd sayings of a portentous character cast in Greek hexameters floated about the Greek world. Jewish writers laid hold of the idea about the middle of the second century before Christ, no doubt embodying not a little pagan material with their own, and continued to express themselves in connected Sibylline poetry on into the fourth Christian century.

Hermas, about A.D. 100, was the first Christian writer to mention the Sibyl, and Justin, Tatian, Athenagoras, and many others did so after him. Christians were already introducing Christian color and passages of their own composing into the Sibylline books, for Celsus, about A.D. 177–78, in his *True Account*, Origen says, charged them with so doing

(*Against Celsus* vii. 53; cf. v. 61). So the Sibylline books came to be a combination of pagan, Jewish, and Christian materials.

They eventually numbered fifteen, of which Books 9, 10, and 15 are lost. While Celsus may be right in saying that Christians were already at work upon the Sibyllines by his day, most of the Christian expansions of them and interpolations in them probably belong to the third century—the time when Christian hands, having previously given a Christian color to the corpus of Jewish apocalypses known to us as II Esdras by providing it with a Christian preface, were adding to it a Christian conclusion.

The exact determination of the Christian additions to the Sibylline books is difficult; Books 1, 2, and 5 have undergone Christian revision and expansion; Books 6, 7, and most of 8 (vss. 217–500) are Christian compositions; the last section begins with the well-known acrostic "Jesus Christ; Son of God, Savior" (vss. 217–44).[6] Books 11–14 also show strong Christian color.

The Christianized Sibyllines had small claims to literary character, being for the most part crude and unskilful in style. While some learned Christians mentioned them, their chief public was among the less educated parts of the churches and may be compared to those who relish the prophecies of Mother Shipton and her successors in modern times. They played little part in the progress of Christian literature.

---

[6] Ἰησοῦς Χρειστὸς θεοῦ υἱὸς σωτήρ. The initials of these words, ιχθυς, spelled the Greek word for "fish" and led to the use of the fish as a Christian symbol.

About the middle of the third century some Gnostic in Egypt composed the curious book known to us,

The Pistis Sophia through a Coptic recast found in the Askew codex, as the *Pistis Sophia*, or *Faith Wisdom*. It represents Jesus as living with his disciples for eleven or twelve years after the Resurrection and telling them a great many things about sin and salvation, especially in response to the questions asked him by Mary Magdalene. The work consists of four books, though the fourth should perhaps be given another name and is evidently earlier than the rest; it deals with matters immediately after the Resurrection.

In the earlier books, especially Books 1 and 2, Jesus' words have to do with the experiences of Pistis Sophia, which evidently typifies the human soul, in her efforts to reach heaven and find salvation. The book recalls passages in Epiphanius' account of certain types of Gnostic teaching, for instance, *Heresies* xxvi. 3, 6; xxxvii–xl. The writer was evidently a Valentinian, a Barbelo Gnostic, of the Ophitic-Sethian type. Five of the *Odes of Solomon* are quoted in the work, as are also the *Books of Jeu*, which Carl Schmidt has identified in the first two books in the Coptic Codex Brucianus.

As the principal authentic work of Gnosticism that has come down to us, the *Pistis Sophia* gives a striking picture of the extraordinary vagaries of Gnostic speculation that were rife in the Christian world from the middle of the second century onward.

CHAPTER IV

GOSPELS

"The church," said Origen, "has four gospels, the sects very many, one of which is entitled 'According to the Egyptians,' another 'According to the Twelve Apostles.' Basilides dared to write a gospel and give it his name. . . . . I know a gospel that is called 'According to Thomas,' and one 'According to Matthias,' and we have read many others."

The Apocryphal Gospels

The gospel is Christianity's first contribution to literary types. The primitive oral gospel may have originated the type, but its first written embodiment was the Gospel of Mark, from which every other gospel inside or outside the New Testament was directly or indirectly descended. To lose sight of this is to miss the originality of the gospel as a literary type, which is the most massive literary fact about the whole gospel literature.

It was not the writing of the individual gospels of Mark, Matthew, and John, however, but the publication of them with Luke in a collection, that stimulated the production of the uncanonical gospels. Luke-Acts was much more than a gospel, and the separation of its first volume from the second not only enriched the great gospel corpus but left the Acts by itself, to form

The Four-fold Gospel

the pattern for the Acta (Actus) literature that was
to come. But the publication of the Fourfold Gospel, probably about A.D. 115–20, set the gospel type,
and while, from one point of view, it seemed to close
the list of gospels with a commanding group of four,
from another it offered a composite of the gospel type
that invited imitation. For one thing it showed the
immense effectiveness of the gospel as a type of literature, by exhibiting a collection of gospels, and for
another, it seemed almost to invite the production of
further gospels by its closing lines: "There are many
other things that Jesus did, so many in fact that if
they were all written out, I do not suppose that the
world itself would hold the books that would have to
be written."

Not that the writer of these lines intended to suggest the writing of further gospels; they are part of the
epilogue of the Fourth Gospel, probably added when
it was combined with the earlier local gospels into the
great quartette. They are in fact the *Finis* of the
Fourfold Gospel and were doubtless intended to anticipate any doubt or opposition that the new gospel
might encounter by its very novelty, since few of the
prospective readers of the combined gospels would
have known more than one or possibly two of them
before and might well be suspicious of the new, un-
familiar material the group of gospels would in-
evitably offer. But as soon as the churches became
familiar with the Four Gospels, this closing sentence
might well suggest that the door was still open to new
gospel narratives. Certainly a whole flock of Chris-

tian writers soon undertook to write new gospels, and none of them seems to have escaped the influence of one or more of the canonical gospels. Indeed, they were all in some degree imitators of them.

The idea that any early Christian anywhere might at any time have set out independently to write a gospel without ever having seen one loses sight of the fact that a gospel was by no means an inevitable thing; still less a commonplace or a matter of course. It was a definite literary origination for which no adequate literary precedents can be found. This is the distinction of the Gospel of Mark. It was soon improved and enlarged by the author of Matthew, and Luke still later imitated it in the first volume of his historical sketch of the beginnings of the movement. Then, twenty years later, John returned to the gospel as a literary form and revived it, and, soon after, the combination of his gospel with the three old ones recalled Christian attention to the gospel type of literature and stimulated literary-minded Christians to cast their work in the gospel form. This is the much-neglected background of the uncanonical gospels.

The makers of the uncanonical gospels probably aimed at unifying the gospels, to rid them of their repetitions and confusions, and at the same time at enriching them. The question at once arises whether they were in possession of any authentic material comparable in historical value with that in the Synoptic Gospels. The apocryphal gospels arose outside of Palestine, in Greek circles which can have had little if any authentic historical material apart from

the canonical gospels. The additions they contain
are seldom remarkable for originality or vigor; some
of the Oxyrhynchus sayings and of those in the *Gospel
of the Hebrews* are exceptions. Sometimes, of course,
they aimed at using the gospel type of literature as
a vehicle for schismatic doctrines, but it would seem
from the fragments that come to light from time to
time that this was not ordinarily the purpose their
writers had in view.

It was in beginning his first *Homily on Luke* that
Origen said, "The church has four gospels, the sects
very many, one of which is called 'According to the Egyptians.'" There seem
to have been at least three uncanonical
gospels that were well known in Egypt
in the second century: the *Gospel accord-
ing to the Egyptians*, the *Gospel according to the Hebrews*,
and the *Gospel of Peter*.

*The Gospel
according to
the Egyp-
tians*

The *Gospel of the Egyptians* and the *Gospel of the Hebrews* seem to have been so called because one circulated among the gentile Christians of Egypt and the
other among the Jewish. Both were written in Greek.
We know them only from a few fragments. *Egyptians*
was mentioned not only by Origen but by his great
predecessor, Clement of Alexandria, at the very beginning of the third century. Clement says it was read
and accepted by the ascetic sect of the Encratites, and
quoted from it a conversation of Jesus with Salome,
of a very ascetic character (*Miscellanies* 3:6 and 9), dis-
couraging the bearing of children. Clement quotes:
"For the Lord himself, being asked by someone when

his kingdom should come, said, 'When the two shall be one, and the outside as the inside, and the male with the female neither male nor female'" Again, "The Lord said to Salome when she inquired, 'How long shall death prevail?'—'As long as you women bear.'" To which she seems to have replied, "Would I have done well then in not bearing?" Salome was the proud and ambitious mother of James and John.[1]

Almost half a century earlier some of these words were quoted in what we know as *II Clement*—perhaps a letter from the church of Rome to the church of Corinth, when Soter and Dionysius were their respective bishops. At any rate, it shows how wide the influence of *Egyptians* had become, even by the middle of the second century. What is most remarkable is that *II Clement* does not dismiss it as heretical or inferior to the Four Gospels, though at this very time, as Justin shows, these latter were regularly read in church as Scripture.[2] It is evident that *Egyptians* was not at first regarded as heretical, that is, as the distinctive document of a sect, but gradually became so. Our own gospels are not wholly free from strongly ascetic utterances, for example, Matt. 19:12.

The "Sayings of Jesus," written early in the third century and found at Oxyrhynchus in 1897, each introduced with the words "Jesus says," have some resemblance to the known fragments of the *Gospel according to the Egyptians*. They are evidently selections from early gospels and show the use of some of the canonical

[1] Matt. 20:20; 27:56, cf. Mark 15:40.   [2] *Apology* lxvi. 3; lxvii. 3.

gospels, but their connection with the *Gospel according to the Egyptians*, while altogether probable, has not been established. The Oxyrhynchus gospel fragment (*Oxyrhynchus Papyri* iv. 655 [third century]), however, is very probably from this gospel, but it consists of only a few sentences.

It seems clear that the *Gospel according to the Egyptians* was written in Egypt in the period of perhaps forty years between the appearance of the Fourfold Gospel there and its rise to supremacy and the position of Scripture. It is easy to understand how with the brilliant example of the Four Gospels before them, and with the virtual invitation to further gospel writing with which they closed, Egyptian Christians might have written such a book, perhaps about 130–40, and for a time have preferred it. It ranked as one more local gospel and was so used in *II Clement*. But by the time of Clement of Alexandria, about A.D. 200, its ascetic tone had led the Egyptian Encratites to adopt it, and a generation later Origen heads his list of heretical gospels with it. Hippolytus of Rome, in his *Refutation of All Heresies* (v. 7. 9 [Eng. v. 2]), written about A.D. 225, says that the Naasenes, or serpent worshipers, support their doctrine of what may be called the fluidity of the soul by appealing to it. Later still, Epiphanius, toward the end of the fourth century, describes the Sabellians as claiming its authority for their teaching that Father, Son, and Holy Spirit are "one and the same" (*Heresies* lxxii. 2). This was, in fact, the central position of their founder Sabellius himself.

A complete copy of this ancient gospel in the original Greek or in an early version is one of the desiderata of patristic study, but it was clearly secondary to the Fourfold Gospel and influenced by it.

The *Gospel according to the Hebrews* is believed to have been so called because of its use by the Jewish Christians of Egypt, but the name may really be no more than an inference from the very Jewish character of some of its contents. Jerome, writing about the end of the fourth century, says that he knew it only in Aramaic and himself translated it into Greek and Latin, but it was certainly current in Greek in the second century and was probably written in that language. We know it only from the quotations made from it by early Christian writers and from a few manuscript fragments which may, with some probability, be assigned to it.

The Gospel according to the Hebrews

Jerome declared that he found the book in Palestine, in use among the Nazarene Christians in Beroea in Syria, and that it was also preserved in the library of Pamphilus in Caesarea. The book was unfortunately confused with the supposed original Aramaic form of the Gospel of Matthew, and Jerome does not entirely escape this error. The fact is, the *Gospel of the Hebrews* borrowed so much from the Gospel of Matthew that they naturally had much in common; but such portions as appear in *Hebrews* are so manifestly elaborated and built up that there can be no doubt that it drew from Matthew, not Matthew from it. The influence of Luke may also be traced in the *Gospel of the He-*

brews;[3] indeed, it is altogether probable that its writer knew the Fourfold Gospel. That he should have independently struck upon the gospel type of literature and created a written gospel without ever having seen one is in itself extremely improbable, and, when his manifest indebtedness to Matthew and Luke is observed, it becomes impossible.

The *Gospel of the Hebrews*, like that of the *Egyptians*, must have been written in the period between the publication of the Fourfold Gospel and its arrival at the status of Scripture, that is, the time when it came to be read in church side by side with the Jewish scriptures, about the middle of the second century.[4] It was about seven-eighths the length of the Gospel of Matthew, containing 2,200 *stichoi*, or lines of Homeric length, against 2,500 in Matthew. It told of the baptism, the temptation, the Lord's Prayer, the man with the withered hand, the rich inquirer, the parable of the talents, and the resurrection. In every case its accounts show literary development as compared with those in the Four Gospels. Jesus is reluctant to go to John's baptism; he says he has no consciousness of sin. This carries the account in Matthew a long step further. In Matthew, John suggests his freedom from sin; in *Hebrews*, Jesus claims it himself. Mark's violent representation of the Spirit "flinging" or throwing Jesus into the wilderness is heightened here: Origen quotes *Hebrews* as saying, "My mother the

[3] See Pierson Parker, "A Proto-Lukan Basis for the Gospel according to the Hebrews," *Journal of Biblical Literature*, LIX (1940), 471–78.

[4] Justin *Apology* lxvii. 3.

Holy Spirit took me by one of my hairs and carried me up to the great mountain Tabor"—evidently for the temptation. This strange saying is usually explained by the fact that, in Hebrew, "Spirit" is feminine; but that does very little to account for an expression so shockingly out of keeping with Palestinian Jewish ways. It presents a divine Holy Family—father, mother, and son—much more like Egyptian religious ideas (Osiris, Isis, and their son Horus) than anything in Judaism. Indeed, it points to Egypt instead of Palestine. The grotesque carrying of Jesus by his hair (indicating his utter helplessness in the grip of the Spirit) recalls Ezekiel, seized by a lock of his hair and carried to Jerusalem (Ezek. 8:3), and the account in the story of Bel and the Dragon (vs. 36), of Habakkuk being lifted up by his hair by the angel of the Lord and carried from Judea to Babylon with the speed of the wind, to take food to Daniel, in the den of lions.

Of the three men intrusted with the talents, in *Hebrews* the first squanders his upon harlots and flute girls, the second increases his, and the third hides his in the ground. This is evidently an effort to improve upon the simpler story.

In dealing with the resurrection, according to Jerome *Hebrews* relates that Jesus said to Peter and those with him, "Feel of me, and see that I am not a bodiless demon" (*On Illustrious Men* 16). This curious saying, which recalls Jesus' words to Thomas in John 20:27, occurs also in Ignatius, *Smyrnaeans* 3:2, and, according to Origen (*First Principles*, prologue 8), in the *Teaching* (probably meaning *Preaching*) of Peter.

The question arises: In which of these works did the saying first appear? It is often assumed that Ignatius (A.D. 110–17) must have been quoting the *Gospel of the Hebrews*. But the *Preaching of Peter* was the earliest of the apologetic efforts of the ancient church and was written very early in the second century. It is much more probable that both Ignatius and the *Gospel of the Hebrews* derived this saying from it than that the *Gospel of the Hebrews* was written before the Fourfold Gospel collection was made and yet contained such marked affinities with both Luke and Matthew as have been pointed out in it. The old view that it may have been a source for Matthew and Luke is negatived by the elaborated character of its presentation of their material; at almost every point *Hebrews* has the ring of the secondary. Moreover, Ignatius describes the saying about the risen Jesus not being "an incorporeal demon" as addressed to "those about Peter," or, as we should say, Peter and those with him—a most natural way to introduce a quotation from the *Preaching of Peter*. The explanation of this perplexing matter seems to be that the *Preaching of Peter* was the tract Ignatius was quoting and that it was later one of the sources of the *Gospel of the Hebrews*, along with the Fourfold Gospel.

Not less singular is the other resurrection incident which Jerome found in this gospel (*On Illustrious Men* 2). It reads: "After the Lord had given the linen cloth to the servant of the high priest, he went to James and appeared to him, for James had sworn that he would not eat bread from the hour when he had drunk the Lord's cup until he should see him risen again from among those that sleep." A little later it goes on: "The Lord said, 'Bring a table and bread,'" and then "He took bread and blessed it and broke it and gave it to James the Just and said to him, 'My brother, eat your bread, for the Son of Man is risen from among those that sleep.'" This is plainly an effort to bring some of Jesus' family into the circle of his followers as early in the story as possible. It is true that, by the time of Paul's letters, James was active in the church at Jerusalem and had become one of the leaders even of the apostles (Gal. 1:19).

Eusebius in his *Church History* (iii. 39. 17) says that Papias, who flourished, about A.D. 135, in Hierapolis in Asia Minor, "related another story about a woman who was accused of many sins before the Lord, which is contained in the *Gospel according to the Hebrews*." This evidently refers to the incident about the adulterous woman which by the sixth century had crept into the Gospel of John at various places in the seventh chapter and later found its way also into some manuscripts of Luke. Its introduction into John was evidently to show that Jesus was not illiterate, as the Jews had intimated (7:15), though, of course, this is far from being the point of the original story. In Eusebius' time it had not yet found its way into any of the Four Gospels and was still known as a passage from the *Gospel of the Hebrews*. It first appears in John in the sixth-century Greco-Latin Codex of Beza.

Clement of Alexandria, writing early in the third century, quotes a very curious saying of Jesus which, he says, is found in the *Gospel of the Hebrews* (*Miscel-lanies* ii. 9. 45; v. 14. 96): "He will not cease seeking until he finds; and when he finds he will be amazed; and when he is amazed he will reign [i.e., enter the kingdom (cf. I Cor. 4:8)], and when he reigns, he will rest." The extraordinary thing is that exactly this saying has been found in the papyrus fragment of Jesus' sayings found at Oxyrhynchus in 1903. This shows that some at least of those sayings, and per-haps all of them, were taken from the *Gospel of the Hebrews* and creates a strong probability that the other Oxyrhynchus logia found in 1897 may have came from the same work. It is true, one papyrus is from a leaf-book (that found in 1897) and the other is from a roll; and that the latter has a title connecting it with the name of Thomas. But recent study inclines to the view that both papyri are from one collection of say-ings and that this collection was principally if not wholly based upon the *Gospel of the Hebrews*.

The second gospel fragment from Oxyrhynchus (*Oxyrhynchus Papyri* v. 840), a tiny parchment leaf, written in the fourth or fifth century, allies itself by its phraseology ("harlots and flute girls") with the *Gospel of the Hebrews* and, notwithstanding its disre-gard of temple arrangements and practices (all discon-tinued, of course, as early as A.D. 70) is probably from that gospel. Its diffuse style and evidently secondary character accord with this identification; and if, as we have argued, *Hebrews* was composed in Egypt, such ignorance of temple conditions would be natural enough. That it should have survived that long is not

strange, for it seems to have contained nothing definitely heretical. The fragment tells of a conversation
between Jesus and a chief priest about spiritual as
against ceremonial purification.

The story of the *Gospel of the Hebrews* would seem,
therefore, to be that it arose in Egypt, in Greek, very
soon after the appearance of the Fourfold Gospel, or
between A.D. 120 and 130. Eusebius implies that it
was known to Papias of Hierapolis, about A.D. 135,
and says that Hegesippus made some use of it in writing his *Memoirs*, A.D. 175–85 (*Church History* iv. 22. 7).
Clement of Alexandria, soon after 200, quotes it with
respect, but Origen is dubious about it: "If any accept
the *Gospel according to the Hebrews*" (*On John* ii. 4). In
the third century Christian opinion in Egypt was evidently going against it, as Origen shows, and this may
have been the reason the Oxyrhynchus collection of
sayings was made, probably early in the century, to
preserve what was most valued in it; the earlier
Oxyrhynchus papyrus, 1, is a leaf from a skil-
fully written book and comes from the first half of
the third century. The Greek form of it seems to have
begun to disappear early in the fourth century, before
the rising authority of the Fourfold Gospel, for Eusebius lists it among the "disputed books" (*Church History* iii. 25. 5). Jerome, toward the close of the century,
could not find a Greek copy of it but saw an Aramaic
text of it in Palestine, which, he says, he translated
into Greek and Latin, probably meaning for the parts
he wished to copy or use in his works. This Aramaic
version, so often regarded as the original, was probably made for the use of the Jewish Christian sects—

perhaps Ebionites, more probably Nazarenes—who in
the third century were using the book, and finally
gave their name to it, so that it came to be known as
the *Gospel of the Nazarenes*. Jerome's contemporary,
Epiphanius (who died in 403), says in his *Heresies*
that the "Nazaraeans," or Gnostic Jewish Christians,
used a gospel resembling Matthew, which they call
"According to the Hebrews" (xxx. 3).

Probably in his days the tiny Oxyrhynchus copy,
miserably written, was produced, in some obscure
quarter, since no Greek text of it came to Jerome's
notice, but only the Aramaic.

This is virtually its last appearance. What Theodoret says about it in the first half of the fifth century
(†458) he derived from earlier writers. The *Gospel of
the Hebrews* fades from sight, as the document of an
obscure sect. The canon list known as the *Stichometry
of Nicephorus* (*ca.* A.D. 850) lists it among the disputed
books, along with the Revelation of John, the *Revelation of Peter* and the *Letter of Barnabas*.

A copy of the *Gospel of the Hebrews*, either in its
Aramaic version or its Greek original, is one of the
desiderata of patristic study.

The feeling that Jesus was too divine to suffer a
humiliating and agonizing death such as the gospels
The Gospel described led many Christians early in
according the second century to resort to the view
to Peter that he only seemed to do so but really
took refuge in another form, leaving his
material body at the mercy of his executioners. This
startling doctrine, as we have seen, was particularly
opposed and condemned in the letters of Ignatius and

the Gospel and Letters of John, which insist that
Jesus Christ has indeed come in the flesh, that is, in
human form (I John 4:2; II John, 7).

The appearance of the Fourfold Gospel, with its
closing words so suggestive of the other gospels that
might be written, may have suggested to some holder
of these Docetic views, as they were called, the idea of
writing a gospel that should embody them and tell the
story, at least of Jesus' passion, from the Docetic point
of view. It was probably in Syria, and between A.D.
120 and 140, that some Docetist produced such a book,
assuming the great name of Peter and writing it in the
first person: "I, Simon Peter, and Andrew my brother,
took our nets and went off to the sea," as the one
fragment of the book that has come down to us reads
in its last lines.

Fifty years ago all that we knew of this book was
gathered from the brief mentions of it in the writings
of Serapion, Origen, Eusebius, and Theodoret. But
in 1886 a fragment of it was discovered by a French
expedition in a tomb at Akhmim, in Upper Egypt, and
in 1892 it was published, along with a Greek mathe-
matical papyrus, which in the eyes of its discoverers
rather overshadowed it. But English and German
scholars were not slow in discovering its extraordinary importance, for here at last was a veritable fragment of this long-lost gospel. It was written upon
five leaves of a little parchment book, which contained also a portion of the *Apocalypse of Peter* and the
first thirty-two chapters of the *Book of Enoch*, the first
appearance of that work in Greek in modern times.

The fragment of the *Gospel of Peter* began abruptly with the handwashing incident at the trial of Jesus, continued with an account of the crucifixion and the resurrection, and broke off as Peter and some other disciples were setting out on a fishing expedition, evidently the one recorded in the last chapter—the epilogue—of John. The use of every one of the canonical gospels, as well as their united form, completed by the addition of John, chapter 21, is unmistakable. Their accounts are often heightened by slight touches, chiefly to enhance the guilt of the Jews, but there is little really new material.

Jesus while being crucified held his peace, as though he felt no pain, and on the cross he cries, "My power, my power, you have forsaken me," and is taken up.[5] After the entombment, two figures descend from heaven in the night and open the tomb and bring Jesus out. Their heads reach to heaven, but his head overpassed the heavens, and a cross followed him. The cross declares that he has preached to them that sleep —an allusion to the Descent into Hades, reflected in Ephesians and I Peter.

Some scholars have suggested that the incident of the adulterous woman (John 7:53—8:11) was derived from this gospel, and some hold that the Oxyrhynchus sayings were taken from it, but we have seen that these are more probably derived from the *Gospel of the*

---

[5] This goes back to a different translation of the Hebrew of Ps. 22:1, which is quoted in Matthew (27:46) and Mark (15:34) in the Aramaic, the spoken language of Jesus' day. The Aramaic *Eloi* means "my God," but the Hebrew *Eli* was sometimes understood, as in the version of Aquila, as meaning "my power."

Hebrews. Dr. Vernon Bartlet refers the Oxyrhynchus gospel fragment 1224, 2, a badly broken papyrus from the fourth century, to this gospel, which he thought emphasized those portions of the gospel story in which Peter was conspicuous, such as his great confession of Jesus as Christ, his denial of him, and his conversation with him on the seashore (John 21:15–20) on the eve of which the Akhmim fragment breaks off.

Justin, who was converted at Ephesus about A.D. 135, and wrote his *Apology*, at Rome, soon after 150, probably knew the *Gospel of Peter*, for he occasionally uses its phraseology. But Serapion, who became bishop of Antioch toward the end of the second century (A.D. 191), is the first Christian writer to mention it by name. He had heard of its currency in the church at Rhossus, near by, and took occasion to examine it. He wrote a letter about it, probably to that church, admitting that it contained much that was in accord with the accepted gospels, but pointing out the heretical character of some of its contents. He recognized it as a work of the Docetists. His letter is unfortunately lost, but an important part of it is quoted in Eusebius' *Church History* (vi. 12).

Although Serapion's great Egyptian contemporary, Clement of Alexandria, makes no mention of the *Gospel of Peter*, Origen, in the first half of the third century, refers to it, along with the *Book of James*, as supporting the idea so popular in modern fiction, that Jesus' brothers were the sons of Joseph not by Mary but by a former wife (*On Matthew* 13:55.

While Eusebius, early in the fourth century (A.D.

326), mentions the *Gospel of Peter* and records Serapion's investigation of it, it is doubtful whether he actually knew the book himself. He classes it among the books cited by the schismatics in the name of the apostles (*Church History* iii. 25. 6) and says that no church writer has made use of it. Still later, Theodoret, a Mesopotamian bishop, early in the fifth century, refers to the *Gospel according to Peter* as in use by the Jewish sect of the Nazaraeans, or Nazarenes, but in this he was probably misinformed; he does not seem to have known the book himself.

When the Akhmim parchment which preserves the fragment (174 lines) of its text was written, the gospel was already disappearing; the little manuscript is complete as it stands and was evidently copied from a fragment. The manuscript has been variously dated, but closer study of its hand shows it is probably not later than the fourth century. The *Gospel of Peter* was evidently already passing out of use and soon completely disappeared. It was almost the only apocryphal gospel written pseudonymously in the first person in the name of an apostle, and one of the few that were produced to present sectarian views in gospel form.

Sometime in the second quarter of the second century a Greek Christian in Egypt wrote a gospel, or

The British Museum Gospel rather he condensed the Four Gospels into one, omitting their numerous duplications of material, which amounted to at least half their total length, and combining with them some new units, either remnants of Palestinian tradition about Jesus and his work, which

had found their way to Egypt, or new products of
Christian reflection. He had no heretical or schismatic
ax to grind but was controlled by a practical purpose
to produce a gospel which should be at the same time
shorter than the fourfold one and also richer. The
possibility of this must have been immediately apparent to the earliest users of the Fourfold Gospel, as
it has been to so many others—ancient, medieval, and
modern. But whereas combiners of the four, like
Tatian and his later successors, in interweaving the
Gospels into one, hesitated to add new elements of
lesson or story, this Greek evangelist embellished his
narrative with new details in the old stories and even
with some stories altogether new. No one had yet
come to think of the gospels as Scripture, like the Law
and the Prophets, and so not to be tampered with, and
the new gospel writer had no inhibitions of that kind.
He saw how the Fourfold Gospel could be improved,
as he thought, and so he blended the four into one.

Who he was we do not know, nor can we as yet
identify his work with any of the numerous new gospels mentioned by early Christian writers. One would
expect it to be the *Gospel of the Egyptians*, but it does
not show the encratite or ascetic leanings which
marked that book. And yet, the five columns of the
work that came to light in 1935 in the British Museum
are, of course, only a small fraction of the whole book,
and other parts of it may have shown heretical bias
of one kind or another; moreover, the *Gospel of the
Egyptians* was not thought of as heretical for a long
time. Neither can we identify it with the *Gospel of*

the Hebrews or with that of *Peter*, though it must have been written in the same generation with them.

Certainly the writer of this British Museum gospel had the Fourfold Gospel in his possession and made use of every one of the four.[6] He may not have used all they had to give him, but he did not hesitate to introduce some new material. There is very little probability that this was authentic Palestinian tradition from Jesus' immediate circle of followers. It was probably the product of Christian reflection, developed in the course of the century that had elapsed since Jesus' day. Its value, if we could recover it, would be for the light it would throw on Egyptian Christianity in its earliest period.

For the fragments of five or six leaves of this old papyrus book that came to light in 1935 cannot have been written later than A.D. 150, and the book of which they are a copy was probably composed ten or twenty years before, that is, about A.D. 130–40. It is surprising to find the Fourfold Gospel in circulation in Egypt at so early a date, and yet such an idea is strongly supported by the recently (1935) discovered Rylands fragment of a leaf from the Gospel of John from a papyrus leaf-book copied certainly before A.D. 150 and probably slightly older than the British Museum gospel fragments. We cannot be sure whether

---

[6] The idea of Professor C. H. Dodd that "as the number of apocryphal Gospel documents increases, it becomes less and less plausible to suppose that they all originated in expansions of material derived from the canonical Gospels, assumed to be already familiar in Egypt" ("A New Gospel," *Bulletin of the John Rylands Library*, Vol. XX [1936]) seems to me the reverse of probable, in view of the amount of canonical material each one contains.

the John leaf is from a Fourfold Gospel or from a Gospel of John circulating by itself, but it is reasonable to suppose that, if John was in use in Egypt by A.D. 150, the other three gospels were also, for they seem to have generally gone together at that time.

The contents of the fragments may be briefly outlined. Jesus tells the rulers that the scriptures bear witness to him, so that Moses becomes their accuser. They protest that they do not know whence Jesus comes. In a second fragment the rulers try to seize him, but he slips from their hands. In another a leper explains how he caught the disease by eating with lepers at an inn, and Jesus cures him. In another the question of paying tribute to Rome is discussed. Another, badly broken, tells of Jesus on the bank of Jordan, but is obscure.

The impulse which the publication of the Four Gospels seems to have given to the writing of gospels was *The Gospel of Thomas* shared by schismatic and sectarian Christians as well as by those of standard types of belief; and, while Marcion (A.D. 140–50) contented himself with revising Luke and adopting it as his gospel, Gnostic leaders produced gospels all their own. One of these was the so-called *Gospel of Thomas*, which told the story of Jesus' childhood from the Gnostic point of view. These people believed that they had received through revelation a peculiar mystical knowledge, including such things as the names of the demons who opposed the soul's progress to heaven and the symbols and formulas necessary to enable it to subdue them on its upward way. A good deal of the old paganism was in this way brought into Christianity.

The best known of the Gnostic leaders were Basilides and Valentinus, and among the latter's followers was a certain Marcus whose adherents formed a sect of their own, which was well known by the time Irenaeus wrote his *Refutation of Gnosticism* (A.D. 181–89). He says that these Marcosians have produced a great mass of apocryphal writings to delude ignorant people. He quotes one curious story of theirs from what was evidently an infancy gospel: "When the Lord was a boy, learning his letters, and his teacher said, as they do, 'Say Alpha,' he answered, 'Alpha.' But when the teacher told him to say 'Beta,' the Lord answered, 'First tell me what Alpha is, and then I will tell you what Beta is.' They explain this as meaning that he alone knew the secret which he revealed under the form of Alpha."[7]

This story meets us several times in the second and third centuries, once as early as the *Epistle of the Apostles;* and, while Irenaeus does not say he found it in the *Gospel of Thomas*, it is most likely that he did.

The gospel is first mentioned by name in Origen, by A.D. 240 (*Homily 1 on Luke*): "There is also current a Gospel according to Thomas." His Roman contemporary, Hippolytus, in his *Refutation of Heresies*, quotes from the *Gospel according to Thomas* the saying, "He who seeks me will find me in children from seven years old on; for I am hidden there, and manifested in

[7] *Refutation* i. 20. 1.

the fourteenth age."[8] This may be an allusion to the dawn of adolescence.

Eusebius, in A.D. 326, mentions this gospel (*Church History* iii. 25. 6), listing it among the books cited by the heretics in the name of the apostles; and Cyril of Jerusalem, twenty-two years later (A.D. 348), says no one should read it, "for it is not by one of the twelve apostles but by one of the three wicked disciples of Mani" (*Catech*. vi. 31). Of course, this will not fit our gospel, for Mani did not begin to preach until about the time Origen ceased to write—A.D. 250. It is interesting to observe that a gospel of this name was connected by different writers with three different sects: with the Marcosians, it would seem, by Irenaeus; with the Naasenes (the serpent worshipers), by Hippolytus; and with the Manicheans, by Cyril.

The last we hear of this old heretical book is a mention of it in the so-called *Stichometry of Nicephorus*, a list of the books of scripture and apocrypha, giving the length of each one in *stichoi*, or lines of Homeric length, and probably dating from about A.D. 850. It lists the *Gospel according to Thomas* among the apocrypha and gives its length as 1,300 lines, or one-half the length of the Gospel of Luke.

This heretical *Gospel of Thomas* has not come down to us, but we possess a gospel of that name in a variety of forms, three Greek and one Latin, more or less closely related. Translations have also been found in

---

[8] *Refutation* v. 7 (Eng. v. 2). Others, it is true, translate in the reverse sense, "There am I manifested, who am hidden in the fourteenth age (aeon)." So M. R. James.

Syriac[9] (much abbreviated), Armenian, and Slavonic. They are full of miracles performed by Jesus while a child from five to twelve years of age. These are sometimes whimsical, sometimes vengeful. But there is nothing clearly heretical in these books, and the longest of them is not half as long as the 1,300 lines which the *Stichometry* gives as the length of the *Gospel of Thomas*. It seems probable that these short forms of the *Gospel of Thomas* were produced by cutting out of it the objectionable heretical matter and by retaining the stories of Jesus' childhood wonders—shaping clay sparrows and making them come to life, striking dead those who annoy him, covering his teachers with confusion, raising the dead, curing people of injuries, even making Joseph's mismeasurements in the carpenter shop come out right. As it stands, the crude little gospel reflects an ancient impulse to push Jesus' miracle-working power back into his boyhood. What remains of it may be read in the translations of M. R. James, in his *Apocryphal New Testament* (pp. 49–70). But a complete form of the second-century *Gospel of Thomas* has yet to be found.

The Acts records the appointment by lot of a twelfth apostle to take the place forfeited by Judas (1:26); his name was Matthias. Nothing more is said about him in the Acts or anywhere in the New Testament, but sometime in the second century a work was written, probably in Egypt, which was given his name and called the *Traditions of Matthias*. There was apparent-

The Traditions of Matthias

[9] Peeters held that all the Greek and Latin forms went back to a Syriac base.

ly nothing particularly heretical about it, for Clement of Alexandria, writing probably about A.D. 190–210, quotes it with apparent approval three or four times in his *Miscellanies* (ii. 9. 45; iii. 4. 26; vii. 13. 82; and perhaps iv. 6. 35).

It is from Clement that we learn all that we really know about the work, though, it is true, he once speaks of the Gnostics as quoting it. Its name may have been suggested by Paul's use of the word in the plural, "traditions" (*paradoseis*), in I Cor. 11:2 and II Thess. 2:15, in a Christian sense, of such Christian instruction as he gave his converts. The work had a decidedly philosophical color, reminding Clement of Plato: "The beginning [of truth, or of the search for it] is to wonder at things, as Plato says in the *Theaetetus*, and Matthias exhorts us in the *Traditions:* 'Wonder at what is present before you.'" The moral solidarity of the Christian society was strongly held in the *Traditions:* "If the neighbor of one of the elect sins, the elect man sins; for if he had behaved as the word (or reason) enjoins, his neighbor also would have respected his manner of life too much to sin."

In a third quotation Clement records that the *Traditions* taught that the physical nature must be controlled and mortified and the soul made to grow through faith and knowledge (iii. 4. 26). This is the text quoted, Clement says, by the Gnostics. This is all we have of this mysterious little book.

The book was evidently written before Clement wrote his *Miscellanies*, and some time before, for

Clement identifies its writer with "the apostle Matthias" (vii. 13. 82). It was probably written in the
days when Christian apologists like Athenagoras were
dipping into Greek philosophy, well after the middle
of the second century.

The *Secret Sayings* which Hippolytus says the schismatic Basilides and his son Isidorus claimed Matthias
had taught them privately (*Refutation* vii. 20 [Eng.
vii. 8]) cannot have been part of the *Traditions* which
Clement speaks of so respectfully. Nor are they to be
identified with another book under his name, the
Gospel of Matthias, mentioned by Origen along with
the *Gospel of Thomas*, as among the schismatic gospels.[10] In fact, nothing is known of such a gospel,
except Origen's mention of it, though it is also spoken
of as heretical by Eusebius (*Church History* iii. 25. 6),
doubtless following Origen. It is mentioned among
the apocrypha at the end of the *List of the Sixty
Canonical Books* (seventh century or earlier) and in the
so-called "Decree of Gelasius," really a product of the
sixth century, though by these times the book must
have disappeared, only its name surviving. This is all
that is known as yet of the *Traditions*, the *Secret Sayings*, and the *Gospel of Matthias*.[11]

[10] *Homily 1 on Luke*.

[11] Theodor Zahn, however, held that the three works were really one,
which was spoken of under different names (*Geschichte des neutestamentlichen
Kanons*, II, 751 f.). Harnack in 1893 thought this might be the case, but in
1896 he held that at least two and probably three works went under the
name of Matthias (*Geschichte der altchristlichen Litteratur*, II, i, 597).

Among the various Christian sects which arose in
the second century, the most Jewish was the Ebionites,
The Gospel of the Ebionites or poor. They seem to have been the
successors of those Jewish Christians of
Palestine, and especially of Jerusalem,
who had not accepted Paul's views and
letters but came to hold a modified Gnostic position,
like that of Cerinthus, who held that Jesus was the
son of Joseph and Mary and that his messiahship,[12]
or the Holy Spirit,[13] descended upon him at his baptism and departed from him before his death on the
cross. They practiced circumcision but they did not
accept the Pentateuch or practice animal sacrifice. We
hear of them from Irenaeus in the second century, from
Origen and Hippolytus in the third, and from Epiphanius in the fourth, when they had revived some of
the ways and views of the old Jewish monastic order
of the Essenes.

Toward the end of the second century these descendants of Paul's Judaizing opponents produced a gospel
embodying their views. It was written in the first
person, singular or plural, Matthew being the spokes-
man in the singular, and the Twelve Apostles speaking
in the plural.[14] This led to its being called, especially
by Epiphanius, by such a variety of names: "Accord-

[12] Irenaeus i. 26. 1; Hippolytus *Refutation* vii. 21 (Eng.).

[13] Epiphanius *Heresies*, xxviii.

[14] In this it resembles the *Gospel of Peter*, in which the apostles speak in
the first person plural ("We the twelve disciples of the Lord wept and
grieved"), and Peter speaks in the first person singular ("I, Simon Peter,
and Andrew my brother took our nets and went away to the sea").

ing to Matthew," "the Gospel of the Hebrews," "the Gospel of the Twelve," "the Gospel of the Ebionites." To the last two only is it properly entitled, for the *Gospel of the Ebionites* was identical with the *Gospel of the Twelve* (Apostles), while the *Gospel of the Hebrews* was another book entirely.[15]

The *Gospel of the Ebionites* was naturally strongly influenced at many points by the Four Gospels, which it was written to combat. It owed most to Luke and Matthew; the Paulinism of John would naturally repel its authors. Its great claim of representing the voices of Matthew and the Twelve was evidently made in opposition to the gentile Christian claim that the Four Gospels were the work "of the apostles and those who followed them," as Justin put it (*Dialogue* ciii. 8).

From the quotations from it preserved in Epiphanius, it is clear that the *Gospel of the Ebionites* opposed animal sacrifice and advocated vegetarianism. One of these quotations, with which this gospel may have begun, reads:

There was a man named Jesus, who was about thirty years of age, and he chose us. And he came to Capernaum, and went into the house of Simon who was called Peter; and he opened his mouth and said, "As I walked by the lake of Tiberias, I chose John and James, the sons of Zebedee, and Simon and Andrew and[16] Thaddeus and Simon the Zealot

---

[15] The *Gospel of the Twelve Apostles* published in 1900 by J. Rendel Harris from a Syriac manuscript is a much later work, written probably in Syriac, well on in the Nicene period, and has no connection with the *Gospel of the Ebionites*.

[16] Philip, Bartholomew, James the son of Alpheus, and Thomas seem to be omitted; perhaps their call had been related earlier in the story.

and Judas Iscariot. And you, Matthew, I called as you sat at the tollhouse, and you followed me. I wish you therefore to be twelve apostles for a testimony to Israel!"

This gospel described the food of John as wild honey and "cakes made with oil and honey." In this way they made John a vegetarian simply by substituting the Greek word *enkris* ("oil cake") for *akris* ("locust") (Mark 1:6). It would seem that they not only used the Greek gospels in writing their gospel but actually wrote theirs in Greek, though it may have passed into Aramaic. Epiphanius is our chief informant on this gospel, through his quotations from it in his *Heresies* (xxx. 13–22). These deal with John's preaching, the baptism of Jesus, the choosing of the Twelve, and the last Passover. They show that the *Gospel of the Ebionites* was not the *Gospel of the Hebrews*, for their accounts of the baptism are very different. It was evidently written to promote the schismatic views of the Ebionite sect.

Symmachus, the first Christian translator of the Old Testament into Greek, in the days of Marcus Aurelius (A.D. 161–80), or (with Epiphanius and the *Paschal Chronicle*) under Severus (193–211), was an Ebionite; in fact, he made his translation for the Greek-speaking Jewish Christians of that sect. It is probable that these two literary products of Ebionism —the gospel and the Greek version of the Old Testament—were produced in the same region, the same period, and the same tongue. Symmachus left his books to a woman named Juliana, who lived in Caesarea in Cappadocia, and she turned them over to

Origen, probably when he took refuge there from
Maximin's persecution (A.D. 235–38).[17]

Origen is the earliest writer to mention the *Gospel of
the Twelve*, as he called it (*Homily 1 on Luke*), and it was
probably written in Greek in Asia Minor, perhaps
fifty years before he visited Caesarea, or around 185.
Our only other information about it comes from Epiphanius, in Cyprus, a century and a half later. Except
for a few fragments preserved by him, the work has
disappeared; but it is one of the early Christian books
that learning hopes may yet come to light.

About the end of the second century a literal acceptance of the Virgin birth of Jesus and a growing

The Book   belief in the perpetual virginity of Mary
of James   led some imaginative believer, probably
              in Egypt, to write a short story in sup-
port of these views. It was hardly a book, for in its
original Greek form it cannot have amounted to more
than fifteen or twenty columns, or pages; but it contained a whole series of striking narratives.

It began with the conception and birth of Mary, in
answer to prayer, and apparently miraculous, very
much like the account of Samuel's birth in I Samuel.
When she is three years old, she is taken to the temple
and kept there through her childhood until her marriage at the age of twelve to Joseph, a widower with
sons. The annunciation, conception, journey to Bethlehem, and birth of Jesus in a cave follow. The mid-
wife who is summoned finds Mary is still a virgin. At
the moment of Jesus' birth all nature, animate and

---

[17] Eusebius *Church History* vi. 17; Palladius *Lausiac History* 147.

inanimate, stops transfixed. The wise men bring their gifts; Herod kills the infant children; the infant John is miraculously preserved, but Herod puts John's father, Zacharias, to death. In the closing lines James, meaning the Lord's brother, declares himself the writer, and Jerusalem the place of writing.

The story about the escape of John and the death of Zacharias is generally regarded as a later addition to the little story; Origen gives other grounds for the martyrdom of Zacharias. This part (chaps. 22–24) probably comes from the century after Origen (A.D. 250–350). The abrupt appearance of Joseph as narrator—"Now I, Joseph, was walking, and walked not" (18:2)—also suggests a change of source; this continues for about a chapter (18:2—19:1) and has the sound of an accretion. The original tract probably consisted of 1:1—18:1; 19:2—21:4; and chapter 25, but had taken on these additions by the year 350.

Even in this earliest form the tract shows a sense of Christian continuity with Jewish religion that did not exist until after the struggle with Gnosticism about the Old Testament was over, and brings us to the beginning of the third century. It was probably written in Egypt; our first mention of it is by Origen, who says that some say Jesus' brothers were the sons of Joseph by a former wife, basing this upon the *Book of James* (*On the Gospel of Matthew* 13:55). Clement of Alexandria, a few years earlier (A.D. 190–210), may have known the book, or at least part of its story, for he states that some say that Mary, after she had brought forth, was found, when examined, to be a virgin (*Miscellanies* vii. 16. 93). This is exactly what is stated in chapters 19 and 20. Half a century earlier, Justin in his *Dialogue* (*ca.* A.D. 155–60) describes Jesus' birth as taking place in a cave near Bethlehem (chap. 78); but this may have been just a bit of current tradition and does not prove the *Book of James* as old as Justin's times. Justin also speaks of Mary as descended from David (*Dialogue* c. 3), as the *Book of James* does (10:1).

Epiphanius certainly knew the book (*Heresies* lxxix. 5), which he calls the story and traditions of Mary, and the "Decree of Gelasius," now assigned to the sixth century, repudiates it as heretical or schismatic along with a considerable list of such gospels, calling it the "Gospel under the name of James the Less."

We have seen gospels that were written to support heretical views; here is one written in support of views that were coming to be held orthodox. The perpetual virginity of Mary, the doctrine that Jesus' brothers were sons of Joseph by a former marriage, and apparently even the idea that Mary herself was miraculously conceived are the views it was intended to promote. It also assumed the continuity of Christianity with Judaism.

But from a historical point of view the *Book of James* leaves much to be desired. No gospel is more completely fiction. The story of Mary's life in the temple from her third to her twelfth year, like some pagan vestal virgin, is altogether impossible; nothing could have been more repugnant to Judaism. The idea of all nature standing still at the moment of the Nativity is an obvious bit of folklore. The book is strongly influenced by the story of the birth of Samuel and shows the use of all four of our gospels as well.

This little work, about the size of a modern short story, has gone by a variety of names; the numerous Greek manuscripts (there is no ancient Latin version) entitle it a narrative, or account; Origen calls it the "Book of James"; the "Gelasian Decree" calls it the "Gospel of James the Less." Its modern discoverer, Guillaume Postel, called it the "Protevangelium," or "Proto-Gospel."

Although frowned upon by church authorities, the *Book of James* survived, probably unaltered after A.D. 350, and had a wide literary influence. It became the source of the Coptic history of Joseph the Carpenter, of the *Gospel of the Pseudo-Matthew*, of the *Nativity of Mary*, and of the Arabic *Gospel of the Infancy*. It was summarized in the thirteenth century (A.D. 1275) in the *Golden Legend* (v. 96), and it has been drawn upon in a number of present-day gospel imitations, such as the Aquarian Gospel. Its scenes were richly illustrated by Italian painters—Giotto ("The Exclusion of Joachim from the Temple"), Raphael ("Betrothal of the Virgin"), Titian ("The Presentation of the Virgin in the Temple"), Ghirlandaio ("The Birth of the Virgin," "The Marriage of the Virgin"), and many others.

A *Gospel of Basilides* is mentioned by Origen (*Homily 1 on Luke*). It seems to have been based principally upon Matthew and Luke and became the subject of a commentary by Basilides, in twenty-four books (the *Exegetica* mentioned by Clement of Alexandria [*Miscellanies* iv. 12. 81]). This was the first gospel commentary. Basilides

Minor Gospels

came from Syria and spent much time in Egypt, reaching Alexandria about A.D. 133. He brought marked elements of Persian religion into his form of Gnosticism. Origen also speaks of songs by Basilides (*On Job* xxi. 11 f.)—perhaps the "incantations" which Irenaeus says were used by his followers (*Refutation* i. 24. 5).

A *Gospel of Judas* is mentioned by Irenaeus (A.D. 181–89) as a production of the Cainites, whom he describes as a variety of Valentinian Gnostics. It embodied the view that Judas had a deeper knowledge of the truth than others, which led him to betray Jesus. The book, if it ever existed, must have been written between A.D. 150 and 175 (*Refutation* i. 31. 1). It is also mentioned by Epiphanius (*Heresies* xxxviii. 1. 3).

The *Gospel of Truth* is another product of the Valentinians, according to Irenaeus, who says it shows no agreement with the "gospels of the apostles," indeed it is totally unlike them (*Refutation* iii. 11. 9). It was probably not really a gospel at all but simply a presentation of Valentinian views. It must have been written in the third quarter of the second century.

A *Gospel of Philip*, "the holy disciple," is mentioned by Epiphanius about 376 as in use among the Egyptian Gnostics of his day (*Heresies* xxvi. 13). He quotes a few sentences, beginning, "The Lord revealed to me what the soul must say as it goes up into heaven, and how it must answer each of the powers above." The answers to be given the powers follows. It is significant that in the *Pistis Sophia* ("Faith Wisdom"), a remarkable Gnostic work of the third century, giving supposed revelations made by Jesus to his disciples after his resurrection, it is Philip who is writing them down, and Philip, Thomas, and Matthew are named as the three witnesess who are to record these revelations (*Pistis Sophia*, pp. 69 f.). This suggests that the *Gospel of Philip* was written by that time and perhaps as early as the close of the second century.

The *Gospel of Nicodemus*, or *Acts of Pilate*, probably belongs to the middle years of the fourth century, for it was unknown to Eusebius (326) but known to Epiphanius (*ca.* 376), who mentions it in his *Heresies* (i. 1). It consists of two parts: one, an account of the trial, passion, and resurrection of Jesus, in which Pilate and Nicodemus are prominent; the other, a later work, an account of the Descent into Hell. The earlier work, an imaginative expansion of what the Four Gospels tell us, aims at proving the resurrection and the responsibility of the Jews for the death of Jesus, a question still being debated in the twentieth century. It was revised by 425 and still later the Descent into Hell was appended to it, especially in the Latin manuscripts. There are Coptic, Syriac, and Armenian versions of Part I, but not of Part II. Part I is current in Greek manuscripts in two forms; Part II appears in two forms, in Latin ones.

A *Gospel of Bartholomew* is spoken of by Jerome in the Prologue to his *Commentary on Matthew*, in a list of uncanonical gospels—*Egyptians, Thomas, Matthias, Bartholomew, Twelve Apostles, Basilides, Apelles,* "and the rest." But it is possible he was making a loose use of Eusebius' statement (*Church History* v. 10. 3) that Bartholomew on his mission to "India" (meaning the

Bosphorus region) found there an Aramaic form of the Gospel of Matthew. Perhaps Jerome knew no more than this about a *Gospel of Bartholomew*. It is true, the "Gelasian Decree" mentions it among the apocryphal gospels, but it may have taken it over from Jerome. A quotation from Bartholomew in Dionysius the Areopagite (*De myst. theol.* 1) may be taken as pointing toward the existence of a gospel bearing Bartholomew's name, but we cannot be sure such a book ever existed.

A Greek work called the *Questions of Bartholomew*, perhaps as old as the fifth century and extant also in two Latin forms, may, as some maintain, contain relics of the gospel Jerome mentions. After the Resurrection, Bartholomew questions Jesus, Mary, and Satan. An English version will be found in M. R. James's *Apocryphal New Testament*.

A *Gospel of Andrew* is mentioned by Augustine (*Contra advers. legis et prophetarum* i. 20) (354–430). It is condemned by Pope Innocent I in a letter written in A.D. 405 (according to some manuscripts), and is listed among the apocrypha in the "Gelasian Decree" of the sixth century. But this is in all probability due to confusion with the *Acts of Andrew*, and there was probably never any actual *Gospel of Andrew*. Certainly no such book has yet been found.

A *Gospel according to Barnabas* is mentioned among the apocrypha in the "Gelasian Decree," now assigned to the sixth century, and also in the *List of the Sixty Canonical Books* (a list as early as the seventh century). In the "Decree" it stands just after, and in the

List just before, the *Gospel according to Matthias*. The curious and interesting *Gospel of Barnabas* published by L. and L. Ragg from the Italian in 1907 is a Mohammedan work of the fifteenth or sixteenth century and has nothing to do with the ancient gospel of that name, about which nothing at all is known.

Numerous other gospels, obscure, perhaps even imaginary, are mentioned or reflected in later lists or writings. A *Gospel of Apelles* is mentioned by Jerome (*Preface to Matthew*); a *Gospel of Cerinthus*, by Epiphanius (*Heresies* li. 7); an unnamed gospel seems to be reflected in the *Pistis Sophia;* a *Gospel of Eve* is quoted by Epiphanius (*Heresies* xxvi. 2, 3), perhaps the same as the *Gospel of Perfection* he mentions in the same passage; etc.

This series of gospels, twenty or more in number, is a massive tribute to the influence of the great Fourfold Gospel, which lies back of them all. That published group created a composite literary pattern which all the later gospel-makers had more or less in mind.

CHAPTER V

ACTS

Christian leaders of the second and third centuries, whether they held the standard or the schismatic type *Religious* of belief, were alive to the values of fic- *Fiction* tion in religion. Not only was fiction useful in propagating their views of truth but it was valuable as a substitute for the tales and stories which the heathen read and which were often immoral in tone. Not only to promote religion but to displace an immoral fiction literature, the later Acts literature was produced.

If the Four Gospels seemed to their early readers to leave gaps in the life of Jesus which might be edifyingly filled, and so led to further gospel-writing, the Book of Acts left a mass of loose ends that invited literary effort. By the middle of the second century the apostles had come to possess great importance for Christian teaching. They were being more and more appealed to against the sects. What became of them? What did they accomplish and what was their fate? In the absence of historical information, Christian imagination was called in, and a group of religious novels resulted.

When the two-volume work of Luke, the Gospel and the Acts, was divided, and the gospel volume was taken out of it to form part of the Fourfold Gospel, toward A.D. 120, the second volume was left to go its own way alone. How soon it came to be called the Acts of the Apostles we do not know; we find it first called by that name in the Muratorian canon fragment about A.D. 200—the "Acts of All the Apostles." But it must have come by the name much earlier than that, for it was that book that unmistakably suggested the apocryphal Acts literature and gave it its name.

In the Acts literature of the late second and early third centuries, Christian literature certainly bloomed with a wild luxuriance.

The sequel most obviously demanded by the Book of Acts is some account of what became of Paul. Its *The Acts of Paul* narrative leaves him in prison, soon to go on trial for his life. Was he convicted or acquitted? The generation for which Luke wrote knew the answer perfectly well, but two generations later hardly anybody knew it. The letters to Timothy and Titus, which were written after A.D. 150, reflect the interest already felt in subsequent movements of his, assuming his release from prison, and from composing such letters as having been written on a later journey, it was a short step to describing such a journey itself.

So it must have seemed to a Christian elder in Asia— we do not know his name—perhaps in Smyrna or Ephesus, who about A.D. 160–70 had come to feel that the Pastoral Letters exaggerated Paul's views on the place of women in the church and needed to be corrected. He also wanted to counteract their strong indorsement of marriage—"train the younger women to

be loving wives and mothers" (Titus 2:4, etc.)—and
to recall the churches to ascetic views and the renunciation of marriage. So he wrote the *Acts of Paul*.

Paul had indeed said in I Corinthians that women
were to keep quiet in church; they were not allowed
to speak (14:34). But I Timothy put this even more
sharply: "I do not allow women to teach; . . . . they
must keep quiet" (2:12). Over against these rather
Jewish views of women in religion some Christians in
Asia felt that women should be allowed to teach and
even to baptize. Montanus had already appeared as a
prophet in A.D. 156, in Mysia, in the north-central part
of the province of Asia, and two women, Maximilla
and Priscilla, were soon exercising the same prophetic
gift as he. Women had long been prominent in
Phrygian religion, and for twenty years this movement, Montanism, was most active in Phrygia, the
eastern part of the province.   5 2 0 6 7

The *Acts of Paul* described one of Paul's women converts named Thecla not only as teaching but as ad-
ministering baptism unrebuked. Paul himself bids her
go and teach the word of God. The author was clearly
seeking to correct the antifeminism of I Timothy,
which he flatly contradicts.

When a few years later the writer of the *Acts of Paul*
was found out and made to admit the writing of this
first Christian novel, as Tertullian relates, he declared
that he had done it out of love for Paul and was forthwith deprived of his office. But his book, though often
officially condemned, achieved great popularity. One
chapter of it in particular, the story of Thecla, has

never been forgotten. It exists in a number of Greek manuscripts and in half-a-dozen versions. Its abrupt beginning turns out to be due to the fact that it is simply one episode in a larger narrative.

But fifty years ago that chapter was about all that was known of the *Acts of Paul*, and we did not even know that it was originally part of those *Acts*, so completely had they disappeared. The old lists of books of scripture, acknowledged and disputed, mentioned the book and gave its length as 3,560 lines, or more than twice that of the Gospel of Mark. Tertullian tells of its origin in Asia and of the elder who wrote it. Origen also mentions it. Hippolytus at Rome early in the third century shows it was highly regarded there in his day. "For if we believe," he writes, "that when Paul was condemned to death, a lion, let loose upon him, fell down and licked his feet, how shall we not believe the things that happened in the case of Daniel?" (in the den of lions).[1] Eusebius, in A.D. 326, speaks of it as one of the books whose place in the New Testament was denied in his day.

But in 1896 a Coptic papyrus of the book was discovered which did much to clear up its story. It was unfortunately incomplete, but it showed that it originally included not only the story of Paul and Thecla but the two letters exchanged between Paul and the Corinthians which had once been extant in Syriac and in fact were actually included in Efrem's Syriac New Testament in the fourth century. A fourth-century papyrus leaf from Berlin and a parchment one of about

[1] *Commentary on Daniel* iii 29.

the same age from Oxyrhynchus (*Oxyrhynchus Papyri* xiii. 1602, 1919) helped to build up the text in the original Greek. But more recently the discovery at Hamburg in 1927 of eleven pages of the book in Greek in a papyrus written about A.D. 300, has given us the concluding part of it in its original language.[2]

As pieced together from these Coptic and Greek papyri and the famous chapter so long known as the "Acts of Paul and Thecla," the story of the *Acts of Paul* ran somewhat as follows:

Course of the Narrative　　1. Paul is at Pisidian Antioch. He restores a Jewish boy to life, and the boy's parents are converted, but the populace becomes incensed, and Paul is driven from the town.

2. Paul reaches Iconium. This is the episode that has survived as the *Acts of Paul and Thecla*. It always seemed to begin very abruptly: "As Paul was going up to Iconium after his escape from Antioch, Demas and Hermogenes the coppersmith were his fellow travelers." This apparent abruptness now disappears; it is just a natural transition from one scene to the next. Thecla is a Greek girl of position who becomes interested in Paul's preaching, breaks off her engagement, is converted and, although thrown to wild beasts in the arena, escapes and lives to teach others her new faith. Paul approves her doing this, in contrast with his reputed unwillingness that a woman

[2] Carl Schmidt and Wilhelm Schubart, *Praxeis Paulou: Acta Pauli* (Hamburg, 1936).

should teach. Thecla subsequently visits Paul at Myra and later retires to Seleucia, where she dies. The leading interests of the book—aversion to marriage and indorsement of woman's place in teaching religion—appear most clearly in this romantic story, which not only survived in Greek and many versions but has been picked up and repeated in a number of modern forms of the life of Paul.

3. At Myra, where Thecla had left Paul, he cures a man of dropsy and thus incurs the enmity of the man's son Hermippus, who had hoped soon to inherit his father's property. The son is smitten with blindness but repents and is cured.

4. Paul proceeds by way of Perga to Sidon. There the people shut him and his friends up in the temple of Apollo, part of which collapses in the course of the night. This further incenses the people, who hurry Paul and his companions to the theater, but what happened there is lost.

5. Paul reappears at Tyre, where he heals the sick and discourses about Judaism.

6. He is next found at some mines, of unknown location, where a certain Frontina, who has been converted, is thrown from a cliff and killed, but Paul restores her to life and leads her home through the town, the people of which are at once won to Christianity.

7. Here belongs the story related by Nicephorus,[3] about 1320, of a visit to Ephesus, not mentioned in the Coptic fragments but now supplied in much detail by

[3] Nicephorus Callisti *Church History* ii 25.

the newly discovered Greek text, which begins with this Ephesian episode. (The Coptic pieces aggregate only about one-half the total length given in the medieval stichometry for the *Acts of Paul*, so that much is certainly missing from them.) At Ephesus, Paul is thrown into prison. Two women who are believers visit him in his prison, seeking baptism, and he escapes from the prison long enough to baptize them on the seashore. Next day, when a huge lion is let loose upon him in the stadium it quietly curls up at his feet like a lamb. (This is the incident referred to by Hippolytus.) The lion speaks to Paul, and Paul asks if this is not the lion he had previously met and baptized. The lion replies that it is. The story of the baptism of the lion (Jerome's "fable of the baptized lion" ["totam baptizati leonis fabulam"], which he not unnaturally rejected[4]) is told in detail in the Ethiopic *Epistle of Pelagia*, which goes on to relate the later encounter of Paul and the lion in the stadium, just as the new Greek portions of the *Acts of Paul* now describe it.[5] A great hailstorm comes on which kills many of the people and of the animals and cuts off the governor's ear. The governor is converted. The lion escapes, and Paul is released and proceeds to Macedonia.

8. The next section is headed "From Philippi to Corinth" in the Greek, the stay at Philippi being

[4] *On Illustrious Men* 7.

[5] This short martyrdom, which I had the good fortune to unearth in an Ethiopic manuscript in the British Museum many years ago ("The Epistle of Pelagia," *American Journal of Semitic Languages*, XX [1904], 95–108), offered the first explanation of the baptized and talking lion. See also my *Ethiopic Martyrdoms* (Chicago, 1931), pp. 92, 102.

passed over. The Coptic, however, relates that it was while in prison there that Paul received a short letter from the Corinthians, reporting the appearance among them of two false teachers, Simon and Cleobius. He writes a letter to the Corinthians in reply. (This is the letter anciently accepted by Syrian and Armenian churches as III Corinthians.) He takes leave of the Philippians; a local prophet and prophetess predict his work and fate in Rome.

9. The Greek proceeds with an account of Paul's stay in Corinth. The brethren are grieved at his conviction that he must go on to Rome. He embarks on a ship the captain of which had been baptized by Peter.

10. On the voyage Jesus, walking on the water, appears to Paul, urges him on to Rome, and goes before the ship, guiding it on its way like a star. As Paul lands, Jesus again appears and says, "I am going to be crucified again." Paul is welcomed by the brethren at Rome and addresses them. He is tried, apparently before Nero, and executed with the sword, but later reappears to Nero and his attendants and declares that much evil will overtake him, in no long time, for the righteous blood he has shed.

Here the title, "Acts of Paul," in the Greek manuscript marks the end of the book.

This is perhaps two-thirds or three-fourths of the *Acts of Paul*. Jerome says, "The Travels of Paul and Thecla, and the whole fable of the baptized lion we reckon among the apocryphal writings." Commodian, the fifth-century Christian poet, says of God's power, "For Paul, when he preached, he made a lion speak to the people with a God-given voice." In the Ethiopic *Epistle of Pelagia*, another of Paul's reputed converts, Paul meets a huge lion on a mountain. They become friends, and the lion asks to be baptized. Paul complies. Later when a woman named Pelagia is converted and leaves her husband, Paul is arrested and a huge lion is set upon him in the "theater." But it is the baptized lion, and he and Paul pray and converse. They let Paul go "with his lion," but Pelagia suffers martyrdom. It is now clear that the lion episodes are from the *Acts of Paul;* here are Jerome's baptized lion and Commodian's talking lion; they are one. The story of Pelagia also exhibits the same aversion to marriage that we find in the story of Thecla.[6]

The Asian elder who wrote the *Acts of Paul* was acquainted with the letters to Timothy and Titus; in fact, they evidently influenced him to write. From them he draws the names of Hermogenes and Onesiphorus; the latter's "household," twice mentioned in the Pastoral Letters, in the *Acts* becomes his wife Lectra and his children Simmias and Zeno. He also knew the Book of Acts, which gave him his model. His work is first mentioned by Tertullian in his work *On Baptism* 17, written at the beginning of the third century. So the *Acts of Paul* was probably written between A.D. 160 and 170. Its feminist views repelled Tertullian, but Origen and Hippolytus used it without prejudice. It begins Eusebius' list of "rejected" writings. In the *Clermont List*, probably formed in Egypt about A.D. 300, it stands between the *Shepherd* of

[6] Goodspeed, *Ethiopic Martyrdoms*, pp. 100, 102.

Hermas and the *Revelation of Peter*. In the *Stichometry of Nicephorus*, about A.D. 850, it leads the list of rejected books (apocrypha) under the title "Journey of Paul."

Most of what has been found of the *Acts of Paul* (excepting only the Greek portion recently discovered) may be read in English in M. R. James's *Apocryphal New Testament*.

Not long after the appearance of the romantic *Acts of Paul* (A.D. 160–70), some Docetist, probably in

The Acts of John

Asia, undertook to embody his views in an imaginative account of the wonders, discourses, and travels of John. He doubtless took his cue from the *Acts of Paul;* certainly he agreed with its author in his disapproval of marriage. John had been a comparatively neglected figure, of whom the Acts had little to say, but to whom tradition was already ascribing the Fourth Gospel and the Revelation. Who the writer of these *Acts* was we cannot say. Later writers spoke of him as Leucius Charinus. He certainly represented himself as a personal disciple of John, who accompanied him on his journeys and witnessed his wonders.

Clement of Alexandria in his *Outlines* (*On I John* i. 1), which may have been written as early as A.D. 189, quotes some sentences that are found in these *Acts*, ascribing them to the "Traditions." If he means the *Acts of John*, as he probably does, they must have been written about A.D. 170–80. The Nicephorus list, about A.D. 850, gives their length at 2,500 lines, or about the size of the Gospel of Matthew. The Greek *Acts of John* as we know it today, however, including the scattered fragments, from various sources, is only about two-thirds that size.

A good deal is evidently lost from the beginning (the first seventeen chapters, as ordinarily numbered, following the example of Bonnet's edition, are from a form of the Greek text very much later than the original) and there are places where gaps are apparent, as in chapter 37 and before chapter 58.

Chapters 18–55 describe John's coming from Miletus to Ephesus and his first stay there. In chapters 58–86 John returns from Laodicea to Ephesus for a second stay. In chapters 87–105 John tells of his first meeting with Jesus, of the transfiguration, of the strange hymn full of paradoxes Jesus taught them on the night of his arrest; of the dance in which he led them; of the strange changes in his body, now hard, now soft, and again quite immaterial; of his appearance to John in a cave on the Mount of Olives, when his body was apparently being crucified across the valley outside Jerusalem; of Jesus' discourse about the cross; and of his ascension. At this point should perhaps be introduced some accounts of John's discourses and wonders preserved in other sources, chiefly Latin; John converts a philosopher, condemns wealth, raises a widow's son, drinks a deadly poison unharmed, and converts the heathen priest. The fourth-century Oxyrhynchus fragment (*Oxyrhynchus Papyri* vi. 850) must belong here; John is threatened with arrest by a soldier and receives a letter, probably a summons, from the emperor.

The Greek text of the *Acts* (chaps. 106–15) concludes with the peaceful death of John; he shows his

disciples where to dig his grave, steps into it, and
after a prayer lies down in it and quietly expires.

While some of this may not have appeared in the
Acts of John as they first existed, about A.D. 175 (the
temple of Artemis in Ephesus, for example [chap. 42],
did not fall until A.D. 262, when the Goths destroyed
it), on the whole it is probably a fair picture of the
work. It is clearly docetic, with its description of
Jesus as appearing to James as a little child, while
John on the same occasion sees him as a full-grown
man (chaps. 88 and 89), and its representation of his
body as sometimes immaterial, and his conversation
with John on the Mount of Olives at the very moment
of the crucifixion (chap. 97). At some points it sounds
decidedly Gnostic; for example, the curious hymn before the betrayal:

> The number Eight (or one ogdoad) sings praise
>   with us. Amen.
> The number Twelve dances on high. Amen.
> The Whole on high joins in dancing. Amen.

This hymn, with its crude paradoxes (chap. 95),

> I would eat, and I would be eaten,
> I would hear, and I would be heard,
> I would be thought, being wholly thought,

certainly reflects mystery forms of worship and
Gnostic ideas. The closing lines of the final prayer
have a Gnostic sound too:

As I come unto thee, let the fire go backward, let the
darkness be overcome, let the gulf be without strength, let
the furnace die out, let Gehenna be quenched. Let angels
follow, let devils fear, let rulers be broken, let powers fall,

let the places of the right hand stand fast, let them of the
left hand not remain . . . . and grant that I may accomplish
the journey unto thee without suffering insolence or provocation . . . . [chap. 114].

It will be remembered that the Gnostics claimed to
know the formulas that would turn aside the demons
that beset the soul's way to God. The book is strongly ascetic; marriage is sternly rebuked, and John in
his dying prayer thanks God that he has been pro-
videntially kept from any union with a woman.

The story is full of marvels; it abounds in the
miraculous. In its effort to be interesting, it descends
to the lurid and the vulgar. When Drusiana dies, in
protest against the marriage relation, a disappointed
admirer makes his way into her tomb to outrage her
dead body. The author even makes some ponderous
attempts at humor; as when in an abandoned inn a
swarm of bedbugs is miraculously halted by the apostle's command (chaps. 60–61).

The story of John playing with the partridge or
watching it playing in the dust probably also formed
part of the *Acts of John*. There is some doubt as to
whether Domitian's having John plunged in boiling
oil, apparently at Rome, did, though it appears in late
forms of the *Acts*, and Tertullian was familiar with it,
for in his book *On Prescription of Heretics* (chap. 36),
written about A.D. 200, he speaks of Rome as the
place "where the apostle John was first plunged unhurt into boiling oil, and then sent back to his island
exile." Curiously enough this story has never been
found in Greek, or in Greek writers, though the

emperor's summons in the Oxyrhynchus fragment may have been leading up to it.

The story of St. John and the Robber Captain, whom he seeks out and leads to repentance, is as old as Clement of Alexandria (*What Rich Man Can Be Saved?* 42) but has never been found in the *Acts of John*. But it is difficult to believe that so good a story about the apostle did not form part of the original *Acts*.

In style the *Acts of John* is wordy and often sluggish. While some scholars seek to date it even before the *Acts of Paul*, this loses sight of important literary facts. (1) The *Acts of Paul* forms a far more natural sequel to the Acts of the Apostles than does the *Acts of John;* when Acts breaks off, interest in Paul is at its height, while John is almost forgotten; he has long since disappeared from the narrative. (2) The *Acts of Paul* is primarily a counterblast to the Pastoral Letters, Timothy and Titus. It is the views they assert as Paul's that the *Acts of Paul* denies. (3) The *Acts of John* is more easily understood as suggested by the *Acts of Paul* than by the Acts of the Apostles; the natural order is: Acts of the Apostles, Pastoral Letters, *Acts of Paul*, *Acts of John*.

In the fourth century the *Acts of Paul* and the *Acts of John* were combined with those of Peter, Andrew, and Thomas into a collection by the Manicheans, who substituted them for the Acts of the Apostles on account of their strong ascetic tone. Photius, the famous patriarch of Constantinople, who read and reviewed this collection about A.D. 890 in his *Bibliotheca* (cod. 114), says that they were all attributed to Leucius

Charinus. Their order as known to Photius seems to have been Peter, John, Andrew, Thomas, Paul. The collection was entitled the "Travels (*periodoi*) of the Apostles."

In the first half of the fifth century a *Life of John* was written, under the name of his supposed disciple Prochorus, which made much use of the *Acts of John* and often throws important light upon its Greek text.

Still later, probably at the end of the sixth century, the so-called *Apostolic History* (*historiae*) of Abdias (published by Fabricius in his *Codex Apocryphus Novi Testamenti* [2d ed., 1719], Vol. II) shows the use of some of the early individual Acts, particularly of Andrew, Thomas, and John.

The *Acts of John* was condemned by the second council of Nicaea, A.D. 787, as it had been appealed to by the Iconoclasts, apparently because of its teaching about the immateriality of Jesus' body. It has played a notable part in popular literature and Christian art; painters and sculptors have shown John holding the poison cup, while the poison leaps out of the cup in the form of a snake. What remains of the work may be read in English in James's *Apocryphal New Testament*, but a complete text of these *Acts* has still to be found.

The rise of the sects in the second century had led the churches to turn back to the apostles as the true exponents of genuine Christian truth and had led to the organization of Catholic Christianity as against the sects, Marcionite, Gnostic, and Montanist, about A.D. 175. We have seen that this increased regard for the apostles

The Acts of Peter

had found expression in such apostolic novels as the *Acts of Paul* and those of *John*.

The name of Peter had long been connected with the early history of the Church of Rome; tradition connected the writing of Mark at Rome with Peter's ministry there; I Peter is clearly a letter from the Roman church written in his name; Hebrews alludes to the former leaders of the Roman church, who had brought it God's message and suffered martyrdom for it, and *I Clement* expands this sentence into a chapter on the fate of Paul and of Peter; the so-called *Preaching of Peter* was the earliest of the literary defenses of Christianity; the *Revelation of Peter* introduced Orphic ideas of heaven and hell into Christianity, and the *Gospel of Peter* was an effort to propagate docetic views under his name. II Peter, written perhaps a hundred years after his death, alludes, 1:14, to the prediction of his martyrdom contained in the epilogue of the Gospel of John, 21:18, 19: "When you grow old, you will stretch out your hands and someone else will put a girdle on you and take you where you have no wish to go."

Gospel, Preaching, Letters, and *Revelation* had already gathered about the name of Peter, and legend had been busy with it too. The rise of *Acts of Paul* and of *John* made it inevitable that someone should write the *Acts of Peter,* especially in Rome, where he had suffered martyrdom and where his memory was therefore especially cherished. The Acts of the Apostles brought Paul to Rome, but not Peter. How did Peter

come to visit Rome and how was their work there related? This was a question that would attract a Christian novelist.

Irenaeus of Lyons says in his *Refutation of Gnosticism*
(iii. 3. 2, 3), A.D. 181–89, that the Church of Rome
had inherited her tradition from the apostles and had
been founded and established by the glorious apostles
Peter and Paul. The Gospel of Matthew contained a
strong commendation of Peter from the lips of Jesus
himself, who named him Cephas, or, in Greek, Peter—
the Rock. "Your name is Peter, a rock, and on this
rock I will build my church, and the powers of death
shall not subdue it! I will give you [singular] the
keys of the Kingdom of Heaven, and whatever you
forbid on earth will be held in heaven to be forbidden,
and whatever you permit on earth will be held in
heaven to be permitted" (16:18, 19). The Roman
bishop Calixtus (A.D. 217–22) ruled that persons who
had been expelled from the church for grievous sins,
even for murder, might after due penance be reinstated,
under these powers of the keys, as they were called,
granted to Peter and, it was assumed, to his successors.

It was natural enough, then, for some Christian
writer early in the third century (A.D. 200–220) to
compose the *Acts of Peter*. Legend had already gathered thickly about the figure of the most picturesque
and spirited of the Twelve. The writer had also a considerable library of Christian books. He shows knowledge of the Four Gospels and the letters of Paul, the
Acts of the Apostles, the *Acts of Paul*, the *Acts of*

John (in chap. 21), the *Preaching of Peter*, the *Apology* of Justin, II Peter, and probably the *Gospel of the Egyptians* (in chap. 38).

His purpose was to entertain and edify his Christian readers with tales of the words and wonders of the great apostle, to whom Roman Christianity was more and more looking back as its great founder and sponsor. He would also indorse asceticism and encourage women to separate from their husbands.

No complete text of these *Acts* has been found, but about two-thirds of it can be recovered from various sources, Greek, Latin, and Coptic. The Nicephorus list gives its length as 2,750 lines, or about that of the Acts of the Apostles.

From one source comes the story of Peter's daughter. Peter has a daughter who is stolen by a rich admirer; Peter prays God to protect her, and she is paralyzed. This story is preserved only in Coptic, but Augustine mentions it,[7] and also the story of the gardener's daughter who fell dead at Peter's prayer for her. This story is told in the apocryphal *Letter of Titus*. The gardener wished her raised to life again, and, when Peter complied, the girl was outraged by a slave and disappeared.

But the main part of the *Acts* is found in a Latin manuscript at Vercelli. It tells how Paul was released from his Roman imprisonment and set out for Spain. Simon Magus comes to Rome, and the church, left without a leader, is reduced to seven members. Peter, at Jerusalem, is warned in a vision that he is needed in

---

[7] *Against Adimantus* xvii. 5.

Rome to resist his old enemy Simon (Acts 8:9–24).
As the twelve years Jesus had told the apostles to remain in Jerusàlem[8] were over, Peter sets out for Rome.
The ship is becalmed, the crew is drunk, and the
captain is converted. Peter goes down by a rope and
baptizes him in the sea. They land at Puteoli and
proceed to Rome. Peter rallies the believers. He
knocks at Simon's door, but the porter pretends Simon
is out. Peter sends his message in by the watchdog,
which is suddenly endowed with speech. Seeing a
dried herring in a shop, Peter puts it in water and
brings it to life. He makes a seven-months-old baby
speak. Peter tells how back in Judea a woman had
been robbed by Simon and his confederates and how
he had been enabled by a vision to uncover the crime
and get back the stolen property.

A woman of bad character brings Peter a large sum
of money. He is warned against accepting it, in view
of her character; it was a case of tainted money. Peter
laughs and says that in reality the money was a debt
owed to Christ (chap. 30).

The senator Marcellus, who had entertained Simon,
is shown his error by Peter and, after sprinkling his
house with holy water, he offers it for use as a church
or convent; the old women and widows are to come
and pray, receiving a piece of gold for the service.
Peter finds the gospel being read in the dining-hall and
preaches in it. He relates the Transfiguration, and in a
vision his hearers see Christ, who appears to some as
an old, to others as a young, man, or even as a child

---

[8] According to the *Preaching of Peter*.

(chap. 21; this rather docetic passage is taken from the *Acts of John*, chap. 87). Platforms are erected in the forum, and great numbers of people pay a piece of gold each to witness the contest between Peter and Simon. The prefect tells Simon to show his power by killing one of his pages; Simon obeys. Peter is then called upon to restore the boy to life and does so. Other resurrections follow.

The rest of the *Acts* is preserved in Greek as well as in Latin. Simon, who has already amazed the Romans by flying over the city, announces that he will do it again. Peter prays that he may fall and break his leg in three places. He does so, disappears from Rome, and dies at Terracina.

Peter's success in prevailing upon wives to leave their husbands arouses leading Romans against him. He is warned and leaves the city but meets Jesus entering it. Peter asks, "Lord, where are you going?" (the famous "Domine quo vadis?"). Jesus replies that he is going into Rome to be crucified again. Peter accepted the rebuke and turned back into the city, where he was crucified, at his request with his head downward.

This noble story of Peter's martyrdom goes far to redeem the trivial and even pagan elements that form so much of the book. Origen says that the *Acts of Paul* contained the saying of Jesus, "I am going to be crucified again," and the newly discovered Greek *Acts of Paul*, as we have seen, contains those words. Evidently the *Acts of Paul* was used by the author of the *Acts of Peter*.

Peter's last words to his wife as she was being led
out to martyrdom are recorded by Clement of Alexandria (*Miscellanies* vii. 11) and repeated by Eusebius
(*Church History* iii. 30. 2): "They say that when the
blessed Peter saw his own wife led out to die, he rejoiced because of her summons and her return home,
and called to her very encouragingly and comforting-
ly, addressing her by name, and saying, 'O thou, remember the Lord.'" Clement does not refer this to the
Acts of Peter, but it may later have formed part of them.

The idea that the apostles were told by Jesus to remain for twelve years in Jerusalem and then go forth
into the world is drawn from the *Preaching of Peter* and
was widely held in the early centuries. That there was
in Rome a statue in honor of Simon Magus, with the
inscription "Simoni deo Sancto" (chap. 10) probably
comes from Justin, who in his *Apology*, about A.D. 150
or soon after, mentions it (*Apology* xxvi. 2). In fact,
Justin is the first writer to suggest that Simon Magus
visited Rome.[9] The inscription was doubtless one in
honor of Semo Sancus, an old Sabine deity; indeed in
1574 the base of a statue of him with such an inscription as Justin and the *Acts of Peter* describe ("Semoni
Sanco deo fidio," etc.) was found at the spot Justin
describes—"in the river Tiber [i.e., on the island] between the two bridges."

[9] That the activity of Theodotus the leather-worker, expelled from the
church for his views by Victor, A.D. 189–98, is covertly assailed under the
guise of Simon is improbable; Simon was still a very real figure to Roman
Christians, as Hippolytus' account of him shows (*Refutation* vi. 2–15) (A.D.
230). Nor do these *Acts* particularly reflect the undoubted evils in the Roman
church under Zephyrinus, A.D. 198–217, and Calixtus, A.D. 217–22, to
which Hippolytus so strongly objected.

Eusebius quotes from the third book of Origen's lost *Commentary on Genesis* a few lines about the apostolic labors of Thomas, Andrew, John, Peter, and Paul that may imply that Origen knew Acts of all five of them (*Church History* iii. 1). The Genesis commentary was written in A.D. 220–30, so that the *Acts of Peter* would naturally fall between A.D. 200 and 220. Eusebius himself says the *Acts of Peter* was not accepted by the church (*Church History* iii. 3. 2), but it does not seem to have been definitely disapproved until sects like the Manicheans made so much of the ascetic elements in it. It is Peter's ascetic influence especially about marriage that leads in the *Acts* to his execution.

The prominent mention of groups of pious widows and virgins in the Roman church and of the support given by the Christian Marcellus to the Christian poor shows that the church is on the way to the state of things described by the bishop Cornelius (†253) when there were fifteen hundred in the Roman church in need of aid.

The earliest list of the heads of the Roman church that has come down to us is reflected in Irenaeus, A.D. 181–89 (*Refutation* iii. 3. 3) and names Linus as the first bishop. The Roman claim of primacy among the bishops for its head began under Victor (†198), progressed under Calixtus, who claimed the "power of the keys," and reached a peak under Stephen (A.D. 254–57), who professed to occupy the "chair of St. Peter."

The Liberian Catalogue of Roman bishops from Peter to Liberius dates from A.D. 354, and, for its earlier portions, from Peter to Pontianus, A.D. 231–

35, has been shown to be derived from the *Chronicle* written about that time by Hippolytus. So by the time of Pontianus Roman writers were thinking of Peter as first bishop of Rome.

The *Acts of Peter* does not go so far as to call Peter the first bishop of Rome, and thus make him head a line of popes, but it clearly contributes to the movement which was under way in the first half of the third century, and was probably written under Zephyrinus or Calixtus, that is, between A.D. 198 and 222.

Early in the third century some Christian novelist, probably at Edessa, wrote the thirteen *Acts of Thomas*, *The Acts of Thomas* completing them with his martyrdom. Tatian had carried the gospel in Syriac into eastern Syria with his *Diatessaron*, or interweaving of the Four Gospels, about A.D. 172, and Bardaisan, A.D. 154–222, had developed some Christian Syriac literature with his poems. Whether the *Acts of Thomas* owes anything directly to him is questioned, but poems of Syriac origin have certainly been wrought into it, for it is rich in liturgical and poetical passages. Most scholars think it was written in Syriac, our numerous Greek manuscripts being a translation from that language; though James and Bonnet argue for a Greek original, now mostly lost. The work, which seems to be complete, is much the most extended of all the really ancient apocryphal Acts. Besides the Syriac and Greek forms of it, it is preserved also in Latin, Ethiopic, and Armenian versions.

The *Acts of Thomas* is strongly ascetic, describing Thomas as laboring to separate wives from their hus-

bands and to abolish the marriage relation. It is full
of strange echoes of Gnostic, Mandaean, and Manichean religion. There is some reason to believe Christianity to have reached southern India early in the
third century, and some of the names in Thomas are
known to history, such as King Gundafor (Hyndopheres), who ruled a part of India in the first Christian
century; but there is no reason to suppose there is
anything historical about these *Acts*. They are, in
fact, full of the ancient popular religious vocabulary
of demon and marvel. The dead are raised, animals
speak, devils are cast out, relics cure.

While the *Acts of Thomas* abounds in long speeches,
prayers, and hymns, there is a good deal of lively narrative, as a summary of its action will show.

1. The apostles draw lots for their mission fields.
Judas Thomas draws India but refuses it. Jesus sells
Course of the   him to a merchant from India who wants
Narrative   a carpenter for the Indian king Gundafor,
giving him a regular deed of sale. (A
king of this name, in Greek Hyndopheres, is known
to have reigned over part of India in the first century.)
The merchant claims Thomas under the deed of sale
and takes him to India. At Andrapolis the king's
daughter is being married. At the wedding Thomas
utters a mystic bridal song. He persuades the bride
and groom to renounce marriage (chaps. 1–16).

2. Gundafor commissions Thomas to build him a
palace and provides the necessary money. Thomas
gives it to the poor and later explains to the king that
he has built him a palace in heaven. The king is

angry, but his brother dies and sees the palace in heaven. He is restored to life and tells the king about it.

3. A serpent has killed a woman's lover. Thomas makes the serpent confess this and all his crimes and restore the man to life. He kills the serpent and converts the youth. The people of the city repent.

4. A colt blesses the apostle, who utters a hymn of praise to Christ (rather like the Oxyrynchus Isis litany). He then converses with the colt and dismisses it. The colt drops dead.

5. A woman long tormented by a lustful devil begs the apostle's help. He rebukes the devil, and it departs in fire and smoke. Thomas utters a prayer to Christ and baptizes the woman and her companions and then administers the communion to them, marking the bread with a cross.

6. A young man confesses having murdered his mistress. The apostle restores her to life, and she tells of the punishments of the lost (chaps. 55–57), in words drawn from the *Revelation of Peter*. The apostle calls upon the people to repent, and they do so.

7. A captain asks Thomas to come and cure his wife and daughter who are harassed by devils; he sets off with him.

8. As they travel, the animals drawing their car give out, and the apostle summons four wild asses to take their places. On reaching the house, Thomas sends one of the asses in to call the demons out. The women come out, and the apostle assisted by the wild ass completes their cure. The apostle sends the four wild asses back to their pastures.

9. A woman of position named Mygdonia is converted and leaves her husband, Charis (or Charisius). He is incensed and has Thomas imprisoned. In prison Thomas utters the Hymn of the Soul, or of Redemption, the finest and most perplexing of the many liturgical pieces that distinguish the *Acts of Thomas:* A prince goes down to Egypt to recover a pearl, but, arrived there, he forgets his errand, until a letter from his own country rouses him to obtain it, resume his royal attire, and return home.

10. The apostle leaves the prison long enough to baptize Mygdonia. The king Misdai (or Misdaeus) releases him with orders to reconcile Mygdonia to her husband.

11. But now Misdai's wife Tertia is converted and decides to leave her husband.

12. The king's son, Vazan (or Iuzanes), joins the disciples of Thomas and follows him back to prison, where the apostle preaches and prays. (But the great prayer, chaps. 144–48, probably belongs in the martyrdom, after chap. 167, where some manuscripts have it.)

13. Thomas' leading converts join him in the prison. They all go to Vazan's house, and Vazan and the others are baptized and are given the communion.

These thirteen *Acts* are followed by the martyrdom of Thomas. Misdai condemns Thomas to death. He is taken up into a mountain and killed with spears. Misdai himself is afterward converted.

The *Acts of Thomas* probably belongs to those Acts which Efrem says were written in Syriac and Greek by the followers of Bardesanes, and it is possible that it was put forth in both languages, as Harnack suggests. The conception of the work seems to be Greek, while some parts of it, like the Hymn of the Soul, are in all probability of Syriac origin. Its use of the *Revelation of Peter*, in chapters 55–57, and of the *Acts of John* (chap. 22), in chapter 53, rather favors a Greek original, for we do not know that these works were so anciently known in Syriac versions. The long series of honorific titles piled up in the prayer in chapters 10 and 39 recalls the style of the Isis litany discovered at Oxyrhynchus (*Oxyrhynchus Papyri* xi. 1380) and the hymn near the end of Clement's *Tutor*. There are traces of the use of the *Gospel of the Hebrews* ("they do rest, and resting do reign," chap. 136) and of the *Gospel of the Egyptians* ("him that was inward have I made outward and the outward inward," chap. 147).

There are even touches of humor in the *Acts of Thomas*, as when Thomas refuses to obey Jesus and go to India, and so Jesus without his knowledge sells him into slavery to the Indian merchant (chap. 2), or when Thomas draws a plan for a palace for the king but gives the money to the poor and explains to the king that he has built him his palace in heaven (chap. 21). When Thomas' ascetic habits were reported to the king, "he rubbed his face with his hands and shook his head for a long time" (chap. 20).

This can hardly be the *Acts of Thomas* that Eusebius intimates Origen knew, for it described Thomas' field as Parthia, not India. The *Acts* was used by the Gnostics and, according to Epiphanius, by the Encratites and the Apostolics (*Heresies* 47, 61). Augustine says it was used by the Manicheans, and Turribius, by the Priscillianists. It entered into the Manichean corpus of apostolic Acts described by Photius (*Bibliotheca* cod. 114) and into the *Apostolic History* of Abdias. It was also revived in a paraphrase by Nicetas of Thessalonica in the twelfth century.

The ascetic ideal of the *Acts* is presented in the description of Thomas himself: "He continually fasts and prays, and eats only bread, with salt, and drinks water, and wears the same garment in fine weather and winter, and accepts nothing from anyone, and gives what he has to others" (chap. 20). This, with Thomas' renunciation of marriage, pretty well sums up the monastic ideal of later days. Indeed it goes beyond it in its abstinence from meat and wine. The estimate of the length of the *Acts* ("Travels") *of Thomas* in the Nicephorus list (about A.D. 850) as 1,600 lines accounts for hardly more than half our present *Acts of Thomas* and is either a mistake or represents an abbreviated form of the work.

About the middle of the third century, perhaps as late as A.D. 260, some Christian, probably in Greece or *The Acts of Andrew* Asia Minor, wrote a story of the wanderings, wonders, and discourses of Andrew, ending with his martyrdom. Its chief purpose seems to have been to discourage marriage and to lead women converts to forsake their husbands. It was probably not heretical, though highly ascetic.

Little remains of the *Acts of Andrew*, and what there is mostly relates to the efforts of a woman named

Maximilla to escape from her husband Aegeas or
Aegeates, the proconsul of Greece, and Andrew's encouragement of these efforts. He succeeds in this, and
the proconsul has him crucified. On reaching the place
of execution, Andrew utters an address to the cross,
reminiscent of Peter's rhapsody before his cross. He
lingers for three days on the cross, refuses release, and
dies. The fragments fall into line with the other
apocryphal *Acts* in their aversion to marriage. They
also exhibit some Gnostic echoes.

In his famous chapter on the New Testament canon
(*Church History* iii. 25. 6) Eusebius speaks of *Acts of
Andrew* and of *John*, which he describes as heretical.
His reference in iii. 1. 1, 2, to Origen's account, now
lost, of the labors of these apostles, John in Ephesus
and Andrew in Scythia, may imply that Origen knew
Acts of each of them. But Eusebius is the earliest
writer to mention them, and we cannot be at all sure
that Origen knew them or that they existed in his
day.

Gregory of Tours (A.D. 538–94) came across the
Greek *Acts of Andrew* and produced a Latin epitome of
them, frankly omitting the tedious parts (the discourses were probably pretty long) and emphasizing
Andrew's miracles. This epitome is in the main embodied in the Andrew section (Book 3) of Abdias'
Apostolic History.

The scene of the story is not Scythia, north of the
Black Sea, which Eusebius said was the field of
Andrew's labors, but Pontus, Bithynia, Macedonia,
and Greece, where Andrew finally suffers martyrdom,

at Patrae, the modern Patras. Gregory prefaced his account of it with a summary of the Egyptian *Acts of Andrew and Matthias* (or Matthew) among the cannibals, who kept any strangers who fell into their hands for thirty days and then ate them, tagging each one with the date of his arrival so as to make no mistake.[10] (This verges on the *Odyssey* and the *Arabian Nights*.) On a ship steered by Jesus himself, Andrew comes and rescues Matthias and their other victims. A sequel to this episode is supplied by the *Acts of Peter and Andrew*, in which Peter causes a camel to go through the eye of a needle. But these were no part of the third-century *Acts of Andrew*. All that we really possess of it is (1) the story in Euodius (*On Faith, against the Manicheans* 38) around A.D. 400, about Maximilla's efforts to escape from her husband; (2) a Vatican Greek fragment, telling of Andrew's discourses in prison, especially encouraging Maximilla to leave her husband; and (3) the martyrdom of Andrew.

Epiphanius (†403), in *Heresies* 47, says that the *Acts of Andrew*, as well as those of John, Thomas, and others, was appealed to by the Encratites, who were vegetarians and total abstainers and renounced marriage, as well as by the self-styled Apostolics, who renounced marriage and private property (chap. 61) and the Origenians or eunuchs (chap. 63). Innocent I, in his letter of A.D. 405, according to some manuscripts, condemns the *Acts of Andrew*, stating that they were written by "the philosophers Neochares and Leoni-

---

[10] This became the basis of an Anglo-Saxon poem, *Andreas*, which has been ascribed to Cynewulf.

das," perhaps a miswriting of Leucius Charinus, the reputed author of the *Acts of John*.

The impulse toward Christian fiction which had found expression in the second and third centuries in

The Clemen-tine Recog-nitions and Homilies

the *Acts* of the individual apostles—Paul, John, Peter, Thomas, and Andrew— in the early years of the fourth century, probably between 313 and 325, produced two considerable works, the *Recognitions* and the *Homilies* of Clement.

The *Recognitions*, in ten books, ostensibly written by Clement of Rome in the first person, describes a jour-ney of Clement to Palestine, his meeting with Peter, and his life with him; the discussions they had about all sorts of religious and doctrinal matters; and the marvelous way in which Clement's long-lost parents and brothers are restored to him. It is to this feature of the narrative that it owes its name, the *Recognitions*.

The twenty *Homilies* relate extended conversations between Peter and Clement, in which spiritual matters are discussed very much as in the *Recognitions*. Both works seem to rest on an earlier piece of fiction about Clement, a sort of Clement romance, written probably about A.D. 260, but now lost; and this in turn proba-bly drew upon two conflicting sources, one Jewish-Christian and Gnostic in color, the other Catholic and anti-Gnostic—the latter probably the *Acts of Peter*, which had so much to say about Simon Magus, who also appears prominently, especially in the *Recogni-tions*. Such sources would explain the strange mixture of heretical and orthodox elements that the *Clemen-*

tines exhibit. The author was no doubt a Catholic Christian, and probably unconscious of the heretical character of some of his materials. The *Homilies* are introduced by letters from Peter and Clement to James of Jerusalem, designed to give them credibility.

While the *Homilies* have come down to us in Greek, the *Recognitions* are preserved in full only in a Latin translation by Rufinus.

CHAPTER VI

THE FIRST APOLOGIES

As Christianity gradually separated from Judaism and came to feel its individual character as a new faith, competing with various ethnic, philosophic, and mystery religions in the Roman world and meeting objection and persecution, it began to be conscious of itself and to frame answers to the criticisms and attacks that were made upon it. This was the beginning of the Christian apologetic literature which soon took shape in a series of apologies and dialogues in defense of the new religion.

Christians were mostly people of little distinction or position, and some things about them and their proceedings aroused suspicion and hostility. They were suspected of incest, cannibalism, atheism, disloyalty to the state, and even setting fire to the capital. Their views, too, were ridiculed, especially their worship of a man who had been crucified.

Jewish writers, seeking to commend their religion to Greek readers, had already produced such books as the Wisdom of Solomon, Philo's treatise *On the Contemplative Life*, and Josephus' two volumes *Against Apion*, all written in the first century. Christian gropings toward such expression begin to appear in Luke's account of Paul's address in Athens in Acts 17:22–31.

But the earliest Christian book or booklet in this field was the so-called *Preaching of Peter.*

Peter appears in the Acts as the first Christian preacher, and it was natural for a Christian writer setting up a pattern of Christian preaching to be followed in carrying the gospel about the Greek world to think first of him. In his name, therefore, about the beginning of the second century, or very early in it, the *Preaching of Peter* was written. The little book itself has long since disappeared, but quotations from it in Clement of Alexandria and in Origen give us some substantial information about it.

The Preach- ing of Peter

It attacked, on the one hand, the prevalent idolatry of its times—the Greek ways of worshiping God— and, on the other, the Jewish ways of worship, with their angels and archangels and their sacred days and seasons, which were governed by the changes of the moon. Christians worshiped God in a new way and, in contrast with Jews and Greeks, formed a third race. For twelve years the apostles were to labor among the Jews; then they were to go out into the world to preach to all men the one God and salvation through faith in Christ. Jesus is both "Law" and "Word." In the writings of the prophets the coming of Christ and his sufferings, death, and resurrection would be found foretold.

These teachings of the *Preaching of Peter* are reported in Clement of Alexandria. Origen, a generation later, seems to be using the same book (in his *On First Principles*, prologue 8) under the name the *Teaching* (or

Doctrine) *of Peter* (the passage is preserved only in Latin) when he says that in that book the Savior is represented as saying to the disciples, "I am not an incorporeal demon." This saying appears in Ignatius' *Letter to the Smyrnaeans* 3:2 (A.D. 110–17), as evidence that Jesus appeared in a material body after the resurrection.[1] The way the saying is introduced in Ignatius ("When he came to Peter and his companions, he said to them, 'Take and handle me, and see that I am not an incorporeal demon' ") sounds very much as though it were drawn from some document associated with Peter's name. Jerome says that this saying stood in the *Gospel of the Hebrews* (*On Illustrious Men* 16), but there is no difficulty in supposing that both Ignatius and that gospel derived it from the *Preaching of Peter*.

If the *Preaching* is quoted in the *Gospel of the Hebrews* (A.D. 120–30) and in Ignatius (A.D. 110–17), it must have been written in the opening years of the second century, A.D. 100–110. Its primitive character accords reasonably well with this date. Its reference to the worship of cats, dogs, and apes has been taken to suggest an Egyptian origin, since idols with the heads of cats and dogs were worshiped in Egypt. Jewish apologetic had been particularly active there, too, in the Wisdom of Solomon, the work of Philo, the *Letter of Aristeas*, and in such attacks on idolatry as the story of Bel and the Dragon and the Letter of Jeremiah, in the Apocrypha.

Some of our earliest mentions of it are also from Egypt—Clement of Alexandria, who accepts it and

[1] Cf. John 20:25–27.

quotes it as Peter's, and Origen, who has found the book quoted in a work of Heracleon's and is very skeptical about its genuineness as a work of Peter. Heracleon was a pupil of Valentinus and flourished between A.D. 145 and 180. Clement says that he was the most distinguished of the followers of Valentinus and quotes some of his comments on the Gospel of Luke. Heracleon wrote a commentary on the Gospel of John, of which Origen made a good deal of use. Hippolytus locates Heracleon in Italy, and so the first reflections of the *Preaching* are widely scattered: Ignatius in Asia in the first quarter of the second century, the *Apology of Aristides* (which it influenced) in Athens and the *Gospel of the Hebrews* in Egypt in the second quarter, and Heracleon in Italy in the third quarter. On the whole, the evidence rather favors Egypt as the place of origin.

The *Preaching* very early became the model for a larger Christian apology, that of Aristides, written in Greece probably between A.D. 138 and 147, for much of what we have of it is reproduced in that book. It may also have influenced the lost *Apology* of Quadratus, A.D. 125–29. The belief that Jesus instructed the apostles to remain in Jerusalem for twelve years after his departure before going out into the world to preach reappears, as we have seen, in the *Acts of Peter*, chapter 5, and seems to have influenced Eusebius to date the Gospel of Matthew in A.D. 41, when Matthew would, according to this belief, be ready to leave Jerusalem and would write his gospel to leave behind him. The

Catholic tradition of Peter's twenty-five years' ministry in Rome also rests upon it.

In his work *On First Principles* (prologue 8) Origen says that the *Teaching* (probably meaning *Preaching*) *of Peter* is not by Peter or anyone else inspired by the spirit and is not counted among the books of the church. Eusebius in his *Church History* (iii. 3. 2, A.D. 326) groups the *Preaching* with the *Acts of Peter*, the *Gospel of Peter*, and the *Revelation of Peter* as not accepted by standard Christianity and not appealed to by church writers.[2] Indeed, of all the works claiming the name of Peter, Eusebius accepted only the first epistle as his work (*Church History* iii. 3. 1).

The *Preaching of Peter* is chiefly significant as the first of the Christian apologies. It is another book of which Christian learning hopes a complete copy may some day be found.

The early Christians were in a most difficult position. Under Roman administration religions had to be recognized—"licensed"—by the state before they could be lawfully practiced. But Christians practiced an unlicensed religion; in fact, Christianity did not obtain the necessary state recognition until early in the fourth century. Christian meetings had sometimes to be covertly, almost secretly, held, and this occasioned suspicion and criticism. Christian ways of describing their proceedings—eating Christ's flesh and drinking his blood—led the uninitiated to think some canni-

The Apology of Quadratus

---

[2] Although Clement of Alexandria accepted the *Preaching* and the *Revelation of Peter* as genuine and quoted from both.

balistic rites were observed by them. It was easy to
think of them as haters of the human race, as Tacitus
put it (*Annals* xv. 44), and to charge them with the
burning of Rome. So to the official hostility of the
government were added the suspicion and detestation
of the public.

It was natural that intelligent Christians should
undertake to repel these attacks and defend themselves
against the hostility of the empire. A beginning in
this direction was made in Egypt, very early in the
second century, in the *Preaching of Peter*. But a more
formal appeal to the emperor himself was soon after
written by a Greek named Quadratus and presented
to the emperor Hadrian, probably at Athens when
Hadrian visited that city in A.D. 125 or later in 129.[3]
Eusebius, who gives us all the information we possess
about Quadratus (for Jerome seems to have simply repeated what he had read in Eusebius about him), con-
nects the presentation of the apology to the emperor
with the year 125. He quotes a sentence from the little
book, which is all that has been preserved of it:

But the works of our Savior were always present, for
they were genuine; those who had been cured, those who
had risen from the dead, who were seen not only when they

---

[3] J. Rendel Harris has advanced the suggestion that Quadratus was replying to the attack of the pagan writer Celsus, the *True Discourse*, a book we
know so well from Origen's detailed answer to it (*Against Celsus* probably
ca. A.D. 246), and that fragments of Quadratus' apology are imbedded in the
Clementine *Homilies* and in the romance of *Barlaam and Joasaph* (*The Ex-
positor*, 1921). But it is most improbable that the *True Discourse* was written
before the middle of the second century, in view of its mention of the *Dialogue of Jason and Papiscus*, which was written about A.D. 140.

were cured and raised, but on all occasions when they were present; and not only while the Savior was on earth, but also after his departure, they were alive for some time, so that some of them lived even to our day [*Church History* iv.3.2].

Eusebius says that, when he wrote, this book of Quadratus' was still in the hands of a great many of the brethren; but no copy of it is now known to exist. It is another of the ancient books the student of Christian literature hopes may somewhere be found.

The writing of apologies for Christianity emerges into clearer light with the figure of Aristides. He was *The Apology of Aristides* a Christian philosopher of Athens and addressed a defense of the new faith to the emperor Antoninus, probably between A.D. 138 and 147, since Marcus Aurelius is not mentioned in the address as coemperor. Up to about sixty years ago all that was known of this book was what Eusebius said of it in his *Church History* iv. 3.3.[4] We cannot be sure that even he had actually seen it, although he says it was still in existence and widely circulated in his day. But in 1878 an Armenian fragment of it (from the tenth century) was published. This confirmed the statement of Eusebius that it was addressed to the emperor Hadrian. In 1889, however, Dr. J. Rendel Harris discovered in St. Catherine's on Mount Sinai an almost complete text of the book in a Syriac version. This gave the title of the emperor ad-

[4] What Jerome says about Aristides (*On Illustrious Men* 20) is probably simply drawn from Eusebius.

dressed more fully: "To the Imperator Caesar Titus
Hadrianus Antoninus Augustus Pius," which means
Antoninus Pius, although it might easily have suggested Hadrian to Eusebius (who sometimes got other
emperors confused) and to the Armenian translator.
Dr. Harris showed his find to his friend J. Armitage
Robinson, who soon after came across large parts of it
in Greek in the medieval romance of *Barlaam and
Joasaph* (or Josaphat), the writer of which had evidently worked practically the whole apology into his
book. This romance (written in the seventh or eighth
century) is the story of a prince of India named
Joasaph who is converted by a Christian monk. The
monk, Barlaam, is later called upon to defend Christianity before the king and his court, and the defense
that is offered is—the *Apology of Aristides!*

In 1922 a few lines of chapters 5 and 6 were published from a Greek papyrus leaf of the fourth century
in *Oxyrhynchus Papyri* xv. 1778. Another fragment,
covering Aristides 15:6—16:1 has been found in the
British Museum and was announced by H. J. M. Milne in
1923.[5] The sources for the text of the *Apology* are therefore the Syriac version, the Greek recast of the work
employed in *Barlaam and Joasaph*, the Greek fragments
from Oxyrhynchus and in the British Museum, and
three short Armenian fragments preserving the opening lines. The Greek, of course, promises to be the
truest witness to the text, but it has been alternately
expanded and condensed for its immediate purpose in
the medieval story, so that in the absence of more

---

[5] *Journal of Theological Studies*, Vol. XXV (1923).

ancient materials the textual problem is almost insoluble.[6]

The apologist begins with an account of the Christian idea of God. He then presents the Chaldean, the Greek, the Egyptian, and the Jewish ways of worshiping God, showing the weaknesses of each.[7] The Chaldeans worship the elements—sky, earth, water, fire, air, sun, and moon. The Greeks worship gods like men, full of frailties and crimes. The Egyptians worship plants and animals—crocodiles, cats, dogs, and snakes. The Jews are too fond of angels and holy days. Finally he presents the Christian way, which he strongly commends, although he speaks of the Christians as well as of the other four groups in the third person. The closing chapters, 15–17, give a fine picture of early Christian practices and morals.

The influence of the Four Gospels is clearly seen in Aristides' account of the Christians; indeed, he probably refers to them when he invites the emperor to examine the Christians' books (16:3, 5). Aristides is also strongly influenced by the *Preaching of Peter*, as we have seen. He sees in the Christians a new race, as the author of the *Preaching* did. He seems to have known the Acts and probably Romans and I Peter. His way of referring to the writings of the Christians as his sources suggests the possession of a larger Christian library.

The book was current in Greek in the fourth cen-

[6] I hazarded a provisional solution in my *Die aeltesten Apologeten* (Göttingen, 1914).

[7] In the Syriac the groups are barbarians, Greeks, Jews, and Christians.

tury, as Eusebius and the Oxyrhynchus fragment show; it passed early into Syriac and later into Armenian, and its Greek form was used in the seventh or eighth century in the romance of *Barlaam and Joasaph*. We may still hope that a complete Greek text of it will sometime come to light.

The dialogue was a Greek literary device for making philosophy easy, and about A.D. 140 Aristo, a man of Pella, in Palestine, laid hold of it for

Aristo of Pella; the Christian Dialogue

Christian purposes. Pella was the city in Perea in which the Christians of Jerusalem were warned to take refuge when the Roman armies gathered about Jerusalem to besiege it in A.D. 66–70 (Eusebius *Church History* iii. 5. 3). It was one of the ten cities that formed the league known as the Decapolis. Aristo may have been a descendant of those Jerusalem refugees. At any rate, his writings, probably this very dialogue of his, supplied some material to Eusebius on the subject of the Bar-Cochba rebellion against Rome (A.D. 132–35), and Eusebius mentions Aristo as the source of some of his information about it (*Church History* iv. 6. 3).

The dialogue was represented as taking place between a Christian named Jason and a Jew named Papiscus and became the model for a whole series of such Jewish-Christian dialogues. The first mention of it is in the famous *True Discourse* which Celsus, about A.D. 150, directed against Christianity. This work has long since disappeared, but Origen in his answer to it (*Against Celsus*, A.D. 246) quoted from it so extensively that we can recover a good deal of it.

Celsus says he knows a *Dialogue of Papiscus and Jason* and that it deserves not so much to be laughed at as to be pitied and hated. Origen finds nothing hateful about the book but defends it as showing how the Jewish prophecies of the Christ apply to Jesus (*Against Celsus* iv. 52).

A few years after Celsus and before Origen, Clement of Alexandria mentioned the book in the sixth book of his *Outlines*. The *Outlines* are now lost, but Maximus the Confessor in the seventh century reports Clement's mention of the *Dialogue*.

Jerome in his *Commentary on Galatians* (3:13) remembers that he has read in the *Dialogue of Jason and Papiscus* that he that hangs is a reproach of God. This was Aquila's translation of a sentence in Deut. 21:23, which is familiar from Paul's quotation of it in Gal. 3:13. Aquila flourished, according to Epiphanius, in A.D. 128–29, so that his translation of the Hebrew scriptures cannot be much earlier than A.D. 130–35. Taken with Aristo's report of the Bar-Cochba War, which ended in A.D. 135, this suggests that Aristo cannot have written before A.D. 140. Jerome also says that the *Dialogue* said: "In the Son God made the heavens and the earth."

Toward the end of the fifth century another man named Celsus made a Latin translation of the *Dialogue*. This has disappeared, but the preface he wrote for it has survived and informs us that Jason was a Jewish Christian and Papiscus an Alexandrian Jew who was finally converted by Jason's arguments.

Maximus the Confessor, a Greek writer of the

seventh century, already mentioned, is the first reader of the *Dialogue* to tell us that it was the work of Aristo of Pella. He reports that it spoke of seven heavens, and, as we have seen, we owe to him our knowledge that Clement of Alexandria mentioned it in the sixth book of his *Outlines*.

In the sixth century another Greek dialogue between a Jew and a Christian—the *Dialogue of Papiscus and Philo*—appeared, and, since it uses the name of one of Aristo's debaters, it is natural to suppose that it made use of Aristo's book; but we cannot be sure of this. Certainly Aristo's idea of using the Greek dialogue as a medium for arguing out the rival claims of Christianity and Judaism was acted upon by a whole series of Christian apologists,[8] beginning almost immediately with Justin's *Dialogue with Trypho*.

This exhausts our present knowledge of Aristo's dialogue, a complete text of which, in either Greek of Latin, would help much toward the recovery of early Christian apologetic.

[8] E.g., the *Dialogue of Simon the Jew and Theophilus the Christian*, a fifth-century work, by the monk Evagrius.

CHAPTER VII

THE AGE OF JUSTIN

Both the early forms of apologetic, the dialogue and apology, were employed by Justin, about the middle of the second century, in defense of Christianity. Justin was a native of Flavia Neapolis, in Palestine, the ancient Shechem, the modern Nablous. He was not a Jew but traveled into the Greek world to complete his education. He visited various philosophical schools—Stoic, Pythagorean, Peripatetic, and Platonist—but found no complete satisfaction until at Ephesus he met a Christian who introduced him to the Jewish prophecies and showed him how they were fulfilled in Christ. This was probably about A.D. 133. A few years later he became a Christian teacher, and by A.D. 150 found himself in Rome, where he wrote the only books of his that have survived, his *Apology*, written soon after A.D. 150, and his *Dialogue*, written between A.D. 155 and 160. He suffered martyrdom in Rome about A.D. 165.

Eusebius (*Church History* iv. 18) lists eight works of Justin—two *Apologies*, *Against the Greeks*, the *Refutation*, *On the Sovereignty of God*, *Psaltes* (perhaps a hymnbook), *On the Soul*, and a *Dialogue against the Jews*. Eusebius also mentions a work of Justin *Against Marcion* (iv. 11. 8), but, when he proceeds to quote from it, he quotes from what we know as the *Apology*. But Justin's contemporary Irenaeus also mentions this work *Against Marcion* and quotes from it a sentence that is not found in the *Apology:* "Justin well says in his work against Marcion that he would not have believed the Lord himself if he had preached another God besides the Creator" etc. (*Refutation* iv. 6. 2; Eusebius *Church History* iv. 18. 9). Eusebius also mentions elsewhere (*Church History* iv. 11. 10), in Justin's own words, a work *Against All Heresies*, which he had probably never seen.

Another list of Justin's writings is given by Photius, about A.D. 890, in his *Bibliotheca* (cod. 125), but it is for the most part taken from Eusebius and adds nothing of value. He does not seem to have seen any of the genuine works of Justin. In general, almost everything said about Justin after the time of Eusebius seems to have been drawn mostly from what he had said in the *Church History* about him.

Of all the works with which Justin has been credited, only two have reached our day: the *Apology* and the *Dialogue*. They are preserved in two manuscripts dated in 1364 and 1541, the latter being a copy of the former. There is also a fifteenth-century fragment, containing *Apology* chapters 65–67.[1] The manuscripts, it is true, offer two apologies, perhaps under the influence of Eusebius, but what they count as the first is now generally recognized as an appendix to the other one, which was evidently the real apology. It is doubtful if there ever was really a second.

[1] These chapters are also preserved in two Latin manuscripts of the sixteenth century.

The *Apology* is addressed to the emperor Antoninus and his colleagues and asks the emperor to examine the charges made against the Christians and to satisfy himself that they are really a decent, law-abiding body who should not be condemned simply for the name they bear. They are not atheists, though they are not idolators. Christ taught a higher morality, and his life and work were foretold by the Hebrew prophets. Persecution and error are the work of the demons. The religious practices of the Christians are pure, pious, and simple. In closing, Justin quotes a letter of Hadrian to Minucius Fundanus, which he thinks favorable to the Christians.

The other so-called "apology" of the manuscripts is really simply an appendix to the *Apology* and was probably added to a second edition of it, a few years later.[2]

Justin was the most voluminous Christian writer up to his time, and his *Dialogue* was probably the longest Christian book thus far written. It describes the discussion, begun on one day and continued on the next, between Justin, speaking in the first person, and a Jew named Trypho, a name perhaps suggested by a well-known Jewish rabbi named Tarphon. Justin makes a great deal of the argument from prophecy. His contention that the Jewish prophecies are fulfilled in Christ is so contrary to the position taken by Marcion in his *Antitheses*, or *Contradictions*, that the *Dialogue*

[2] In the manuscripts the *Dialogue* stands first, then comes the Appendix, entitled the first apology, then the *Apology*, entitled the second apology. Eusebius, while he lists two apologies, quotes from both *Apology* and Appendix as the "first apology." It is not likely that there were two; the scribes may have been led to think there were by the remarks of Eusebius.

may be regarded as a counterblast against Marcion's book. Justin naturally allegorizes the Jewish scriptures in the manner of interpretation customary with Jews, Greeks, and Christians in antiquity. In the end, while Trypho is not converted, they part, with courtesy and good feeling. This irenic note is characteristic of Justin, whether he deals with Jewish prophecy or Greek philosophy.

In the *Apology* (xxvi. 8) Justin speaks of his treatise *Against All Heresies*, which may have been the work *Against Marcion* which Irenaeus mentions and quotes and which Eusebius had confused with the *Apology*. Justin is frequently mentioned by later Christian writers, beginning with his own pupil Tatian, who speaks of him as the ''most admirable Justin'' and refers to his martyrdom as brought about by the Cynic Crescens, who may have reported him to the authorities.[3] His *Apology* manifestly influenced later apologists like Athenagoras, Theophilus, Tertullian, and probably Minucius Felix. Hippolytus (*Refutation* viii. 9 [Gr. 16]), and other Roman writers knew his work, though Clement and Origen do not mention him. How far he may have influenced subsequent writers on the heresies we cannot certainly say, but, beginning with his contemporary Hegesippus, they probably owed much to his lost work *Against All Heresies*. Eusebius quotes a dozen passages from his *Apology*, and Methodius, about A.D. 300, in his book *On the Resurrection*, describes him as a man ''neither in time nor virtue far removed from the apostles.''

[3] *Address to the Greeks* 18:2; 19:1.

Justin flourished in what Harnack has called the blooming time of the sects, the middle of the second century, and it was natural that he should be the first to undertake a literary counterattack upon them which led to such notable works as those of Hegesippus, Irenaeus, Hippolytus, and Ephiphanius. He also laid hold of both apology and dialogue in the service of Christian truth. Not only the bulk but the breadth of his literary work gives him importance. And, in seeking to bring Greek philosophy to the aid of his Christian faith, he is, as Staehlin has pointed out, a forerunner of the Alexandrian theology.

We are most grateful to Justin for his account (*Apology*, chaps. 65–67) of early Christian worship as practiced in the church at Rome in the middle of the second century, when the memoirs of the apostles or the writings of the prophets (67:3) were read to the congregation as long as time permitted. Even after his conversion, he continued to wear the philosopher's cloak, which drew Trypho's attention to him, in the opening scene of the *Dialogue*, and, like Aristides, he was called a "Christian philosopher," which seems to have been a sort of primitive Christian honorary degree.

But, notwithstanding all his influence and fame, Justin's works have for the most part disappeared, and even those we have rest on the slenderest manuscript tradition—a single fourteenth-century manuscript and a copy made from it in the sixteenth century. Even this is, for the *Dialogue* at least, somewhat dilapidated, for there is a manifest break at 74:4, where one leaf or more was missing from the text from which our oldest manuscript was copied. What follows seems to belong to the second day of the debate, 78:6, etc. So for Justin, too, we should welcome new manuscripts of his works, whether extant or lost.[4]

Out of a number of works preserved in Greek manuscripts under the name of Justin, but quite certainly not written by him, three may be mentioned here. The *Exhortation (Cohortatio) to the Greeks* appeals to the Greeks to turn from Homer and the poets to Moses and the prophets and to accept the truth of Christianity. It shows the use of the *Chronography* of Julius Africanus (A.D. 221) and was probably written in the latter part of the third century, somewhere about the Aegean.

In the *Address (Oratio) to the Greeks*, a Greek who has become a Christian offers a justification of his course, exposes the immoralities of Greek mythology and of pagan festivals, and urges the Greeks to follow him into the Christian faith. It is probably a work of the early years of the third century.

On Sovereignty makes use of quotations from the Greek poets to show the truth of monotheism. Justin

---

[4] The older of the two Justin manuscripts, Paris. 450, was a corpus of twelve works ascribed to Justin and included such pieces as the *Letter to Zenas and Serenus* and the *Exhortation to the Greeks*, ending with a work *On the Resurrection*, really written by Athenagoras, but here evidently regarded as a work of Justin. Robert Curzon, in his *Visit to the Monasteries in the Levant* (London, 1840), reports seeing at Caracalla (Caracallou) on Mount Athos in 1837 a Greek manuscript of Justin, "a small thick octavo, on charta bombycina" (pp. 378, 388), which was given to him but which he forgot to bring away. Dr. Martin Sprengling, visiting the convent in 1914, made a special search for the manuscript, but it could not be found. It may have been only a collection of the works falsely ascribed to Justin.

is said to have written a work on the *Sovereignty of God*, but his method of proof was rather different, as he sought to establish it from the scriptures as well as from the books of the Greeks—so Eusebius tells us (*Church History* iv. 18. 4). The present work gives little evidence of its date, but it may be as early as the closing years of the second century.

Six other works have come down to us under the name of Justin, but all except possibly the *Letter to Diognetus* are as late as the fifth century.

In a Strassburg manuscript of some Greek writings falsely ascribed to Justin which was destroyed in the
The Letter to Diognetus burning of the cathedral library during the siege of 1870, there stood a *Letter to Diognetus*. It has never been found in any other manuscript, nor has any reference to it been identified in Christian literature. The text is broken at two points (7:6 and 10:1), and the final chapters (11 and 12), are evidently from another work altogether, perhaps from a homily of Methodius or someone belonging to his circle, though some have thought them a fragment from Hippolytus.

Diognetus was the tutor of Marcus Aurelius, and he may be the individual ostensibly addressed in the opening lines: "Since I perceive, most excellent Diognetus, that you are exceedingly zealous to learn the religion of the Christians." The ten or twelve short pages of the *Letter* proper reveal a decidedly rhetorical style, which sometimes seems to be concerning the writer more than what he has to say. It bristles with antitheses; in short, it is so full of art that it verges on the artificial. The letter lacks entirely the convincing and gripping quality of early Christian literature and has even called forth the conjecture that it is not a work of antiquity at all, but a Renaissance composition, simulating an ancient situation, though its apparent acquaintance with the work of Aristides is against this view.

The writer elaborates the idea that the Christians are in the world as the soul is in the body. He assails the folly of idolatry and the crudity of Jewish material sacrifice. If the *Letter* is an ancient work at all, and most scholars agree that it is, it probably belongs to the third century; but, if so, it is little more than a showy piece of Christian apologetic in an age when such things no longer met a vital need.

About the middle of the second century another man from the East, Syria or Assyria, journeyed westward, to Greece and Rome, in the pursuit of his
Tatian   studies. His name was Tatian. He says he came from Assyria, but Clement of Alexandria calls him a Syrian (*Miscellanies* iii. 12). He seems to have traveled widely about Greece, though some would explain his apparent familiarity with its works of art from his supposed possession of some Greek book describing them.[5] In Rome he met Justin and became a Christian. He returned to Greece and there, probably about A.D. 152–55, wrote his *Address to the Greeks*. It is usually classed as an apology, but it is quite as much a bitter attack upon Greek pretensions to leadership in

---

[5] R. C. Kukula, *Altersbeweis und Kuenstlerkatalog in Tatians Rede an die Griechen* (Vienna, 1900).

arts and letters. Tatian declares that all the great inventions really came from the barbarians. He points out the disagreement among Greek philosophers and ridicules their plays and sports. He declares that Moses is more ancient than Homer and dwells upon the immoralities celebrated in Greek sculpture. With all this polemic he interweaves a sketch of Christian views and morals and declares himself a champion of this barbarian philosophy.

Tatian is a sprightly, if somewhat intemperate, writer, and he leaves out a great deal that was certainly lofty and true in Greek thought. But it must be remembered that he wrote under great provocation, for the Greco-Roman world was equally blind to what was lofty and true on the Christian side of the debate and contemptuous of Christian character and principles. Tatian writes with the utmost rhetorical vigor and shows a keen satirical delight in exposing the foibles and faults of Greek philosophy, art, and religion.

Tatian had previously written a book *On Animals*, of which nothing is known (*Address* 15:2). He later returned to Rome, attaching himself to Justin, whom he greatly admired. There he must have written the book of *Problems*, which Eusebius knew of from the mention of it by Rhodo, an Asian writer of the time. In it, Rhodo said, Tatian promised to explain the obscure and hidden parts of the scriptures (*Church History* v. 13. 8). Rhodo, who was converted to Christianity by Tatian, wrote two or three books, one *Against the Heresy of Marcion* and one a commentary *On the Six Days'*

Work of Creation. He expressed the intention of writing
also a book of *Solutions* of Tatian's *Problems*, as Eusebius relates (*Church History* v. 13. 1–8). This sequence
of teacher and pupil, Justin-Tatian-Rhodo, all seeking
to express their views in books is a striking illustra-
tion of the vigorous literary activity of second-century
Christianity.

After the death of Justin, Tatian broke with the
church and returned to the East, where he became the
leader, if not the founder, of the Encratite sect, dis-
couraging marriage and denying the salvation of
Adam. Irenaeus discusses his heretical views in the
Refutation i. 28. 1. Clement of Alexandria in *Miscellanies* iii. 12 mentions and quotes another book of
Tatian, written in this Encratite period, *On Perfection
according to the Savior*, which J. Rendel Harris with
some plausibility identified with an Armenian tract on
the subject long ascribed to Efrem the Syrian (†373).[6]
Rufinus says that Tatian wrote a *Chronicon*, or chronological work (*Church History* vi. 11), but of this
nothing further is known.

Eusebius somewhat hyperbolically says that Tatian
left a great multitude of writings. Tatian seems to refer
to a work of his *On Demons* (*Address*, chap. 16). In
chapter 40 he seems to contemplate writing a treatise
"Against Those Who Have Discussed Divine Things,"
but nothing is known of either of these books. In fact,
the *Address* is the only creative writing of Tatian's that
has come down to us.

[6] *Tatian: Perfection according to the Saviour* (reprinted from the *Bulletin of
the Rylands Library*, Vol. VIII [1924]).

Eusebius had also heard (iv. 29. 6) that Tatian had ventured to paraphrase certain utterances of Paul in order to improve their style, but whether this means that he had translated Paul's letters into Syriac, or had made a commentary on them, or had merely revised and improved their text cannot certainly be made out. It is strange to think of Tatian as so concerned for Greek style, when he so loudly derides Greek literary refinements in his *Address*. It is pretty clear that Paul's letters were not known in Syriac in the second century. There is some irony in the fact that modern editors of Tatian's *Address* have made great efforts to improve *his* Greek style into conformity with Attic models.[7]

Tatian's great work, however, was his *Diatessaron*, or interweaving of the Four Gospels into one continuous narrative. This was probably made in Greek, for a Greek fragment of it, written probably early in the third century, was discovered at Dura-Europos on the Euphrates in 1933;[8] but its chief significance was in the Syriac version into which Tatian immediately put it, apparently for missionary use in Syria. It had a remarkable success, became the first Christian scripture of the Syriac-speaking Christians, and was not displaced from their scriptures until the appearance of the Peshitto New Testament in A.D. 411. Tatian with his Syriac *Diatessaron* seems to have been the founder of Syriac Christianity. Eusebius and Epiphanius both

[7] Cf. *Tatiani Oratio ad Graecos*, ed. Ed. Schwartz (Leipzig, 1888). His numerous emendations have been criticized by C. L. Heiler, *De Tatiani Apologetae dicendi genere* (1909).

[8] Carl H. Kraeling, "A Greek Fragment of Tatian's *Diatessaron* from Dura," in *Studies and Documents*, III (London, 1935), 1–37.

mention Tatian and the *Diatessaron*, but our best glimpse of it comes from Theodoret, who was bishop of Cyrrhus, west of the Euphrates. In his *Epitome* of heresy written about A.D. 453 he relates (1:20) that he found more than two hundred copies of the *Diatessaron* held in honor among the churches, which he gathered up and replaced with the gospels of the four evangelists. This process was probably generally followed after the introduction of the Peshitto version in 411, and the result is that, although Peshitto manuscripts are numerous, not a single copy of the *Diatessaron* in Syriac has yet been found.

It has survived, however, in an Arabic version, published by Ciasca in 1888, and a Latin form of it in the Vulgate text takes the place of the Four Gospels in the Codex Fuldensis, A.D. 541–46. Efrem (†373) wrote a commentary on it in Syriac, and, although this work has disappeared, a sixth-century Armenian version of it was published in a Latin translation by Moesinger in 1876. An Old German version of the Fuldensis Latin and a Dutch version made from the Syriac itself have also appeared. The recent discovery of a small Greek fragment at Dura-Europos has already been mentioned and encourages the hope that substantial parts at least of the early Greek or Syriac forms of this remarkable work may yet be found.

Tatian must have been a strong personality, as not only Rhodo but Clement of Alexandria seem to have been among his pupils; for when, at the beginning of the *Miscellanies* i. 1. 11, Clement speaks of his teachers, the first of them, whom he describes as born in Assyria

and heard by him in Greece, is generally identified as
Tatian. In the so-called *Little Labyrinth* Hippolytus
mentions Tatian as an apologist. But numerous writers refer to him as a heretic—Irenaeus, Clement of
Alexandria, Tertullian, Origen, Eusebius, and the author of the *Acts of Archelaus*. What the Fathers found
most unpardonable in Tatian was his idea that Adam
was not saved—a view that he was said to have originated, though later writers, like the author of the
Acts of Pilate, held that Adam was saved when Christ
descended into Hades and preached the gospel to the
dead (24:2). Medieval miniatures show Christ emerg-
ing from Hades, leading Adam by the hand.

One of the most dynamic characters in Christian history in the second century was Marcion. While he
Marcion wrote little himself, books were written
about him and against him, and for a time
he seemed to bid fair to dominate the Christian movement and to reshape its scripture, organization, and
views. Certainly in organization and scripture, standard Christianity learned much from Marcion, and his
influence can be traced in the later effort to organize
Christianity into one great body and to add the letters
of Paul to its scripture. Marcion was the first man, as
far as we know, to attempt these things.

Marcion was the son of the bishop of Sinope in Pontus. He was born about A.D. 85 and grew up to be a
man of affairs, a well-to-do shipowner of Sinope. He
felt the incongruity between the picture of God the
Creator in the Jewish scriptures, which were the Bible
of the churches, and the merciful and loving Father

revealed by Jesus. He concluded that they were different beings and, since the Jewish Bible was so largely concerned with the Creator, that it should be dislodged from its place in Christian worship and replaced by really Christian books—the Gospel of Luke and the ten letters of Paul. He went to Rome about A.D. 138, gave money to the church there, but left the church about 144, though he continued his efforts to prevail upon the western churches to unite upon his platform. He almost succeeded, for Justin, writing in Rome some ten years later, says that he was still at work and had attracted followers from every race (*Apology* 26:5; 58:1).

Marcion wrote but one book, his *Antitheses*, or *Contradictions*. It was written about the middle of the second century or soon after. In it he sought to show how different Christianity was from what the Jewish prophets had foretold; how history and prophecy had, in fact, contradicted each other. (This idea had been broached as far back as the writing of Matthew, which was written in part to meet it.) The Law and the Gospel were set forth as irreconcilable opposites. Passages in Jewish and Christian writings were set up in contrast to each other and probably interpreted, but not by the allegorical method then so popular, for Marcion strongly condemned it. Justin's *Dialogue with the Jew Trypho*, written in Rome within five or ten years after Marcion's book, has this position in mind in its insistence that Jewish prophecy *was* fulfilled in Christian history. In fact, the *Dialogue* may be regarded as a counterblast to Marcion's *Antitheses*, so directly does it oppose the central idea of Marcion's book. The letters of Timothy and Titus, too, written in Paul's name about this time, mentioned and denounced the *Antitheses* and Gnosticism (I Tim. 6:20, 21). They were clearly intended in part to repudiate Marcion's views and so make Paul's genuine letters more acceptable to the churches. This is why they reassert that God is one, the scriptures are inspired, and marriage is not wrong; Marcion had discouraged marriage.

Marcion was also immediately opposed, as we have seen, by Justin, who presumably dealt with him faithfully in his book *Against All Heresies* and who is also said to have written a special treatise *Against Marcion*. Theophilus of Antioch, who flourished about A.D. 181–190, wrote a treatise *Against Marcion* which is mentioned by Eusebius (*Church History* iv. 24. 3) and was very probably made immediate use of by Irenaeus, but is now lost. Irenaeus tells of Marcion in the same decade (A.D. 181–89) in his *Refutation* (i. 27. 2; iii. 3. 4) and more than once declared his intention of writing a special treatise against him (i. 27. 4; iii. 12. 12). Eusebius quotes this promise, *Church History* v. 8. 9, and in iv. 25 speaks as though Irenaeus had written such a work; but, if he did so, nothing is known of it, and Eusebius may be referring to his treatment of Marcion along with the other schismatics in the *Refutation*. He associates him with an otherwise unknown Philip of Gortyna, who "wrote a most elaborate work against Marcion," and a certain Modestus, who, Eusebius says, "exposed the man's error more clearly than the rest." He also mentions Rhodo, a convert of Tatian's, as writing a book *Against Marcion*, probably at Rome, about A.D. 180–90, now lost (*Church History* v. 13. 1).

Few fragments of Marcion's book have been identified, but among them is its opening sentence. Marcion is speaking of the Gospel: "O wealth of riches! Folly, power and ecstasy!—Seeing that there can be nothing to say about it, or to imagine about it, or to compare it to!"[9] It was evidently a book rich in paradox and fraught with strong emotion.

What with Justin, Rhodo, Theophilus, Irenaeus, Philip, and Modestus there was evidently a whole barrage of books against Marcion. That none of them survived was due in part to the decline of Marcion's movement and hence of zeal for its correction but perhaps also to the massive and satisfying way in which Tertullian dealt with it. For Tertullian devoted one of his major works to him—the five books *Against Marcion*, the first edition, in three books, written about A.D. 200 (198–202). This was soon revised and then again revised ten or twelve years later; a fact which suggests its popularity and influence. This book remains our best source of information about Marcion, of whom Tertullian characteristically inquires, "What Pontic mouse ever had such gnawing powers as he who has gnawed the gospels to pieces?"

Hippolytus, about A.D. 230, deals with him briefly

[9] From a Syriac and Armenian "Exposition of the Gospel," especially the Parables, published by J. Schaefer (1917); as revised by Harnack, *Das Evangelium vom fremden Gott* (2d ed., Leipzig, 1924), p. 256*, and Burkitt, *Journal of Theological Studies*, XXX (1929), 279–80.

in his *Refutation* (vii. 17; x. 15), bracketing him with Cerdo, the Syrian Gnostic who had come to Rome a little before him and influenced him a good deal, although Marcion never became a real Gnostic; he was too devoted to Paul and his doctrine of faith for that. Clement of Alexandria occasionally mentions Marcion, always to oppose his views. Origen, too, assails him now and then, as in *Against Celsus* 6:53. Eusebius has a good deal to say about Marcion, principally about the controversial literature he provoked.

While Marcion's book and his sect disappeared after a few generations, his influence upon Christianity was enduring. It was from him that standard Christianity seems to have gained the great idea of a Christian church with a world-wide organization. The churches were already reading the Fourfold Gospel in their public worship, as Justin shows (*Apology* 67:3), but it was Marcion who proposed a Christian scripture that should include not only the Gospel but the Apostle, who was, of course, Paul. When standard Christianity framed the first New Testament, Paul's letters found their place in it beside the Four Gospels, although they were now accompanied by a supplement, the Pastoral Letters, which disclaimed Marcion. As Harnack once observed, in the second century Marcion was the only man who tried to understand Paul—and he misunderstood him!

CHAPTER VIII

MANUALS, MEMOIRS, HYMNS
AND HOMILIES

To Jewish Christian minds Paul's idea of substituting an inward attitude of faith for all the old controls
The Teach-   of Law and Tradition seemed intolerably
ing of the   lax and free, and he himself frequently
Apostles—   supplemented the attitude of faith with a
the Doctrina   group of precepts of a somewhat legal
cast. But one early Christian, probably
of Antioch, undertook to formulate briefly, as embodying the teaching of the Twelve Apostles (doubtless over against Paul), the rules of conduct the Christian should observe. It was hardly more than a leaflet,
of less than a thousand words, but it was destined to
attain a wide influence and to be wrought into one
body of rules for Christian conduct after another. One
form of it had been found appended to the *Letter of
Barnabas*, and another, interpolated with material
from Matthew, began the *Didache*, or *Teaching of the
Twelve Apostles*, as discovered by Bryennius and published by him in 1883. But the original tract itself, in
a Latin version, came to light in 1899 in a Munich
manuscript of the eleventh century and at once corrected a number of impressions that had been formed
about it.[1]

[1] A Latin fragment of the text (*Doctrina Apostolorum*), covering about one-
fifth of the whole, was published from a Melk manuscript of the twelfth

For it was not, as most scholars had assumed, a Jewish document, which the writers of the *Didache* and of Barnabas had turned to Christian uses; it was a Jewish Christian tract, setting forth, without the slightest attempt at art, rules for the Christian life under the title, the *Teaching of the Apostles* (*De Doctrina Apostolorum*).

The *Teaching* begins by saying that there are two ways in the world, of Life and Death and of Light and Darkness. It goes on to list some seventy brief commands, mostly prohibitions, including some of the Ten Commandments, and occasionally introducing a short sentence in support of the command or in explanation of it. "This is the Way of Life." It proceeds to sketch the Way of Death under a list of almost forty sins—adultery, murder, false witness, etc.—in most cases simply naming the sin forbidden, and closes with a warning against them and an admonition to observe this teaching and thus attain the crown, "through our Lord Jesus Christ, who with God the Father and the Holy Spirit lives and reigns for ever and ever."

It is at once apparent that the *Teaching* reduces religion to conformity to a series of legalistic precepts. While the opening statement of the Way of Life at once suggests the influence of Jesus' teaching, the series of precepts that follows is precisely in the style of the Ten Commandments. To this original form the

century (1:1—2:6*a*) by Bernard Pez, librarian there early in the eighteenth century. It was reprinted by Gebhardt and, as far as it goes, agrees closely with the Munich Latin.

full title of the later form of the work, *The Teaching of the Lord through the Twelve Apostles to the Heathen*, is entirely appropriate, and it is probable that the full title belongs to the original work. That title fairly describes the original *Teaching* and its intention. It purports to be a summary of Jesus' teaching on life, as handed down by the Twelve Apostles, evidently in contrast with Paul, and as intended for heathen converts. The Pauline emphasis upon faith and an inner spiritual life is wanting. But those superstitious practices—magic, astrology, etc.—which were so congenial to heathen religion and so repugnant to the higher Judaism and to Christianity, are forbidden, while an unmistakably Jewish emphasis is laid upon giving to charity. The encouragement of corporal punishment is clearly reminiscent of Proverbs and Ecclesiasticus, as much of the *Teaching* is, in both matter and manner. The *Teaching* stands nearer to James and Proverbs than to almost any other ancient writings, but it altogether lacks the skill and variety with which those two books present a very similar ethical message.

This artless little tract, written about the beginning of the second century, probably in the circle of Antioch, as a brief code of Christian morals, was later added, somewhat rearranged, to the *Letter of Barnabas;* it was freely enriched with material from Matthew and with the addition of a short manual of church life—how to baptize and pray, when to fast, how to observe the Lord's Supper, etc.—formed the larger *Didache* published by Bryennius in 1883. In its primitive, or in this secondary, form, it became a part of the

Apostolic Church Ordinances, of Book vii of the *Apostolic Constitutions*, of the Athanasian *Summary of Doctrine*, of the pseudo-Athanasian *Fides Nicaena*, and of the Arabic *Life of Schnudi the Monk*.[2]

The *Didache* found by Bryennius may be regarded as an enlarged edition of this tract and had a somewhat distinguished history, as we shall see. We must add that a Greek text of the original *Teaching* would be a welcome discovery.

In the second quarter of the second century there lived in Hierapolis in Phrygia a Christian named

Papias of Hierapolis

Papias who lost no opportunity to meet and talk with any older Christian who came his way who might have known anyone who had heard the apostles. For from such living witnesses to Jesus' words and doings Papias felt he could learn more than from Christian books. And finally out of such interviews with his elders, about A.D. 140, or a little later, Papias produced a work of his own, in five books, which he called the *Interpretations of Sayings of the Lord*.

This work has disappeared, but Irenaeus and Eusebius knew it and made use of it, and what they and later writers quoted from it shows that it contained traditions of the utmost value about the beginnings of Christian history and literature. Harnack has suggested that the elders of whom Irenaeus, between A.D. 181–89, occasionally speaks in his *Refutation*,[3] were just these elders whom Papias had so faithfully interviewed, and this may be true.

---

[2] Harnack, *Theologische Litteraturzeitung*, 1900, p. 639.

[3] Lightfoot has collected seventeen such passages, or "Reliques of the Elders Preserved in Irenaeus," in his *Apostolic Fathers*, pp. 539–62.

A long list of Christian writers use and mention Papias—Irenaeus (A.D. 181–89), Eusebius (326), Jerome (†420), Philip of Side (*ca.* 430), Andreas of Caesarea (late sixth century), Maximus the Confessor (†662), Anastasius of Sinai († *ca.* 700), Georgius Hamartolus (*ca.* 842), and Photius (890). There are also scattered references to him in anonymous pieces.

It is from Papias that we learn the early Christian tradition as to the origin of the Gospel of Mark:

Mark having become the interpreter of Peter wrote down accurately everything that he remembered, without however recording in order what was either said or done by Christ. For neither did he hear the Lord speak nor did he follow him, but afterwards, as I said, attended Peter, who adapted his instructions to the needs of his hearers, but had no design of giving a connected account of the Lord's oracles. So then Mark made no mistake while he thus wrote some things as he remembered them, for he made it his one care not to omit anything that he heard, or to set down any false statement therein.[4]

This statement, obscure as it is, has proved of great value in dealing with the vexed question of the origin of Mark. Much more perplexing is Papias' statement about Matthew: "So then Matthew composed the Sayings in the Aramaic language, and each one translated them as best he could."[5] The only possible meaning of this is that Matthew the apostle was believed to be the author of the *oral* gospel.[6]

[4] Eusebius *Church History* iii. 39. 15.

[5] *Ibid.*

[6] Goodspeed, *Introduction to the New Testament* (Chicago, 1937), pp. 129–32.

Eusebius calls Papias a man of very limited understanding, but this is perhaps due to Papias' crass millennialism, which rather attracted Irenaeus but so repelled Eusebius:

The days will come in which vines shall grow each having ten thousand shoots, and on each shoot ten thousand branches, and on each branch again ten thousand twigs, and on each twig ten thousand clusters, and on each cluster ten thousand grapes, and each grape when pressed shall yield twenty-five measures of wine. And when any of the saints shall have taken hold of one of their clusters, another will cry, "I am a better cluster; take me, bless the Lord through me!"

Such millennial calculations outrun even astronomical figures, but under it all lay the dream of a time when nature would respond freely and richly to man's needs.

Papias did not agree that Judas hung himself and died, as Matthew reported (Matt. 27:5), but held that, like the traitorous Nadan, in the Story of Ahikar, he swelled to a hideous size. This tradition of his fate is reflected in Acts 1:18. He speaks of Aristion and the Elder John as disciples of the Lord who were among his informants (so Eusebius and Jerome say). He quoted the daughters of Philip, mentioned in Acts (21:9), as saying that Barsabbas, who was called Justus—the man mentioned in Acts 1:23 as nominated to take Judas' place—"when challenged by unbelievers drank serpent's poison in the name of the Lord and was shielded from all harm." He says that some persons raised from the dead by Christ lived on until the time of Hadrian, who became emperor in the summer of

A.D. 117. He also says that John and James were killed by the Jews. These statements are preserved in Philip of Side, who wrote about A.D. 430; the last one is also reported by Georgius Hamartolus, about A.D. 842.

Papias is quoted by Andreas of Caesarea as the earliest witness to the Book of Revelation, and as time went on he was pushed further and further back toward John the Evangelist, in the Middle Ages becoming not only his disciple but the scribe to whom John dictated his gospel.

Most of these writers indicate in which of the five books what they report from Papias is found, so that it is fairly clear that his work was still in existence at the end of the ninth century. Indeed the book is listed in the inventory of the sacristy of the church at Nismes, written in A.D. 1218, and it appears in the catalogue of the library of the convent at Stams, written in A.D. 1341. We may still hope that the whole text of this primitive and curious work will yet be found. The fragments we now possess can be read in English in Lightfoot's *Apostolic Fathers*.

Before the churches had agreed upon a Christian scripture, when Christian practices of prayer and worship were in their infancy, a need was felt for a little manual that should give directions as to baptism, fasts, prayer, and the celebration of the Lord's Supper. Rural churches in particular might need to know what their responsibilities were as to itinerant apostles or missionaries. Prophetic claims, too, might need looking into, and the demands of visit-

The Teaching of the Twelve Apostles— the Didache

ing brethren in the way of hospitality should be controlled. Sunday worship and church officers were also matters that called for some definition.

To meet this demand, someone in the second quarter of the second century, probably toward A.D. 150, produced the *Didache*, or *Teaching of the Lord through the Twelve Apostles for the Heathen*. It was really, as its name reveals, an expansion of the little tract on Christian morals produced a generation before under that name; its opening chapters, 1–6, reproduce all that material, but now enriched and amplified with additions chiefly from the Gospel of Matthew, especially the Sermon on the Mount. These commands may have been intended for the instruction of people awaiting baptism. They close with a warning against eating meat that has been offered to idols (6:3).

They are followed by instructions as to how to baptize. It is to be in running water, if possible; if not, in other water, preferably cold. Failing that, however, "pour water three times on the head, in the name of the Father and Son and Holy Spirit." Fasting must be on Wednesdays and Fridays, not on Mondays and Thursdays, for the hypocrites (the Jews) fast on those days. This harsh designation of the Jews is also found several times in the Gospel of Matthew. Three times a day they are to utter the Lord's Prayer, in the form we find in Matthew. Instructions for celebrating the Eucharist, or giving of thanks, follow, with special prayers for the Cup and the Bread; the order is that of Luke 22:17, not that of

Paul and Mark, which have the cup following the bread.

The treatment given traveling missionaries (or apostles) and prophets is to be "according to the rule of the gospel," evidently meaning Matt. 10:40, 41, where we read: "Whoever welcomes you [the apostles], welcomes me, and whoever welcomes me, welcomes him who sent me. Whoever welcomes a prophet because he is a prophet will have the same reward as a prophet," etc. The *Didache* (*Teaching*) goes on to say that every missionary ("apostle") who comes must be welcomed as the Lord but must not be allowed to stay more than two days at the most. "If he stays three days, he is a false prophet." Evidently the prophetic office has begun to be abused. Prophetic utterances, too, must be carefully checked; a prophet who while under the influence of the Spirit asks for money for himself is not to be listened to. Christian travelers are to be entertained for two days or at the most three, then they should go to work. The true prophet, on the other hand, should be liberally supported.

Christians are to meet on the Lord's Day, break bread, and hold their thanksgiving, or Eucharist. They are to appoint overseers, or bishops, and assistants, or deacons, and these officers are to be honored along with their prophets and teachers. Their prayers and charity and all their acts are to be done in accordance with what they "find in the Gospel of our Lord," another reference to Matthew (6:1–15).

The final chapter, 16, warns that the end is at hand and mentions the signs that shall precede and attend it. While it is chiefly drawn from Matthew, especially chapters 24 and 25, there is one sentence unmistakably taken from *Barnabas* 4:9.

The use of the Gospel of Matthew, the original *Teaching of the Apostles (Doctrina)* and the *Letter of Barnabas*, shows that the enlarged *Didache* must have been written toward the middle of the second century, or not far from A.D. 150. It was probably written in Syria, where Matthew and the primitive *Teaching* in all probability appeared. It shows little if any influence of any other gospel than Matthew, which it speaks of as the Gospel of the Lord. The Fourfold Gospel had evidently not yet come into general use in the region where the *Didache* was written.

As a whole, the little work is less suited to candidates awaiting baptism than to Christians in general; it is a miniature manual of Christian morals and church life, from times and circles where church procedure had not yet developed. It shows Christian hospitality, organization, ritual, and liturgy in a very early stage, when bishops (in the sense of elders) and deacons are just rising into such esteem as prophets and teachers already enjoyed. Its twofold ministry, bishops and deacons, is that of the Pastorals, Timothy and Titus, except that here the prophets and teachers are still in the picture, though beginning to fade from it.

The Greek *Didache* was well known to some early Christian writers. Clement of Alexandria quotes its language as scripture, but without actually mentioning its name (*Miscellanies* i. 20. 100). Eusebius puts "the so-called Teachings of the Apostles" among the books that are disputed and rejected (*Church History* iii. 25. 4). Athanasius in his *Festal Letter* of A.D. 367 omits it from the New Testament but says that it and the *Shepherd* of Hermas may be read by new converts and persons preparing for baptism. The *Teaching* is listed among the "apocrypha" or rejected books, in the *List of Sixty Canonical Books* and in the *Stichometry of Nicephorus*.

But it had completely disappeared and been lost for centuries when Bryennius in 1875, in publishing the complete Greek text of the *Letters of Clement* from an eleventh-century manuscript (A.D. 1056) then in Constantinople, revealed the fact that the same manuscript contained a work called "The Teaching of the Apostles." It is a little strange that Bryennius did not himself first publish the *Didache*, so much the most important of the pieces contained in the manuscript. He seems to have found the manuscript in 1873, and in 1875 published the *Letters of Clement*, previously known only from the Codex Alexandrinus, which had lost a number of leaves. The manuscript Bryennius found was almost a medieval edition of the Apostolic Fathers, for it included principally the *Letter of Barnabas*, the two letters ascribed to *Clement*, the *Teaching of the Twelve Apostles*, and the *Letters of Ignatius* in the long form (twelve letters). Bryennius supplied the readings of *Barnabas* to Hilgenfeld for his edition of 1877 and at length in 1883 published the *Didache*. It at once called forth a flood of books and articles, all the principal patristic scholars of the time contributing.

Two small Greek fragments of the *Didache* (two

parchment leaves of the fourth century) have since been discovered among the *Oxyrhynchus Papyri* (xv. 1782, 1922); they cover 1:3*b*–4*a;* 2:7*b*—3:2*a*. A British Museum Coptic fragment from early in the fifth century, published in 1924, preserves substantially 10: 3*b*–12:2*a* in that language, apparently excerpted from the little work for some immediate purpose. Of even more importance was the Latin version of the original *Didache* (the *Doctrina*), discovered by J. Schlecht and published by him in 1900. It has been discussed under *The Teaching of the Apostles*, of which it evidently represents the primitive form.

Many scholars seek to explain this shorter Latin *Teaching* (*Doctrina*) as a reduction of the *Didache*, made by omitting 1:3—2:1 and 6:2—16:8, but it is obvious that early Christian literature generally moved in the opposite direction, and its documents grew by inclusion, not by omission. It was perhaps natural at first to suppose that the document so obviously underlying *Barnabas* and the *Didache* was a Jewish "Two Ways," but the discovery of the Latin *Doctrina* has changed the situation by putting in our hands a Christian "Two Ways," calling itself the "Teaching of the Apostles" and marked by many Christian touches, which clearly served as source for *Didache*, chapters 1–6, and *Barnabas*, chapters 18–21. There is no longer any reason to postulate a Jewish "Two Ways" source for all three. The primitive Greek *Didache* reflected in the Latin form of chapters 1–6 found by Schlecht was the source of *Barnabas* and the *Didache*.

While the *Didache* as such seems to have disappeared

from Christian consciousness somewhat early, it was only because it was absorbed or expanded into such church manuals as the *Didascalia*, of the second half of the third century, the *Apostolic Church Ordinances*, written about A.D. 300,[7] and the *Apostolic Constitutions*, Book vii, about A.D. 380.

From the very beginning of the Christian movement, hymns and songs were part of its life. These *The Odes of Solomon* were at first the psalms of Judaism; at the end of the Last Supper, Jesus and the disciples "sang the hymn"—the second part (Pss. 115–18)—of the Hallel. Paul recommends the use of psalms, hymns, and sacred songs to the Colossians (3:16). In the canticles of Luke—the Magnificat, the Benedictus, the Gloria in excelsis, and the Nunc dimittis—we begin to see the dawn of a Christian hymnology, and we catch other glimpses of the same movement in the great arias, antiphonies, and choruses of the Revelation.

Nothing like a collection of early Christian hymns seemed to have survived, however, until Dr. J. Rendel Harris, the discoverer of Aristides, in 1909 found among some Syriac manuscripts gathered in the neighborhood of the Tigris a group of Christian hymns which he soon identified as the so-called *Odes of Solomon*, mentioned in the *Synopsis of Holy Scripture* that goes under the name of Chrysostom, which may be as late as the sixth century, and in the *Stichometry of*

---

[7] The *Apostolic Canons* probably reflect the primitive, not the expanded, form of the *Teaching*.

Nicephorus (*ca*. A.D. 850). In both these lists the *Odes* appear not by themselves but as the *Psalms and Odes of Solomon*, and in Nicephorus their length is given as 2,100 lines. It is interesting to observe that in Dr. Harris' manuscript the *Psalms of Solomon* accompany and follow the *Odes*.

The *Psalms of Solomon* are the well-known Pharisaic hymns, composed in the last century before Christ and extant in Greek in a few manuscripts. They once stood at the end of the fifth-century Codex Alexandrinus, after the New Testament and the two *Letters of Clement*, for they are listed in its table of contents, though they have long since been lost from the manuscript.

But the *Odes of Solomon* had never been found in modern times until Dr. Harris discovered them in his Syriac manuscript on January 4, 1909. A second manuscript of the *Odes and Psalms* was soon after identified by Dr. F. C. Burkitt in the British Museum. Neither manuscript is entirely complete, however. The *Pistis Sophia*, a Coptic product of Egyptian Gnosticism of the Ophite or Sethite type, about A.D. 250–300, quotes five of the *Odes*, one of which, the first, is missing in both Syriac manuscripts. The nineteenth ode is quoted by Lactantius in his *Divine Institutes* 4:12 (A.D. 311). He introduces his quotation with the words, "Thus Solomon speaks."

The *Odes*, forty-two in number, are followed in the Syriac manuscript by the eighteen *Psalms of Solomon*, which are numbered continuously with them, from 43 to 60. The *Odes* introduce us at once to a very well-marked religious atmosphere which pervades them all but is utterly unlike that of the *Psalms of Solomon* that follow them. The *Odes* are spiritual, mystical, imaginative, and boldly, even harshly, figurative, a trait they share with the *Letters of Ignatius*, with which they have other affinities. They sometimes recall characteristic touches in the Gospel and Letters of John, and, of course, they owe much to the Hebrew Psalms. In fact, some scholars regard them as Jewish hymns made over by revision and expansion to serve Christian purposes; but the Christian strain in them is too deep to be thus explained. "Love," "light," "life," and "truth" are words often on the lips of the odist; his spirit aspires and expands in communion with God; he rejoices in his sense of trust and salvation. The *Odes* reflect, as Dr. Harris put it, "Christian experience upon the highest levels of the spiritual life."

Why were these hymns of devotion and aspiration ascribed to Solomon? Probably for the same reason that the Song of Songs and the Psalms of the Pharisees were; which was that Solomon was credited among the Hebrews with five thousand songs (I Kings 4:32). Certainly their amalgamation with the Psalms of the Pharisees which went by his name carried the fiction of his authorship with it. Judaism had long enjoyed these sweeping literary verdicts—all the Law by Moses, all the Psalms by David, all the Proverbs and Wisdom writings by Solomon. Only the closing of the Psalter as finished turned new song writers to Solomon, in view of his record in that field announced in Kings. Such verdicts were, of course, no more than dedications, or gestures of respect, to great figures of the past.

Who really wrote these *Odes* no one can say. They have come to light only in Syriac, and some scholars have thought they might be the work of the Syriac poet Bardaisan (Bardasanes), A.D. 154–222. But they were almost certainly written in Greek, at some time near the middle of the second century, before Christian theology had begun to assume something like fixity of form. Justin seems to have written a hymnbook about that time, but the *Odes* do not sound very much like him. The use of them in the *Pistis Sophia* shows that they were acceptable to some groups of Gnostics but does not prove that they were of Gnostic origin, though what looks very much like Gnostic influence can be traced here and there in them. Probably some imaginative and devout Greek Christian, perhaps of Ephesus (the Johannine atmosphere) or even more probably of Antioch (for they sometimes make us think of Ignatius), poured out his soul in them. Certainly they seem to be all from the same hand.

Soon after Dr. Harris discovered these *Odes*, he described them in a letter, as "redolent of antiquity and radiant with spiritual light." It would be difficult to characterize them better. And when Augustine uttered his famous words, "Join yourself to the eternal God and you will be eternal," it is now clear that he was quoting the third ode: "He that is joined to him that is immortal will himself become immortal."

We have yet to find the original Greek text of these early Christian hymns.

The main activity of the early church was not writing but preaching; the sermon was its characteristic expression. One such early homily is preserved in the Epistle of James. Another has survived as the *Second Letter of Clement*, although it is obviously not a letter at all and not by Clement. But it follows the *Letter of Clement* both in the Greek manuscripts of that work and in the Syriac one, though not in the Latin or Coptic versions of it. Eusebius is the first writer to mention *II Clement* (*Church History* iii. 38. 4), but he is careful not to acknowledge it as really a letter of Clement.

II Clement

This sermon is an appeal to its hearers to repent and serve God with their whole hearts, live pure and holy lives, and cling to their hope of the resurrection of the body. Its true character as a sermon is plain from some words in 17:3: "Let us not merely seem to believe and pay attention now, while we are being exhorted by the elders, but also when we have gone home let us remember the commandments of the Lord, and let us not be dragged aside by worldly lusts, but let us try to come here more frequently, and to make progress in the commands of the Lord." It is evidently, like James, a sermon that has come to be treated as a letter, and a letter of Clement of Rome.

It owes this connection with Clement evidently to the fact that it was preserved at Corinth, which was the destination of *I Clement*, the genuine letter of the Roman church to the Corinthians, written about A.D. 95. It must either have been preached in Corinth or sent there for some purpose. At any rate, it came to be associated with the *Letter of Clement*, which was preserved there and occasionally read in church, as Dionysius of Corinth says in his letter to Soter, bishop of Rome, about A.D. 165–75. He is replying to a letter from Soter recently received by the Corinthians and indicates their purpose to preserve it and read it from time to time. "From it," he writes, "whenever we read it, we shall always be able to draw advice, as also from the former epistle, which was written to us through Clement" (Eusebius *Church History* iv. 23. 11). This prompt associating by the bishop of Corinth of Soter's letter with Clement's led Hilgenfeld and Harnack to think that *II Clement* was probably Soter's letter and that immediately on its arrival in Corinth it had been filed with the *Letter of Clement* as making two letters from the church at Rome to that at Corinth, from which the Corinthians would read from time to time for their edification. This is certainly an attractive suggestion, for it solves two problems: How did *II Clement* ever come to be grouped with *I Clement?* and What has become of the letter from Soter, which Dionysius said the Corinthians would keep and read with the *Letter of Clement?*

The difficulty with this view is that *II Clement* is not really a letter but a homily or sermon and conveys nothing in the way of a message from Rome to Corinth that might not have been sent from any church to any other. In fact, it does not sound like a church letter at all. That it lacks the name of Soter does not matter; *I Clement* has no mention of Clement. It is, of course, hard to see why the church of Rome should send a sermon, of no particular applicability, to the church of Corinth, except as a gesture of interest and good will, and that is perhaps, in view of Dionysius' words to Soter, the best explanation of it.

This difficulty has led scholars like Lightfoot to the view that the homily was really written in Corinth, perhaps at a time when crowds were gathering for the Isthmian games, and that these are reflected in chapter 7: "Many are landing for the corruptible contests." It may have been a favorite sermon with the Corinthians which was kept and read occasionally in church, like *I Clement*, and so came to be associated with it.

Others have thought *II Clement* might have been of Alexandrian origin, partly because of its apparent use of the *Gospel of the Egyptians*, especially in 12:2: "For when the Lord himself was asked by someone when his kingdom would come, he said, 'When the two shall be one, and the outside as the inside, and the male with the female neither male nor female.' " This closely resembles Jesus' words to Salome, as quoted by Clement of Alexandria from the *Gospel of the Egyptians* (*Miscellanies* iii. 6, 9). Other curious sayings ascribed to Christ in the sermon are probably derived from that gospel, but the writer is also familiar with the Four Gospels, the principal letters of Paul, and I Peter. This list of Christian books with which he is acquainted, especially his knowledge of the *Gospel of the Egyptians*, brings the date of the sermon well into the third quarter of the second century. From another curious book, which he does not name, but merely describes as "the word of prophecy," he quotes a strange saying: "Miserable are the double-minded who doubt in their hearts and say, 'These things we heard long ago, and in the days of our fathers, but we have waited from day to day and have seen none of them.' You fools! Compare yourselves to a tree; take a vine; first it sheds its leaves, then there comes a bud, after that an unripe grape, then a full cluster," etc. This passage appears also in *I Clement* (23:3, 4), but in *II Clement* it is carried a sentence further, so that the writer is not quoting *I Clement* but the word of prophecy from which it drew, possibly the mysterious *Book of Eldad and Modat*, which is mentioned in Hermas (*Vis*. ii. 3. 4). Hermas quotes from it the saying, "The Lord is near those who turn to him," and describes Eldad and Modat as those "who prophesied to the people in the wilderness" (Num. 11:26).

Nothing is really known of this work, though it is mentioned in the *Stichometry of Nicephorus* among the Old Testament apocrypha.[8] But, at any rate, *II Clement* is certainly quoting the same book as *I Clement*, and that suggests that both were written in the Roman church. If the book they quoted was the *Book of Eldad and Modat*, mentioned and quoted in Hermas, the link between *II Clement* and Rome becomes still stronger, for Rome would appear to be the one place where that little apocryph was known and valued. But of this we cannot be certain.

[8] There is also a somewhat dubious reference to it in the *Targum of Jonathan*, on Num. 11:26 f. The *Stichometry* gives its length as 400 *stichoi*, or about that of Galatians.

While the place of *II Clement*'s origin remains uncertain, its value as a piece of Christian preaching from the third quarter of the second century is considerable. For the time of its origin is reasonably clear; the *Gospel of the Egyptians* is current but not yet suspected as heretical; it may be used along with the great quartette of gospels. The movement to organize worldwide Christianity into a Catholic church has not yet come. This would date the writing of *II Clement* between A.D. 150 and 175. As to place, it must certainly have been written in a circle remarkably well provided with Christian books—five gospels, the principal Pauline letters, I Peter—and the "book of prophecy," now lost. This points to one of the major Christian centers of the time, such as Antioch, Alexandria, Ephesus, Corinth, or Rome. And while the *Gospel of the Egyptians* is mentioned by Clement of Alexandria and by Origen, it is also discussed by the Roman Hippolytus, about A.D. 230, so that it was known far beyond the borders of Egypt, and its use does not necessarily connect *II Clement* with Alexandria.

II Clement was translated along with *I Clement* into Syriac, but it did not follow it into Latin and Coptic versions, so that *I Clement* must have begun to circulate widely before *II Clement* became attached to it.

Under the shadow of *I Clement*, *II Clement* passed in the fifth century into the Alexandrian manuscript of the Greek Bible, as the last book of the New Testament; and the two are mentioned as part of the New Testament in the *Apostolic Canons*, a Syrian work of about A.D. 400. The *Stichometry of Nicephorus*, about

A.D. 850, lists them among the rejected books, its "apocrypha." But they stand in a twelfth-century Syriac manuscript of the New Testament, between the Catholic, or general, letters, and those of Paul; and Abu'l Barakat, who died in 1363, in his account of Christian literature in Arabic speaks of them as belonging to the New Testament.

While Luke's two volumes on Christian beginnings had pointed the way for the Christian historian, for a *The Memoirs of Hegesippus* long time little was done to carry on the work of a history of the church. The first writer to take any steps in that direction was Hegesippus. He came from the East, and his knowledge of Aramaic and Hebrew led Eusebius to think he must have been of Jewish birth, but this is more than doubtful. Probably he was a gentile Christian of Syria. He traveled from the East to Corinth, and spent some time there, proceeding thence to Rome, perhaps about A.D. 155–60, and later returning to the East to write, or at least to finish, his book, which he completed while Eleutherus was bishop of Rome, A.D. 174–89—probably about A.D. 180.

The real motive of Hegesippus in writing his five books of *Memoirs* was not so much historical as polemic. He wrote to prove the superior claims of Christian apostolic tradition against the vagaries of the sects. Agrippa Castor, about A.D. 135, had begun the literary warfare against Gnosticism, with his *Refutation*, which was particularly directed against Basilides (*Church History* iv. 7. 6–8). Later Justin carried on the fight with his lost book *Against All Heresies*, and Dionysius, bishop of Corinth (*ca.* A.D. 170), wrote a letter to the church of Nicomedia, in Bithynia, attacking Marcion's views, as Eusebius informs us (*Church History* iv. 23. 4). Eusebius reports a whole series of books *Against Marcion* about this time, as we have seen in connection with Justin and Tatian.

Hegesippus was widely traveled and knew the East as well as the West, and he made use of a variety of historical materials, most uncritically, of course, in championing apostolic Christianity as he understood it against the sects. He said that on his journey to Rome he met many bishops and received the same doctrine from them all (*Church History* iv. 22. 1). Hegesippus gives a list of the Christian sects and describes the Marcionites and Gnostics as arising from a Jewish sect, the Masbotheans. He lists the seven Jewish sects, as Justin had done (*Dialogue* lxxx. 4), but agrees with Justin in only four of the seven named.[9] But it is likely that he made use of Justin's book *Against All Heresies*, which had appeared some twenty-five years before (*ca.* A.D. 150).

The *Memoirs* have unfortunately disappeared, but Eusebius made a good deal of use of Hegesippus, especially valuing the pieces of Christian Palestinian tradition that he supplied. He often quotes him at length, his most notable use of Hegesippus being the latter's account of the life and martyrdom of Jesus' brother James, who was thrown from the pinnacle of the tem-

[9] Other early Christian writers who attempted lists of Jewish sects were Hippolytus (*Refutation* ix. 13 [Eng.]), the author of the Clementine *Recognitions* (1:54), Eusebius, who repeats Hegesippus' list (iv. 22. 6), Epiphanius, and the author of the *Apostolic Constitutions* (6:6).

ple and then stoned and beaten to death by the Jews
(*Church History* ii. 23. 3–18). Of almost as much interest is his story of Domitian and the grandsons of Jesus'
brother Jude. He says that the emperor was seeking
out any descendants of David, as possible leaders of
insurrection, and his agent found two grandsons of
Jude who were farmers, cultivating a little farm of
thirty-nine acres, worth about fifteen to seventeen
hundred dollars. They showed their toil-worn hands,
and were so manifestly inoffensive peasants that the
emperor let them go (*Church History* iii. 20. 1–8). So,
however careless Hegesippus was, his book would be
of great interest to students of primitive Christianity
if it could be found.

It was used almost immediately by Irenaeus, A.D.
181–89, in his great *Refutation of Gnosticism*, and by
Clement of Alexandria, in his lost *Outlines*, as Eusebius' references to the two writers show (*Church History* ii. 1. 3, 4; 23. 3). Neither Clement nor Origen actually mentions Hegesippus, in such of their writings
as are extant, but Eusebius owed much to him, perhaps
even more than he credits him with. Indeed both historical and polemical writers were indebted to Hegesippus. But his work does not seem to have long survived; as Staehlin suggests, as the sects disappeared,
books about them, like those of Justin, Hegesippus,
Irenaeus, and Hippolytus, likewise disappeared; they
were no longer of interest. Jerome and Sozomen (*ca.*
440) probably knew Hegesippus only from Eusebius'
account of him. But Philip of Side made use of his
work in his *Christian History*, written about A.D. 430

but now for the most part lost;[10] and Photius, about A.D. 890 (*Bibliotheca*, cod. 232), quotes a passage from Hegesippus which he had found in the work of Stephen Gobarus, now lost.

It would be difficult to name a lost book of early Christian literature that would be more warmly welcomed than the five books of the *Memoirs* (*Hypomnemata*) of Hegesippus. They may possibly be preserved somewhere under the name of Josephus, which was sometimes confused with Hegesippus in the Middle Ages.

[10] Philip said that Hegesippus gave the names of Jesus' relatives who were called before Domitian as Zoker and Jacob.

CHAPTER IX

THE SUCCESSORS OF JUSTIN

The Lydian city of Sardis, in Asia, was the seat of a Christian church before the end of the first century, as the Revelation shows (3:1-6), and in the *Melito of Sardis* time of Marcus Aurelius its bishop was one of the ablest and most prolific writers of his day—Melito of Sardis. He is credited with having written eighteen and perhaps twenty works, chiefly on the evidence of Eusebius, who in *Church History* iv. 26. 2 gives this list: *On the Passover* (two books), *On the Conduct of Life and the Prophets, On the Church, On the Lord's Day, On the Faith of Man, On His Creation, On the Obedience of Faith, On the Senses, On the Soul and Body, On Baptism, On Truth, On the Creation and Generation of Christ, On Prophecy, On Hospitality, A Key* (to the scriptures), *On the Devil and the Revelation of John*, and, finally, the *Apology*. He later mentions the *Extracts* (iv. 26. 13), or *Selections from the Old Testament*, of which Jerome says there were six books. Eusebius preserves the opening paragraph of this work. It was addressed to a brother Onesimus and gives the list of the Hebrew scriptures as current in Palestine.

The *Apology* was written probably between A.D. 169 and 176, certainly by 180. Three passages from it, making about a page in all, are quoted by Eusebius (*Church History* iv. 26. 5-11). Another small fragment

—a part of a sentence—is preserved in the *Paschal Chronicle*. Melito points out to the emperor that the church had proved a benefit to the empire and should be regarded as a bulwark and ally of it, not as a hostile force. Even these are enough to show that Melito's *Apology* influenced Tertullian's.

Small fragments of at least six other works have been recovered from various sources; the longest, of little more than a page, from the work *On Baptism*. One is preserved in Origen and two in Anastasius of Sinai, altogether a meager record of so copious a writer.[1]

Anastasius of Sinai, in the seventh century, credits Melito with a work *On the Incarnation of Christ* in three or more books. He also mentions a work *On the Passion*, from which he quotes a single line: "God suffered under an Israelitish hand." It is an extraordinary thing that this homily of Melito should have gone unmentioned until the seventh century and now in 1940 have come to light almost entire in Greek. For among the papyri recently obtained from Egypt by Mr. A. Chester Beatty and the University of Michigan is one written in the fourth century and preserving no less than seventeen pages of its text, mostly in good condition, and headed with the name of Melito. In it we find almost the very words quoted by Anastasius (sec. 96): "God has been murdered! The king of Israel has been slain by an Israelitish hand!"[2]

[1] The so-called *Apology of Melito* current in Syriac is now recognized as a Syriac composition, having no connection with Melito.

[2] Campbell Bonner, *Homily on the Passion by Melito, Bishop of Sardis* (*Studies and Documents*, Vol. XII [London, 1940]).

This extraordinary discovery gives us at last one substantial work of Melito, and it has been buttressed by the detection of three further fragments of the same homily, one in Greek (*Oxyrhynchus Papyri* xiii. 1600, a fifth-century leaf, covering secs. 57–63), one in Coptic (fourth century, now in the British Museum, covering secs. 12–14), and one in Syriac in the British Museum, which has long been assigned to Alexander of Alexandria (†328), but is really a part of Melito's homily, covering sections 94–98. This last confirms an idea of Gustav Krueger, who as long ago as 1888 suggested that this fragment was really from Melito.

It has been maintained that Hippolytus and Origen were the first orthodox Christian preachers to make full use of Greek rhetorical techniques in their sermons, but that distinction must now go to Melito.[3] He revels in the ornate artificialities of Greek rhetoric—exclamation, apostrophe, antithesis, rhetorical questions, startling forms of statement, dramatic impersonations, beginning sentence after sentence in the same way, etc. These overconscious habits of style weary the modern reader, and yet the earnestness and power of the preacher can still be felt, after all these centuries of oblivion. And, as a matter of fact, these same traits appear in the familiar fragment, a page long, from the work *On Baptism*, which has long been included among Melito's literary remains.[4]

The homily interprets the Passover, in the usual

[3] Norden, *Antike Kunstprosa*, II, 547; cf. Bonner's ed., p. 20.

[4] Printed as No. viii among the remains of Melito in Goodspeed, *Die aeltesten Apologeten* (Göttingen, 1914), pp. 310–11.

early Christian way, from Paul down (I Cor. 5:7) as symbolic of the redemptive death of Christ. Melito relates the slaying of the firstborn in Egypt and the preservation of the Hebrews; explains the Jewish Law as simply a temporary sketch or model for Christianity, which is the true and enduring work of the Great Artist; finds the sufferings of Christ foreshadowed in those of many Old Testament worthies; and bitterly condemns the Jews for their responsibility for his death.

Like most Asian bishops, Melito was a Quartodeciman; he celebrated the Passover on the fourteenth of Nisan, whatever the day of the week, so that this would be comparable with a Good Friday sermon today. His work *On the Passover* was evidently a contribution to the debate as to the date of Easter, which so divided the church. It was written, as its opening lines indicate (they are quoted by Eusebius *Church History* iv. 26. 3), in A.D. 167–68. Polycrates of Ephesus, writing to Victor of Rome when the controversy was resumed about A.D. 190, speaks of Melito as no longer living (*Church History* v. 24. 5, 6), so that his literary work as far as we can trace it fell between A.D. 167 and 190.

The new use of Greek rhetoric made by Melito in introducing it into nonschismatic Christian preaching (the Gnostics were already using it in theirs) was soon taken up by Hippolytus and Origen, and Bonner has traced the influence of this particular homily upon the work of Melito's contemporary Apollinaris of Hierapolis *On the Passover* and upon the work of Hippolytus

On the Passover, recently identified by Charles Martin in a sermon long erroneously ascribed to Chrysostom.[5] Clement seems to have written his work *On the Passover* (now lost) in reply to Melito's. Jerome says that Tertullian derided the declamatory elegance of Melito's style, though he was even more addicted to that sort of thing himself and should have recognized a kindred spirit in Melito. We have noted the influence of Melito's *Apology* upon Tertullian. That he influenced such men as Tertullian, Clement, and Hippolytus is sufficient proof of Melito's powers.

It is very evident that if the discovery of one fairly complete work of Melito can so alter the picture of one phase of early Christian literature, the finding of the whole library of his writings would throw a flood of light upon it. But, as yet, probably nineteen-twentieths of his work remains lost.

The defense of Christianity against misrepresentation and persecution took a variety of forms; Justin had done it in one way, and Tatian in quite another. The friendly and understanding way which Justin had tried to take was followed even more successfully by Athenagoras of Athens, who is described in the title of his book as a Christian philosopher. Athenagoras holds that Christians should be entitled to the same liberty to practice their faith that is enjoyed by the other miscellaneous groups that make up the population of the empire and appeals to the emperor Marcus Aurelius to see that justice is done them.

Athenagoras

[5] *Mélanges Franz Cumont* (1936), pp. 321–63.

Athenagoras repels the stock charges of atheism, cannibalism, and incest that were brought against the Christians; shows that their worship and teaching are more reasonable and moral than those of their accusers; and appeals again and again to Greek philosophers and poets in support of his claims. Indeed, over and over again Athenagoras by his quotations preserves to us a few lines of Greek poetry that have nowhere else survived, thus contributing a whole series of precious items to the Greek anthology. He is better versed in Greek literature and thought than his predecessors in Christian literature. He writes earnestly and competently and in good temper, not as an advocate but like a reasonable man.

He produced his *Apology*, or *Appeal on Behalf of Christians*, probably at Rome, between A.D. 177 and 180. It and he went unmentioned for a long time in Christian antiquity; Methodius, who died in A.D. 311, is the first writer to speak of him, quoting freely a passage from the *Apology*. Philip of Side (*ca.* A.D. 430) also mentions him as flourishing in the times of "Hadrian and Antoninus" and addressing to them an apology for the Christians. But the *Apology*—the Greek manuscripts call it *Presbeia*, or *Embassy*—shows by its opening lines that it was addressed to Aurelius and Commodus, as joint emperors, a state of things that existed only in A.D. 177–80.

In A.D. 914 Arethas, the learned bishop of Caesarea, the reviser of the commentary of Andreas on the Revelation, had a manuscript written which proved of great importance. The scribe was Baanes, but Arethas himself revised and corrected the text, and the book is known as the Arethas Codex. This manuscript, now in Paris,[6] although it contained other items as well, was practically a corpus of early Christian apologies; it contained works of Clement, Justin (as was supposed), Tatian (now lost from it but preserved in the three copies early made from it), Eusebius, Athenagoras (*Apology* and *On Resurrection*), and Eusebius again. It seems to have been copied from a seventh-century manuscript and was itself the parent of three copies made from it in the eleventh, twelfth, and fourteenth centuries, portions of the Arethas manuscript having disappeared meantime. From each of these, further copies were made in later centuries, the whole relationship constituting one of the clearest manuscript genealogies known. This fact, together with the unique importance of its contents and the scholarly care taken in its preparation, gives the Arethas Codex great significance.

The treatise *On the Resurrection of the Dead* which accompanies the *Apology* of Athenagoras in the Arethas manuscript exhibits very much the same philosophical attitude that appears in the *Apology*. Athenagoras presents the reasons for believing in resurrection, basing his argument on general considerations, rather than on the narrative of the gospels about the resurrection of Jesus. Athenagoras argues not only for the possibility and actuality of resurrection but for its necessity.

Zahn suggested that Athenagoras was the philosopher of that name to whom Boethus of Alexandria dedicated his work on Plato, not long after A.D. 180,

[6] Paris. Graec. 451.

but, while this is possible, it cannot, of course, be established.

Among the notable Christian writers who sprang up in such numbers in the last third of the second century *Theophilus of Antioch* was Theophilus, the sixth bishop of Antioch (Eusebius *Church History* iv. 20). He wrote a number of books of varied character. He describes himself as of Eastern origin, coming from near the Tigris and Euphrates (*To Autolycus* 2:24), and indicates that he had grown to manhood before he became a Christian. Eusebius gives a short list of his works: three "elementary" works addressed *To Autolycus*, one *Against the Heresy of Hermogenes;*[7] some catechetical books—that is, instructions for those wishing to enter the church—and, finally, a discourse *Against Marcion* (*Church History* iv. 24. 1–3). Jerome (*On Illustrious Men* 25) adds a gospel harmony, or a commentary on one, besides a commentary on Proverbs,[8] and from Theophilus himself we learn (3:30) that he had also written a work *On History*.

Of all these, the only one that has survived is the defense of Christianity, in three books, addressed to Theophilus' pagan friend Autolycus. As it assumes the death of Marcus Aurelius (3:27), which took place in A.D. 180, it must have been written after that time. But the earliest mention of it is in Lactantius, a Western writer, who died about A.D. 325, who in his *Divine*

---

[7] The heresy of Hermogenes was that God created the world not out of nothing but out of matter eternally existent like himself; so Tertullian and Hippolytus described it (see A. C. McGiffert, *Eusebius* [New York, 1890], p. 202, n. 3).

[8] *Epist. ad Algasiam* 121.

Institutes 1:23 speaks of such a work of Theophilus
addressed to Autolycus and quotes from it (3:29).
The work is preserved in an eleventh-century manuscript and in two copies made directly or indirectly
from it.

The three books are really independent of one another and belong to different literary categories. The
first is a direct personal address, put as though Theophilus and Autolycus were face to face. It deals with
the existence of God, the frailties of heathen gods, and
the absurdities of idolatry and offers some analogies
for the resurrection. The second is a treatise. It continues the attack upon pagan religion and contrasts
the contradictory doctrines of Greek writers with the
messages of the prophets. The Genesis accounts of the
Creation and Fall are taken up and explained. The
third book begins like an ordinary Greek letter—
"Theophilus to Autolycus, greeting." It shows the
superiority of Christianity to paganism, exposes the
immorality of pagan writers and the falsity of their
charges against the Christians, and gives evidence for
the great antiquity of Moses and the Jewish religion,
of which Christians felt they were the true heirs.

Theophilus shows a good deal of familiarity with
Greek literature, quoting numbers of poets and philosophers, as well as the Sibylline books, which, of
course, were really more Jewish than Greek. He is also
familiar with Greek rhetorical devices and uses them
freely. He had a deep reverence for the Jewish Bible—
the Holy Scriptures, as he often calls it. He also had a
high regard for the gospels and once definitely co-

ordinates them with the Law and the Prophets, "because they all spoke inspired by one spirit of God" (3:12). Theophilus gives us the first express quotation of one of the gospels that has come down to us; it is from the Gospel of John, whom he describes as inspired (2:22).

Eusebius is the first and only Eastern Christian writer to mention Theophilus, as far as our information goes, but Theophilus' contemporary Irenaeus in his *Refutation* seems to make use of the second book (chaps. 25 and 26), where Theophilus alludes vaguely to the schismatics,[9] though it is possible that Irenaeus was really using the lost work of Theophilus *Against Marcion* instead. Indeed, it has been argued that not only Irenaeus but Tertullian, Adamantius, Minucius Felix, Clement, Hippolytus, Julius Africanus, and Novatian were all influenced by one or another of the works of Theophilus (*Against Hermogenes*, *Against Marcion*); but, until further discoveries bring more of his writings to light, the extent of his contribution to Christian thought cannot be determined. Even the rather shadowy picture of his work that we possess shows that Theophilus must have been a many-sided writer—harmonist, commentator, apologist, opponent of heresy, and religious teacher. But probably fourfifths of the writings of Theophilus have yet to be found.

[9] Harnack, *Texte und Untersuchungen*, I, 1 (1882), 292–93.

CHAPTER X

IRENAEUS

Toward A.D. 180 Christian leaders, hard pressed after half a century of schismatic movements, Docetic, Gnostic, and Marcionite, by the extrav-
The Catho- agant claims and eccentric activities of
lic Church the Montanist sect, took a leaf from Marcion's book, as it were, and agreed to organize the scattered churches into one General, or Catholic, church, to maintain a standard type of Christianity. The idea was as old as Ephesians, but its practical application to the problem of the perplexed and harassed churches had not been made before. Of this new movement, fraught with such significance, our first reflections are in the writings of Irenaeus.

Irenaeus is further remarkable in that he binds together the Eastern and Western Christianity of his day. For he was born in Asia Minor and lived in his youth in Smyrna, where he had seen Polycarp and heard him speak. He tells of this in a letter which was virtually a treatise *On Sovereignty*, addressed to his old friend Florinus, a Roman presbyter inclined to the views of Valentinus. But Irenaeus' middle and later life was spent in Lyons, in Gaul, where he succeeded Pothinus as bishop and carried on an active mission among the Gauls, preaching to them in their own tongue. While still a presbyter at Lyons, when Mon-

tanism was at its height, he was sent to Rome with a
letter of introduction to the bishop Eleutherus from
the confessors who had survived the persecution of
A.D. 177 there. So Irenaeus knew Christianity East
and West, Asian, Gallic and Roman, and participated
in the controversies over Gnosticism, Montanism, and
the Quartodeciman question.

Irenaeus was not only an active missionary churchman; he was also one of the leading Christian writers
The Refu- of his day, and his work describing and
tation condemning the heretical movements of
his times is the most important work of
the kind that has come down to us from the second
century. He set out, it is true, to deal with the Gnostic
heresy and called his book a *Refutation of Gnosticism*
("Gnosis falsely so called," cf. I Tim. 6:20, where the
same phrase is used). But, as he advanced, the work
grew under his hand, and, before he had finished, he
had covered not only Gnosticism in its various forms
(Books i and ii) but had presented the sound Christian
position as he understood it (Books iii–v).

Irenaeus appeals to the fact that some churches of
apostolic foundation had maintained an unbroken tradition of sound Christian teaching and so should,
when he wrote, be trustworthy centers of the faith as
the apostles had taught it. As he was writing in the
West, he pointed to the Roman church as such a center
and appealed to its tradition of Christian truth
through an unbroken line of bishops in support of the
standard type of Christianity (*Refutation* iii. 3. 2). He
gives a list of these Roman bishops reaching down

from the days of the apostles to his own contemporary
Eleutherus (iii. 3. 3), in whose episcopate, A.D. 175–
89, he evidently wrote this third book, and probably
all five books, of the *Refutation*.

Irenaeus also appealed to a Christian scripture, not
only an Old Testament and the Four Gospels (iii. 11.
8) but the Acts (iii. 12. 15) and the letters of Paul. In
fact, Irenaeus is the first Christian writer who can be
shown to have had something like what we understand by the New Testament, at least in its earliest
form of twenty-two books—four gospels, the Acts,
thirteen letters of Paul (including the three Pastorals,
to Timothy and Titus), I John and I Peter, the Revelation of John, and the *Shepherd* of Hermas. With Irenaeus, Christians began to call these books "scriptures" just as they did the Jewish books of our Old
Testament.

In these more constructive books of his *Refutation*
Irenaeus still has his eye on the heretics, for he occasionally deals with the positions of Marcion, the
Ebionites, etc. His book has been well described as a
treasure-house from which later writers on the heresies
drew. He himself was indebted for material to Justin,
from whose book *Against Marcion* he quotes (iv. 6. 2),
to Hegesippus, and probably to Theophilus. His own
work, on the other hand, was later used by his pupil
Hippolytus, by Clement of Alexandria, and by Epiphanius. He was, as McGiffert says, the most important of the polemical writers of antiquity. His practice of quoting characteristic passages from the writings of leading schismatics which have since disap-

peared makes him an invaluable source of information about them. And the positive statement of Christian views that forms more than half his great book reveals him as a notable definer and developer of Christian thought.

It is a curious fact that so important a book as Irenaeus' *Refutation* should have disappeared, but in its original Greek form it has nowhere been found; except for quotations from it in later writers, for our knowledge of it we are largely dependent upon an early Latin translation of it, which is extant in numerous manuscripts. There is also an Armenian version of Books iv and v (*Texte und Untersuchungen*, Vol. XXXV, 2 [1910]), besides fragments of a Syriac translation. Some portions of the Greek original are known, quoted in the pages of Hippolytus, Eusebius, and Epiphanius or unearthed in fragmentary papyri now chiefly at Jena. But one, found at Oxyrhynchus, is believed to have been written in the late second or early third century, so that it is almost contemporary with Irenaeus.[1]

In addition to the *Refutation*, Irenaeus wrote a number of other books. Eusebius mentions one *On Knowledge*, "written against the Greeks," as he says (*Church History* v. 26. 1). Jerome mistakenly thought this was two books (*On Illustrious Men* 35). Eusebius also mentioned a book dedicated to a certain brother named Marcianus, entitled *In Demonstration of the Apostolic Preaching*, and a "book of various dissertations." This *Demonstration*, long lost, was discovered in 1904, at Eriwan, in Ar-

Other Writings

[1] *Oxyrhynchus Papyri* iii. 405; iv. p. 264.

menia, in an Armenian translation, and published with a German translation in 1907 (*Texte und Unter-suchungen*, Vol. XXXI, 1). An English translation of it, by Dr. J. Armitage Robinson, appeared in 1920. The book is a short one, of seventy-five or eighty pages and was designed to give the intelligent Christian a summary of the Christian positions and the grounds for them. It gives new evidence of Irenaeus' debt to Justin Martyr but shows the advance Christian thought was making in the hands of men like Irenaeus.

Irenaeus also wrote a number of letters which, to judge by their names, must have been almost treatises. Eusebius mentions one to Blastus *On Schism*, one *On the Ogdoad*, and one to Florinus *On Sovereignty* (*Church History* v. 20. 1). From this he quotes an important passage bearing on Polycarp, and Irenaeus' memories of him (*Church History* v. 20. 2–8).

Irenaeus himself says in the *Refutation* that he intends to write a book devoted to exposing the errors of Marcion (i. 27. 4; iii. 12. 12), and Eusebius (*Church History* iv. 25) lists him among the writers against Marcion. The others he mentions are Philip of Gortyna and Modestus, and, of the three, he declares Modestus the most effective. But all these works on Marcion have disappeared.

Irenaeus participated in the paschal controversy, so bitter in his day, between Polycrates of Ephesus and Victor of Rome. The important letter written by Polycrates to Victor on the subject is preserved in part in *Church History* v. 24. 2–8. Victor replied by excommunicating all the churches of Asia, which were represented by Polycrates. Irenaeus sought to calm the storm with a letter to Victor, pointing out that the East had long differed from the West in this matter, and yet the churches had respected and tolerated these differences of practice, and urging that they continue to do so. Parts of this wise and temperate letter are preserved in Eusebius (*Church History* v. 24. 12–17). Eusebius adds that Irenaeus corresponded with most of the other Christian leaders of his day on this matter. He rightly held that Victor should not excommunicate whole churches of God.

A few other fragments of Irenaeus have been discovered in later writers like John of Damascus, A.D. 675–749, but some of the fragments ascribed to him have been found to be modern forgeries, in particular those published in the middle of the eighteenth century by C. M. Pfaff (†1760).[2] It is evident that a great service would be done to the study of early Christian literature by the finding of any one of the works of Irenaeus in the original Greek.

[2] See Harnack, *Texte und Untersuchungen*, XX, 3 (1900), 1 ff.

CHAPTER XI

CLEMENT OF ALEXANDRIA

The first school established by Christians of which we have any knowledge was one at Alexandria, de-

The First Christian School signed to instruct converts from paganism in Christian truth. Just when it was instituted we do not know, but it must have been in operation soon after the middle of the second century. For a long time it was headed by Pantaenus, a man of piety and force, but a teacher rather than a writer in the Christian cause. To this school came probably about A.D. 180 a young man named Titus Flavius Clemens, who took up his studies with such vigor and ability that he became the assistant of Pantaenus and finally his successor. His later career as teacher and writer was so identified with Alexandria that he came to be known as Clement of Alexandria.

Most of what we know of his master Pantaenus we learn from Clement, who seems to refer to him when

Pantaenus he speaks of the "blessed presbyter"; he very rarely mentions his name. Alexander of Jerusalem, Origen, Pamphilus, and Eusebius all mention Pantaenus and speak of him with respect. Eusebius and Jerome went so far as to credit him with a good deal of writing, probably through a misunderstanding of what Clement had said. Clement himself

199

shows that Pantaenus left no writings behind him (*Miscellanies* i. 1:11).

It was Pantaenus ("the blessed presbyter") who taught Clement that Paul was the author of Hebrews (*Church History* vi. 14. 4), and it was through Clement that this idea became established in the Eastern church and extended finally, two centuries later, to the West as well. Alexander of Jerusalem was another of his pupils and admirers (*Church History* vi. 14. 8). Lightfoot suggested that Pantaenus might have been the author of the work from which, he thought, the last two chapters of the *Letter to Diognetus* were taken and pointed out that such language on the part of Pantaenus might have led Photius (*Bibliotheca* 118) to say, quite erroneously of course, that Pantaenus had heard the apostles preach.[1] But Clement clearly implies in *Miscellanies* i. 1 that he had to depend on his notes and his memory for the teachings of his masters, the elders, or presbyters, as he calls them, and in *Selections* 27 he distinctly says, "The elders did not write." Of course, if Tatian was actually one of Clement's teachers, Clement certainly did not have him in mind when he wrote this.

Pantaenus was the last of Clement's teachers and the one who gave him most satisfaction: "When I came upon the last (he was the first in power), having tracked him out, concealed in Egypt, I found rest. He, the true Sicilian bee, gathering the spoil of the flowers of the prophetic and apostolic meadow, en-

[1] J. B. Lightfoot and J. R. Harmer, *The Apostolic Fathers* (2d ed.; London and New York, 1893), pp. 488 and 489.

gendered in the souls of his hearers a deathless element of knowledge."

Origen appeals to the practice of Pantaenus in defense of his own custom of dealing with the teachings
of the philosophers as a proper part of Christian studies (*Church History* vi. 19. 13). Both Eusebius and
Jerome say that Pantaenus went on a mission to India
(*Church History* v. 10. 3; *On Illustrious Men* 36).

Clement was himself a native of Athens and was
probably of pagan parentage. He traveled widely
Clement   about the world, pursuing his studies under a series of masters, of whom he speaks
half-playfully, but most obscurely, in the opening
pages of his *Miscellanies*, which were in part at least
the result of years of diligent note-taking:

Now this work of mine is not a writing artfully con-
structed for display, but my notes are stored up for old age,
as a remedy against forgetfulness, an image without art, and
a rough sketch of those powerful and animated discourses
which it was my privilege to hear, and of blessed and truly
remarkable men.

Of these, one was in Greece, an Ionian; another in Magna
Graecia; another of them from Coele-Syria, and another
from Egypt. Others were in the East, one born in Assyria,
and another, a Hebrew, in Palestine.

Clement seems to have had six teachers before he
found his way to Pantaenus, but it is difficult to name
any of them, except probably the Assyrian, who must
have been Tatian. That Tatian's later views were very
objectionable to Clement does not conflict with this.

Clement probably began to assist Pantaenus about

A.D. 190, and was head of the school from about 200 to 202, doing most of his writing in these twelve years. The outbreak of the persecution of Severus drove him from Alexandria, and we do not know that he ever returned. When Alexander (later bishop of Jerusalem) wrote his letter from prison to Antioch, A.D. 211, he sent it by Clement (*Church History* vi. 11. 6), so that Clement was still alive at that date, but we cannot trace him after that time. Alexander tells of the useful work that Clement "the blessed presbyter" has been doing for the church at Caesarea (in Cappadocia) while its bishop, Alexander himself, was in prison. In another letter, written to Origen not later than A.D. 217, Alexander speaks of Clement as deceased (*Church History* vi. 14. 9). Clement's death must therefore have occurred not far from A.D. 215. Our last glimpse of him is in Cappadocian Caesarea in A.D. 211, strengthening and building up the church there.

Clement had traveled and studied widely; he seems to have visited Ionia, Middle Syria, Palestine, southern Italy, and Egypt in his pursuit of learning. And he had studied well. His firsthand acquaintance with scripture and classics exceeds that of any Christian writer before him, and of this lore he made good use in his literary efforts to propagate the gospel.

For Clement was not content, like his beloved master Pantaenus, with lecturing to his pupils; he committed his views to writing and expressed himself in the form of books, and books on a grand scale. Whether he planned a great cycle, after the threefold organization of the pagan mysteries—Purification, In-

struction, Revelation—may be doubted. Certainly
such a plan was never completed, if he ever contem-
plated it.

Eusebius gives a long list of Clement's works:
The *Miscellanies* (*Stromateis*), in eight books
The *Outlines* (of holy scripture), in eight books
The *Address to the Greeks* (the *Protrepticus*)
The *Tutor* (the *Paedagogus*), in three books
What Rich Man Can Be Saved?—a tract, or sermon
On the Passover
On Fasting
On Evil-speaking
On Patience, a discourse to the newly baptized
Against the Judaizers, on the rule of the church

Beside these ten works listed by Eusebius, Clement
wrote one *On Providence* (two books) of which some
fragments exist, and one, Palladius says,[2] *On the Prophet Amos*, but of this there are no remains.

Of these twelve books, the majority have almost
entirely disappeared, but three of Clement's major
works survive: The *Miscellanies*, the *Address*, and the
Tutor. We have also the tract or sermon, *What Rich
Man Can Be Saved?* and part of the *Outlines*. All these
books seem to have been written while Clement was
still at Alexandria, that is, by A.D. 202.

The *Protrepticus*, or *Address*, was addressed to pagan
readers and designed to clear the way for the presentation of Christianity by showing the folly of idolatry
and the failure of their old faiths and philosophies to
bring them the salvation they needed. The immorali-

---

[2] *Lausiac History* 139.

ties of Greek mythology, the prostitution of Greek art, and the vagaries of the philosophers are unsparingly set forth, with an extraordinary amount of direct quotation, often of Greek classics now lost. Yet these philosophers, Clement goes on to say, sometimes did find the truth and spoke by divine inspiration—Plato and Socrates and Cleanthes and Pythagoras. In the Greek poets, too, Clement often finds divine truth expressed. But the true teaching is to be found in the prophets. Clement calls upon the pagan Greeks to repent and accept the salvation offered them through Christ. The *Address* is a spirited, richly illustrated, penetrating, and moving appeal.

The *Tutor*, the second book in Clement's sequence, for to that extent at any rate, his sequence did extend, frankly regards its readers as children in spiritual matters and proceeds to teach them in the name of Jesus, the divine Instructor. "We are the children," says Clement. The true basis of morality is set forth and intemperance, extravagance, frivolity, luxury, matrimonial relations, dress, and personal habits are frankly and fully dealt with. Incidentally, an extraordinarily bold and detailed, almost photographic, picture emerges of ancient life, its vanities, foibles, and fashions, as the background against which a Christian morality was being developed. Modesty, frugality, simplicity, and decency are to be the Christian practice. Clement shows how the Christian is to dress, walk, talk, look, and even laugh, and what his attitude should be to jewelry, cosmetics, amusements, and public spectacles. After a veritable final volley of scripture texts bearing on the good life, Clement closes with an extraordinary hymn, addressed to Christ. The hymn is uttered ostensibly by children, but really, of course, by all believers, thought of by Clement as children. It may have formed part of the liturgy of the Alexandrian church and, with its string of disconnected epithets, twelve of them at one time, recalls the Isis litany found some years ago at Oxyrhynchus.[3] It marks another step in Christian hymnology already developing, as we have seen, in the *Odes of Solomon*.[4] It has been made the basis of a modern children's hymn widely used, beginning "Shepherd of tender youth."

If Clement meant to produce a trilogy culminating in a *Didascalus*, or *Teacher*, as some have thought, he never reached his goal, though his tract called *What Rich Man Can Be Saved?* has been thought possibly a part of such a work, but without much plausibility. In that short work Clement argues that it is not the possession of wealth so much as its misuse that is to be condemned. Still less can the *Miscellanies* be identified as such a third book.

The *Miscellanies*, or *Scrapbooks* (*Stromateis*), as we have seen, disclaims any literary or orderly intention. It does this in its very title: "Scrapbooks of Gnostic Notes after the True Philosophy." Into it Clement crammed things he wished to say or at least to preserve. The fact that the book does not seem to come to

[3] *Oxyrhynchus Papyri* xi. 1380.

[4] Cf. H. Jordan, *Geschichte der altchristlichen Literatur* (Leipzig, 1911), pp. 458–59.

an end accords well with this; he kept putting things into it perhaps as long as he lived or kept at work. The eighth book has a very different air. It begins with a fragment on logic, which Westcott thought was part of the introduction to the lost *Outlines*. It includes also the *Excerpts* from the Valentinian Theodotus[5] and the *Selections* from the Prophets which are evidently incomplete notes and materials which Clement never found time or inclination to write up.

The *Miscellanies* have been well described as "a heterogeneous mixture of science, philosophy, poetry, and theology," controlled by the conviction that Christianity can satisfy man's highest intellectual yearnings.[6] Clement is a great reconciler of the intellectual with the religious, as his hospitality to truth wherever he met it among the writings of the philosophers shows. He argues for the greater antiquity of Moses as against Homer and tells, in language evidently drawn from Tatian,[7] what the Greeks owed to other peoples. Like Tatian, too, he speaks of Christianity as a barbarian philosophy. He thinks that philosophies and in a sense even heresies help on the finding of the truth (vi. 15). Clement is not afraid to describe the true Gnostic, who attains Gnosis (knowledge) through virtue and does right because he loves what is right, as the perfect man. Clement's wide acquaintance with books and his numerous quotations

[5] Recently edited with commentary by R. P. Casey, *Excerpta ex Theodoto of Clement of Alexandria* (*Studies and Documents*, Vol. I [London, 1934]).

[6] A. C. McGiffert, *Eusebius* (New York, 1890), p. 259.

[7] *Address*, chaps. 1, 31.

from all sorts of sources come out most strongly here, as do his breadth of view, his tolerance, and his genial good will. The *Miscellanies* makes a decidedly positive impression, but interwoven with its argument is an undercurrent of apologetic and also of antiheretical polemic, as Clement seeks to regain the honorable title of Gnostic from the sects that had appropriated and abused it.

In the *Outlines*, Eusebius says, Clement gave concise accounts of the whole scriptures, "not passing over the disputed books;—I mean Jude and the rest of the Catholic letters and Barnabas and what is called the Revelation of Peter." It was in the *Outlines* that he declared Hebrews to be the work of Paul and quoted the authority of "the blessed presbyter," Pantaenus, for that view. This book, which would be of the utmost interest, has never been found, but a considerable fragment, covering I Peter, Jude, and I and II John, is preserved in a Latin translation by Cassiodorus, under the name of the *Adumbrations of Clement*. Clement's method seems to have been to deal with an occasional sentence, allegorically or doctrinally. Smaller fragments are found in Eusebius and others. Photius says that irreligious and fabulous passages occurred in them (*Bibliotheca* 109) and this may have led to their disappearance.

Of the homilies *On Fasting* and *On Evil-speaking* no pieces have been found, but there are fragments of the works *On the Passover* (called forth by Melito's book of that name), *On Patience*, and *Against the Judaizers*. There are also traces of some of his letters.

In the course of his writings Clement indicated his intention to write five other books, on various subjects, and some of these he may have written; but, if so, they have disappeared.

Clement saw in Christianity the true philosophy and found in the works of Greek philosophers and poets an armory for its defense. It was not the least of his distinctions that he abandoned the types of Christian writing that had been customary and in the *Address* and the *Tutor* cast his views and arguments in literary forms more familiar to the Greek paganism he was seeking to reach.

Clement's liberality was illustrated in his Christian scripture, to which he admitted not only Hebrews, but *I Clement*, *Barnabas*, the *Shepherd* of Hermas, the *Revelation of Peter*, the *Preaching of Peter*, and the *Teaching of the Twelve Apostles;* at any rate, he quotes these books as scripture. In fact, he goes further and sometimes quotes as scripture works now quite unknown. "Take away from you the heavy yoke, and take up the easy one, says the scripture." "Ask, says the scripture, and I will do; think and I will give." "The scripture exhorts us, Be ye skilful money-changers."

Clement sometimes quoted the Sibylline books and spoke of the Sibyl as a prophetess: "Let the Sibyl prophetess be the first to sing to us the song of salvation" (*Address* 8). He knew the *Gospel of the Hebrews*, the *Gospel of the Egyptians*, and the *Traditions of Matthias*, and, though he did not accept them as scripture, he did not dismiss them as heretical.

Clement was no rigorous churchman or theologian;

he was a Puritan in morals, as he had to be, in the
Greek world of the second century. But his literary
and religious sympathies were far from narrow, and
his ideal for the intelligent Christian, in thought and
life, was a noble one.

We are fortunate in possessing, almost complete,
three of his major works; the beginning of the first
book of the *Miscellanies* is missing, and the so-called
eighth book, as we have seen, is a group of unrelated
pieces, plainly unfinished. Of the *Outlines* we have little more than what Cassiodorus has left us in his translation, as the *Adumbrations*. Whatever the value of
Clement's lost minor works might be, the recovery of
the *Outlines* would have the utmost value for many
phases of biblical study.

CHAPTER XII

TERTULLIAN

In the latter part of the first century the writing of Latin literature was already passing into the hands of *Provincial Latin* provincials, men from North Africa and Spain, like Seneca, Martial, and Quintilian. The district about Carthage was particularly active in literary lines, and it is not strange that it was there that the Bible began to be translated into Latin. It was there, and not in Rome, that Latin Christianity had its beginning and that it soon began to express itself vigorously in Latin books.

The first great figure in Latin Christianity was Tertullian, or Quintus Septimius Florens Tertullianus, to *Tertullian* give him his full name. He was born in Carthage, about A.D. 155–60, of good family, and seems, from what he says in his writings, to have visited Athens and Rome in early life, studying to be a lawyer and entering fully into the excesses of heathen life in those centers. At Rome he seems to have practiced law and taught rhetoric, with marked success. There, it appears, he was converted, and he returned to Carthage a Christian. Jerome says he became a presbyter in the church there. At any rate, he threw himself into the Christian cause with tremendous vigor, especially in the crises which persecution now and then brought on for the church. These attacks called forth the notable apologetic pieces which were among his earliest writings, but a wealth of other books, practical, doctrinal, and polemic, soon followed.

The heroic behavior of Christian martyrs deeply impressed Tertullian. He may have had glimpses of it in the first year of Commodus, A.D. 180, when twelve Christians—seven men and five women—from the neighboring town of Scilli suffered martyrdom in Carthage. The simple story of their trial and fate is the earliest of Latin martyrdoms.

In A.D. 197–98 there was another outbreak against the African Christians. Their habit of holding aloof *Apologetic Writings* from public shows, which were both pagan and brutal in character, kept them away from the public celebration of the victory of the emperor, Septimius Severus, over his rivals, and precipitated a fresh persecution. Tertullian came to the defense of his harassed brethren with the fiery vehemence and fervor that always characterized him. In a work addressed *To the Heathen (Ad Nationes,* two books) he vigorously protested against the laws condemning Christians simply as such and without first examining their behavior and manner of life. He protests also against the calumnies heaped upon them and the charges of incest, child murder, and disloyalty to the empire that were made against them. He refers to the ancient pagan practice of exposing undesired children and throws back the charges upon those who made them.

A second book of this same year, A.D. 197, was his

great *Apology* (*Apologeticus*). It was addressed to the Roman governors of provinces and presents a similar argument, though in a more restrained and legal tone. He repels again the stock charges of child-slaying, incest, and cannibalism and admits that Christians do not worship the old gods but holds that they are not disloyal to the empire; though they cannot call the emperor God, they respect and revere him and are good Romans. Here Tertullian points out that persecution simply advances Christianity: "We multiply every time we are mowed down by you; the blood of Christians is seed"—the most famous of all his famous observations.

These writings were preceded in the same year, 197, by a short address *To the Martyrs* already in prison, encouraging them and cheering them on. But the *Address to the Heathen* and the *Apology* form Tertullian's main contribution to Christian defense literature, and they are powerful reinforcements of it.

Upon the death of Severus, fourteen years later, A.D. 211, and the accession of Caracalla, persecution began again, and once more, in 212–13, Tertullian wrote a short but vigorous apology addressed *To Scapula*, the proconsul of Africa, warning him, in view of well-known Roman precedents favorable to Christians, not to proceed against them.

Trenchant and timely as were his writings in the apologetic field, his practical, doctrinal, and polemic works were no less so. No ancient list of his writings has come down to us, but in the oldest manuscript we have of Tertullian, the Codex Agobardinus, given by

Agobard, bishop of Lyons, who died in A.D. 840, to a church there, there is a list of twenty-one of his works, which that manuscript originally contained. From other sources, however, this list can be increased to forty-three, and possibly even to forty-five.

The majority of these were practical in character, dealing with Christian morality and true Christian be-

Practical Works havior in situations of certain kinds or in relation to special groups and matters. Tertullian defends the Christian soldier who refuses to wear the chaplet or wreath on his head, regarding it as a heathenish practice (*On the Chaplet*). He condemns public games, shows, and theatrical and gladiatorial exhibitions as brutal, immoral, and interwoven with pagan rites (*On Idolatry*). He also wrote *On Veiling Virgins*, *On the Adornment of Women*, *On Baptism*, *On Patience*, *On Prayer*, *On Modesty*, and *On Repentance*.

In the doctrinal field Tertullian was not markedly creative, for he owed much to Irenaeus and Melito.

Doctrinal Works He was also much influenced by Stoic philosophy and by what he had been taught by the church at Rome, where he was converted. Yet his work *Against Praxeas* is a notable defense of the doctrine of the Trinity, particularly against the followers of the Roman Sabellius, who flourished late in the second and early in the third century and held Monarchian and modalistic views. Praxeas in his solicitude for the divine unity identified Father, Son, and Holy Spirit, so that it was the Father himself who was born of a virgin and suffered on the cross. Tertullian wrote also *On the Flesh of Christ*, *On the Resurrection of the Flesh*, and *On the Soul*—a work which Harnack calls the first book on Christian psychology.

Closely related to these were his polemic writings, attacking the positions of heretics and schismatics. In *Polemic Writings* his book *On Prescription of Heretics*, which Hort called a most plausible and most mischievous book,[1] he argues that, after exhausting reasoning with such people, one must simply say, "What we hold is the belief of the church, handed down from the apostles, from bishop to bishop, in all the historic centers of Christianity, so it must be true, and there is no more to be said." This shows that when he wrote this book, at least, Tertullian was a strong adherent of the Catholic movement, which Irenaeus reflected. He was, in fact, much influenced in his polemic writings by Irenaeus, and Tertullian and Irenaeus are the first Catholic Fathers.

This appeal to the great apostolic churches, as faithful depositories of Christian tradition, naturally directed North African Christians to Rome, the only church in the West of apostolic foundation:

Since you are close upon Italy, you have Rome, from which there comes even into your hands the very authority [of the apostles]. How happy is its church, upon which apostles poured forth all their doctrine, along with their blood! Where Peter endures a passion like his Lord's! Where Paul wins his crown in a death like John's! Where

[1] F. J. A. Hort, *Six Lectures on the Ante-Nicene Fathers* (London, 1895), p. 103.

the apostle John was first plunged unhurt into boiling oil, and then returned to his island exile! . . . . The Law and the prophets she unites with the writings of evangelists and apostles, from which she drinks in her faith [chap. 36].

This is very much what Irenaeus says in his *Refutation* (iii. 3. 2, 3) about the position of the Roman church, which he in Lyons looked up to from Gaul, just as Tertullian looked up to it from Africa.

But Tertullian's greatest polemic work was that *Against Marcion*, in five books, written over and over again, until his work upon it spread over ten or twelve years of his life, from about 200 to 212. This elaborate work gives us our principal information about Marcion, and especially about his effort to put a Christian scripture consisting of the Gospel of Luke and ten letters of Paul in place of the Jewish scriptures which then made up most of the Bible of Christian churches. Other polemic writings were *Against the Jews, Against Hermogenes*, and *Against the Valentinians*.

We have grouped Tertullian's writings as apologetic, practical, doctrinal, and polemic. But there is also a value in surveying them in the order in which they were written, for they reveal the gradual shift in his religious views, which carried him in the course of ten years from the bosom of the Catholic church into that of the Montanist sect. He was a strong Puritan in feeling and, whatever direction he took, was pretty sure to go to extremes. His devotion to the Catholic movement and his aversion to heretics are very marked in the *Prescription of Heretics*, which he wrote in his first period, when he was a thoroughgoing Catholic. It covers the years 197 to 202. He had become a Christian probably by A.D. 195, perhaps a little earlier. In 197, as we have seen, he wrote his principal apologetic books, *To the Martyrs*, *To the Heathen*, the *Apologeticus*, and also the *Testimony of the Soul*, which he thought essentially Christian by nature and itself a witness to Christianity.

In the course of the next five years, 198–202, he wrote twelve other books and treatises: *On Shows* (two editions), *On the Dress of Women*, *On Baptism*, *On Repentance*, *On Patience*, *On Prayer*, *To His Wife* (against remarriage of women), *On Idolatry*, *On Prescription of Heretics*, *Against Marcion* (two editions), *Against Hermogenes*, and *Against the Jews*.

The edict of Severus in 202, forbidding anyone to become a Christian, marks a shift in Tertullian's attitude. He now begins to see truth and value in the Montanists' position—their Puritan morality, in contrast with the growing laxity of the Roman church; their spiritual emphasis, in contrast with the political cast that was coming over Roman Christianity. For five years Tertullian works to build these Montanist values into his Catholic Christianity. He is still a Catholic, but he sees the worth of Montanism, too, and strives to realize them both and to unite them.

In this period of tension he probably wrote three works now lost: *On Ecstasy*, in seven books, dealing with Montanism; *On the Hope of the Faithful* including the millennial expectations, which he shared; and *On Paradise*—these probably in 202–3 to 204–5. The *Ex-*

hortation to Chastity and the book *On Veiling Virgins* also belong to this time, 204–5 to 206–7.

But by 207–8 the tension had become unbearable, and Tertullian with other Montanists left the church. He now produced a third edition of the first four books *Against Marcion*, his longest work, 207–8. He also wrote now *Against the Valentinians* and *Against the Followers of Apelles*, the Marcionite leader, a work now lost. These belong to 207–8. In 210 he wrote *On the Cloak* (which he wore instead of the toga), in 211 *On the Chaplet*, and in 211–12, *On Flight in Persecution*, holding it inadmissible.

In the following five years, 208–13, he wrote also the books *On the Flesh of Christ*, *On the Testimony of the Soul*, *On the Soul*, *On the Resurrection*, and the fifth and final book *Against Marcion*, completing his discussion of Marcion's proposed scripture, Luke and Paul. In Books i and ii, Tertullian had dealt with Marcion's doctrine that the Creator and the Father of Jesus were different beings; in Book iii he argued that the Christian movement does not contradict the prophets but fulfils them; in Books iv and v he uses Marcion's own scripture, Luke and Paul, to establish this.

About 212 he wrote his short apology to the proconsul, *To Scapula*, and in 212 or 213 his *Scorpiace*, warning against the scorpion sting of heresy and encouraging to martyrdom, which some Gnostics taught was unnecessary. In the course of the next five years he wrote *Against Praxeas* his defense of the Trinity, and soon after 217–18 his book *On Monogamy*, protesting against second marriages, and his work *On Fasting*. And finally, not long before 222–23, he wrote the work *On Modesty*, bitterly assailing the action of Calixtus, bishop of Rome, in declaring that the sins of adultery and fornication, though committed after baptism, could be forgiven by the church; it had previously been held that while God could forgive them, along with murder and idolatry, the church could not. Tertullian's invective against this action stands in sharp contrast to his rhapsody upon the Roman church, in his *Prescription of Heretics*, chapter 36, written twenty years before, in 198–202/3:

The Pontifex Maximus, that is the bishop of bishops, issues an edict: I remit, to such as have discharged the requirements of repentence (or penitence), the sins both of adultery and of fornication. O edict which cannot be inscribed "Good deed!" [chap. 1].

All three of these last works of Tertullian, in fact (*Monogamy*, *Fasting*, and *Modesty*), are bitter in their denunciation of the laxity that was pervading the Roman church under Zephyrinus and Calixtus. He felt strongly that it had forfeited the spiritual heritage of Christianity. "You have quenched the spirit," he cried, "You have driven away the Comforter (Paraclete)."

At the time of Tertullian's death, soon after A.D. 222–23, he had left the Montanists and organized a little sect of his own, for Augustine, almost two hundred years later, found a group of Tertullianists still meeting independently in Carthage and brought them back into the church.

Some of Tertullian's writings, like the one *On Veil-*

ing Virgins, he wrote first in Greek. Whether he was the author of the *Martyrdom of Perpetua and Felicitas*, women of Carthage who suffered in the persecution of A.D. 202–3, is not certain; it is extant in both Greek and Latin and is a work of moving simplicity. Perpetua was a woman of position, while Felicitas was a slave. The account is written from a Montanist point of view. Jerome also mentions a book *On the Difficulties of Marriage* addressed "to a philosophic friend," which may have been written early in life and possibly even in a lighter vein, for Jerome speaks of him as "playing" (*lusit*) with the subject.

Of the works of Tertullian, thirty-one have been preserved, and the names of more than a dozen others can be gathered from references to them in Tertullian himself, in Jerome, or in the table of contents of the Codex Agobardinus. The Greek form of the book *On Baptism* dealt also with the question of heretical baptism and was evidently a different book from the Latin work of that name. Other lost writings are the *Hope of the Faithful, Paradise, Against the Followers of Apelles,* the *Origin of the Soul, Fate, Ecstasy,* the *Garments of Aaron, To a Philosophic Friend, Flesh and Soul, Submission of Soul,* and the *Superstition of the World.* The Greek forms of the works *On Shows* and *On the Veiling of Virgins* have also been lost. He may also have written *On Clean and Unclean Animals* and *On Circumcision,* as Jerome intimates (*Epist.* 36:1).

Tertullian is always the advocate; there is nothing judicial about his attitude; he sees only one side. His style is impetuous, dramatic, direct, varied, often richly illustrated, sometimes full of apostrophe and exclamation, gifted, but uncontrolled, except by overwhelming conviction. It reveals unmistakably one of the most powerful personalities of the early church, whose works have for the most part survived even though he had withdrawn from the Catholic church years before his death.

The Latin version of the Bible was just coming into being in North Africa in Tertullian's day, and he was *The Latin Bible* well versed in scripture, probably both Greek and Latin. Like Irenaeus, he had a New Testament, and these two are the first Christian Fathers of whom this can be said. Tertullian's included the Four Gospels, the Acts, and thirteen letters of Paul, besides I Peter, I John and Jude, the Revelation of John, and at first the *Shepherd* of Hermas, though later in life he repudiated that book with great scorn, for what he considered its moral laxity.[2]

Tertullian also knew early Christian literature very well, especially Justin, Tatian, Melito, Irenaeus, and Clement. His own influence was very marked upon Minucius Felix and upon Cyprian, his great literary successor in North Africa, the bishop of Carthage from A.D. 250 to 258. Jerome reports that he once met an aged man who in his youth had known one of Cyprian's assistants, who said that Cyprian made it a rule to read something of Tertullian's every day and would often say when he wanted to consult Tertullian, "Give me the Master."

[2] *On Modesty* x. 20.

In connection with Tertullian we may discuss also the admirable work of another gifted Latin, the *Oc-*

Minucius   *tavius* of Minucius Felix. For in the *Oc-*
Felix   *tavius* Minucius Felix wrote the finest of all the Latin apologies for Christianity— Renan called it the pearl of apologetic literature—and he wrote it in reply to an attack on Christianity made by one of the leading pagan Latin writers of the second century, M. Cornelius Fronto. For what Celsus did so ably in Greek in A.D. 178, in his critique of Christianity, had already been done, though less effectively, in Latin by Fronto.

We know much more about Fronto than we do about Minucius. M. Cornelius Fronto (*ca*. 100–175) was a native of Cirta in Africa who had come to Rome in the time of Hadrian and found fame and fortune there as a lawyer, orator, and writer. He became a senator and was consul in A.D. 143 but declined the proconsulship of Asia. He undertook to reform Roman literary style, advocating a return to the earliest Latin models; he exalted oratory as the greatest of arts and was himself considered second only to Cicero. He was invited by Antoninus to become the tutor of the princes Marcus and Verus. His writings had completely disappeared, however, when in 1815 Angelo Mai found in a sixth-century palimpsest at Milan part of a collection of Fronto's letters, written to the emperors Antoninus and Aurelius, among others, from A.D. 143 on. The rest of the manuscript Mai afterward found at Rome. It also contained some of Fronto's smaller literary pieces, but his attack on Christianity has never been found. It may possibly have been part of an address to the senate, uttered when Christianity was beginning to show strength, about A.D. 150–60.

Sixty or seventy years later a Latin Christian named Minucius Felix, probably a lawyer in Rome, replied to
The Octavius   Fronto with a dialogue entitled the *Octavius*. It twice mentions Fronto as an assailant of Christianity (chaps. 9 and 31), and it is not unlikely that it reproduces some of his attack in the first third of it, in which the pagan case against Christianity is presented. Fronto's was the only literary attack on Christianity made in Latin.

The scene of the *Octavius* is laid in Rome. Minucius, or Marcus, as his friends call him, tells how his friend Octavius has come from Africa to visit him, and, as the weather is fine, they and a pagan friend Caecilius go on a pleasure trip to Ostia for the sea baths. As they go, they pass a statue of Serapis, and Caecilius throws it a kiss. Octavius rebukes his superstition, and Caecilius declares he is ready to defend his attitude, if they will hear him. They agree and sit down, Minucius, as a sort of umpire, sitting between Caecilius and Octavius.

Caecilius then presents the popular case against the Christians: Christians are too ignorant to know the things they profess to know. As a matter of fact, there is no reason or providence in the universe. Rome flourished as long as it piously worshiped the gods; it is wrong for the Christians to revile them. They themselves worship a crucified man and indulge in hideous, evil, and wanton orgies. They conceal their practices and are really a wretched lot of secretive, ignorant, miserable people, unequal to the demands of this life and utterly unfitted to forecast the life to come (chaps. 5–13).

Challenged by Caecilius and encouraged by Minucius to reply, Octavius does so. Wisdom and intelligence, he declares, depend upon natural endowment, and the Christians' possession of them is not determined by the measure of wealth or advantages they may enjoy. Reasonable men have always seen reason and order in the universe and perceived that these imply a divine ruler controlling it all. Such a ruler is too great to be understood or even named; any name would fall short of him. Poets and philosophers have agreed that he is man's father and that he is one. Against such views, old fables and the worship of dead heroes as gods ought not to weigh at all. The heathen gods were really deified men, images of whom the people worship. The very birds and animals know that these images are not gods. Their rites are grotesque and absurd, even inhuman and immoral. Roman success has been won not by piety but by violence. Demons, not gods, are behind the auguries and oracles, and they inspire the hideous slanders against the Christians— that they worship monsters, devour infants, and indulge in incest at their feasts. It is really the heathen themselves who practice murder and incest. God cannot be contained in a temple. The Jews themselves admit in their writings that they forsook him before he abandoned them. The philosophers have long maintained that the universe will eventually perish, and

God, who created man, can bring him back to life, and reward or punish him, as he deserves. What Christians now suffer is not a punishment but a discipline, heroically endured. They avoid pagan shows and practices as impious, cruel, and absurd (chaps. 16–38).

Caecilius acknowledges himself defeated by the arguments of Octavius and forthwith accepts Christianity (chaps. 39–41).

It is generally agreed that in elegance of style Minucius' defense of Christianity decidedly excels Fronto's attack upon it, if we may judge the latter from the clumsy and affected pieces of Fronto discovered in the past century. The absence of scripture or of mention of Christ by name in the *Octavius* is natural enough in a work addressed to pagan readers, as, of course, the *Octavius* was.

We owe the preservation of the *Octavius* to the fact that it was mistaken in the Middle Ages for the eighth (*octavus*) book of Arnobius *Against the Heathen* (*Adversus nationes*) and preserved as such, appended to the seven books of that work, and with no title of its own, in the Paris manuscript of the ninth century, which is our sole independent witness to the text of Arnobius. It was first published, as a part of Arnobius, in 1543, but was soon recognized (1560) by Balduinus as the long-lost *Octavius* mentioned by Lactantius (in his *Divine Institutes* 1:11 and 5:1, begun about A.D. 303) and by Jerome (*On Illustrious Men* 58 and *Epist.* 70:5). Jerome mentions a work *On Fate* as ascribed to Minucius but says the style is very unlike that of the *Octavius*. No trace of it has been found.

No problem in the field of early Christian literature has been more hotly debated than the relative dates of the *Octavius* and of the *Apology* (*Apologeticus*) of Tertullian; more than two hundred articles and monographs have been devoted to it. The *Apologeticus* was written in A.D. 197 and so much resembles the *Octavius* in so many points that it is clear that one was strongly influenced by the other. Jerome repeatedly speaks as though Tertullian preceded Minucius, and it would be strange if the Roman writer could think so disparagingly of the state of the empire in the course of the splendid era from Trajan to Aurelius; his attitude accords much better with the days of its palpable decline, in the middle of the third century. In the third century, moreover, the empire was getting into the lawyers' hands, and that might suggest making them the participants in the debate.

The *Octavius* was later made use of by Novatian in his work *On the Trinity*, for example, written toward A.D. 250, and also by Xystus II, bishop of Rome, if he wrote the discourse *To Novatian*, written between A.D. 253 and 258 and preserved under the name of Cyprian.[3] So the *Octavius* was probably written sometime between A.D. 238 and 249, when the empire was at a low ebb.[4] If Novatian's work *On the Trinity* was written about A.D. 245, the *Octavius* may be dated about 240.

[3] Another work preserved under Cyprian's name, the treatise *That Idols Are Not Gods*, also shows the influence of the *Octavius*, and it, too, may be a work of Novatian.

[4] See A. Harnack, *Geschichte der altchristlichen Litteratur* (3 vols.; Leipzig, 1893–1904), II, 2, 325–30.

Its mention by Lactantius, about A.D. 303, and by Jerome has been noted.

The *Octavius* is very different from the Greek apologies; it swings away from the earlier biblical apologetic toward the more sophisticated philosophical Christianity of Lactantius; it is much more like a hearing before a magistrate or, particularly, a philosophical debate before an umpire. It was modeled on Cicero's disputations—the *Orator*, the *Nature of the Gods*, and *Revelation*. The pagan side is first presented with brutal frankness, and then the Christian side is just as unsparingly given.

It seems idle to look for historical characters in the persons who take part. Octavius is introduced as an old friend and teacher from Africa, and he and Caecilius are dead when the book is written, but in a work so full of art all this is probably simply part of the literary guise of the book. The appearance of the latter name, Caecilius Natalis, in a number of Cirta inscriptions of A.D. 211–17, as belonging to a leading citizen there at that time is probably little more than a coincidence.

CHAPTER XIII

HIPPOLYTUS

Among the young men whom Irenaeus taught, probably in the years he spent at Lyons, was one named

His Life

Hippolytus, who came to be his great successor as the foremost figure of Greek Christianity in the West. He was born about A.D. 170 (165–75) and spent his mature life in Rome, where he became a presbyter. When Origen visited Rome, about 215, he heard Hippolytus preach. Hippolytus was active in the campaign against the sects and was a prolific writer. He strongly opposed the laxity of Zephyrinus, bishop from 198 to 217, and his assistant Calixtus, regarding them both as mercenary and self-seeking, and upon the election of Calixtus as bishop made such a protest that the Roman church divided into two factions, one of which actually chose Hippolytus as bishop. He continued to hold this office in opposition to Calixtus and his successors, Urbanus (222–23 to 230) and Pontianus. In fact, in 235, in Maximin's persecution, Hippolytus and Pontianus were sent into exile together to the mines of Sardinia, where Pontianus seems to have died. Whether Hippolytus, too, died there or survived his exile and died in Rome the following year is uncertain. But he was buried on the road to Tivoli (Via Tiburtina) on August 13, probably A.D. 236.

On this road, and probably near his grave, a statue of Hippolytus, or what was left of it, was found in 1551, and while the head and upper part of the body were gone, the marble chair proved of great importance, because a list of the works of Hippolytus was carved on the back of it. Upon it were also carved the tables for calculating the date of Easter, but as these proved erroneous by as much as three days, as early as 237, the statue can hardly be of later date than that year and was probably made and set up in 236 or 237. The schism in the church was evidently healed before the death of Hippolytus.

The Statue

A hundred years ago the works of Hippolytus had almost entirely disappeared, but a series of discoveries has gone far to remedy this. One of his most notable works was his *Refutation of All Heresies*, which seemed to have perished. But in 1701 a Greek work surveying the views of the Greek philosophers, the Brahmins and the Druids, was printed by Gronovius as the *Philosophumena* of Origen. In 1842 a Greek named Minas Minoides found on Mount Athos a fourteenth-century manuscript of Books iv–x of the same work, of which the part previously published was evidently Book i. These eight books E. Miller published in 1851 as Origen's *Philosophumena or Refutation of All Heresies*. But it was soon perceived that they were not the work of Origen at all but of Hippolytus, being his long-lost *Refutation of All Heresies*, mentioned by Eusebius (as *Against All Heresies* [*Church History* vi. 22. 2]) and by Jerome (*On Illustrious Men* 61), and they were republished under the name of Hippolytus by Duncker and

Schneidewin in 1859. One scholar, d'Alès, has endeav-
ored to show that Book iv really contains Books ii and
iii and part at least of Book iv, but this cannot be said
to have been proved. As it is, however, these discoveries and researches have given us one of the major
works of Hippolytus almost complete.

A long series of other discoveries has brought vari-
ous lost works of Hippolytus to light in Latin, Syriac,
Coptic, Arabic, Ethiopic, Armenian, Georgian, and
Slavic translations. The remarkable thing is that so
few of them have been preserved in Greek, but Hip-
polytus had been out of harmony with the dominant
element in the Roman church most of his later life, and
Greek very soon ceased to be the language of Roman
Christianity; in fact, Hippolytus is really our last
Greek writer in the Western church.

His literary work was done principally between
A.D. 200 and 235. The inscription on the back of the
chair lists at least ten of his works, but two lines are
probably lost at the top, with the upper part of the
chair back.[1] Eusebius lists eight works but says that
many others were current in his day. Jerome names
nineteen, and Photius, who seems to have confused
Hippolytus with Gaius, mentions a number of his
works (*Bibliotheca* 48, 121, and 202) but does not attempt a unified list. Upon the basis of these and the
manuscript discoveries of recent years, a list of no less
than forty works of Hippolytus can be reconstructed,
covering the fields of scripture interpretation, polemic

[1] The list on the chair may have purposely omitted works which would
have been offensive to the rival faction in the Roman church.

and doctrinal writing, church law, and chronology. Harnack listed forty-three, of which eight are preserved, complete or nearly so, in Greek or in ancient versions; twelve are lost; and twenty-three are represented only by fragments, few or many.

Fully half of the books of Hippolytus of which we know were devoted to the interpretation of the scrip-

Scripture Interpretation tures. His interest extended all the way from Genesis to the Revelation, but he covered very few individual books completely—Ruth, Proverbs, Song of Songs, Daniel, Revelation—usually contenting himself with discussing particular narratives or prophecies here and there.

Of some twenty-six such commentaries and homilies, we have six, either in the original Greek or in early versions, the most extended being the commentary *On Daniel* in four books, written in A.D. 203–4, which is complete in Old Slavic but is preserved in large part in Greek also. We have also the commentary *On the Song of Songs* (in Georgian); *On the Blessing of Jacob* (Genesis, chap. 49) (in Greek, Armenian, and Georgian); *On the Blessing of Moses* (Deuteronomy, chap. 33) and the *Story of David and Goliath* (I Samuel, chap. 17) (these two in Armenian and Georgian); and *On the Raising of Lazarus* (John, chap. 11), preserved in Greek among the sermons of Chrysostom but in Armenian as a work of Hippolytus. These Eastern versions show how highly the Eastern churches regarded the work of Hippolytus, although he was generally forgotten in the West. Hippolytus' method of interpretation was, of course, highly allegorical; Susanna, in Daniel, symbolized the Christian church, threatened by Jews, pagans, and heretics but saved by Christ. Yet he was less atomistic and more historical in his interpretation than his Alexandrian contemporary Origen.

The sermon which Origen on his visit to Rome heard Hippolytus preach has disappeared, but Jerome says it was *On the Praise of the Lord Our Savior* (*On Illustrious Men* 61). The work *On the Passover* was found in 1936 by C. Martin among the sermons of Chrysostom.

We can name at least eighteen other exegetical writings of Hippolytus, which are either entirely lost or represented only by fragments, and it is worth while to mention them, if for no other reason than to facilitate their discovery, in case they still exist. For we shall find them sooner if we know what we are looking for, and some of them can probably be found.

From our various sources, already mentioned, we know that in this field he wrote on:

The Six Days of Creation. There are some Greek fragments of this and the four following

What Followed the Six Days

The Blessing of Isaac (Genesis, chap. 27)

The Blessing of Balaam (Numbers, chaps. 23 and 24)

Moses' Song (Deuteronomy, chap. 32)

The Book of Ruth. A Greek fragment

Elkanah and Hannah (I Samuel, chap. 1). Four short Greek fragments

The Witch of Endor. A Greek fragment

The Psalms (some of them). Four Greek fragments

Proverbs. Twenty-nine fragments

Ecclesiastes. One fragment
Part of Isaiah. One Greek fragment
Parts of Ezekiel. One Greek and one Syriac fragment
Zechariah (lost)
Parts of Matthew. Possible Greek and Syriac fragments
The Parable of the Talents. One Greek fragment
The Two Thieves. Three Greek fragments
The Revelation. Some Arabic fragments

It is as an anti-heretical writer, however, that we naturally think of Hippolytus, because, of his works *The Refutation* that have come down to us, his *Refutation of All Heresies* is the longest and most interesting. The succession of discoveries that has restored at least eight of its ten books to us in Greek has already been described. Long before he wrote it, or soon after A.D. 200, Hippolytus had written a shorter work *Against All Heresies*, also known as the work *Against Thirty-two Heresies*. (This was afterward used by various writers on heresy—Epiphanius, Philastrius [A.D. 383], and the author of an anonymous work *Against All Heresies*, long ascribed to Tertullian.) He had also written a work against the Alogi, or opponents of the Logos doctrine of John—the work *In Defense of the Gospel and Revelation of John*, probably about A.D. 204–5. This book is sometimes identified with the *Heads against Gaius*,[2] which was more probably an independent work, written a little later to de-

---

[2] There are several Syriac fragments of this work in Bar-Salibi's commentary on the Revelation, written in the twelfth century.

fend the Revelation against the claim of a Roman Christian, perhaps a presbyter, named Gaius who in his *Dialogue with Proclus*, the leading Montanist in Rome, had maintained that the Revelation was really written by the early heretic Cerinthus.[3]

But the *Refutation* was Hippolytus' great work in this field. It made use of the earlier *Refutation* written by Hippolytus' teacher Irenaeus and also of Hippolytus own earlier work *Against Thirty-two Heresies*, written a quarter-century before. Hippolytus seeks to show that the heresies had their source in Greek philosophy and in pagan religions; this is why he devoted his first book to a survey of Greek philosophies, his (lost) second and third, probably, to the mystery religions, and his fourth to astrology and magic, in preparation for his discussion of the heresies, which begins with the fifth book. His picture of the Gnostics has been criticized as based upon secondary and biased sources and as seriously misrepresenting their views. The *Refutation* was written in the years 225–30.

Two other polemic works of his are known, at least by name: one *Against Marcion*, now lost, and one *Against Artemon*, written about A.D. 230—certainly after the *Refutation*, which makes no mention of Artemon. It was also called the *Little Labyrinth*, perhaps because it formed a sort of supplement to the *Labyrinth* (as Hippolytus seems to call the *Refutation*, x. 5 [Gr.]), bringing it up to date. This, too, is lost, except for

[3] A Greek fragment of the *Dialogue* is found in Eusebius *Church History* ii. 25. 7.

three substantial fragments preserved in Eusebius
Church History v. 28.[4]

Hippolytus did not neglect the field of Christian
doctrine. Perhaps the earliest of his works was that

Works on Doctrine — On Christ and Antichrist, written about
A.D. 200. It was written in reply to cer-
tain topics ("heads") or questions raised
by his friend Theophilus about the signs of the end.
Hippolytus did not regard Rome as the kingdom of
Antichrist but as the fourth of the kingdoms described
in the Book of Daniel. In it he made some use of the
great work of his old master Irenaeus. It is often mentioned in his Daniel commentary, written in 202–4,
and is extant in full in Greek.

A work *On the Resurrection*, addressed to the empress
Julia Mamaea, was composed sometime during the
reign of her son Alexander Severus, A.D. 222–35. Only
a few Greek and Syriac fragments remain of it.

A work *On the Universe, against the Greeks and Plato*, is
mentioned by medieval writers (Photius, Philoponus)
as the work of Josephus or Gaius but was pretty certainly written by Hippolytus, for he mentions it as his
in *Refutation* x. 28 (Eng.), so that it was evidently written before 225. It was in two books, but only a few
Greek fragments remain.

We have also the titles of two other works—the
Address to Severina and *On Good and the Source of Evil*—

---

[4] A work *Against Montanism* written in Rome in the time of Hippolytus
has been conjectured from its apparent use in Epiphanius *Against Heresies*
48:2–13. It seems to have made use of Tertullian's work *On Ecstasy*, written
in A.D. 202–3 to 204–5, and to have been in turn attacked by him in his work
On Monogamy. But it can hardly have been the work of Hippolytus.

but both are lost, and there seem to be no identifiable fragments, so that their dates cannot be determined.

The curious little anonymous *Letter to Diognetus* shows such a change of style and subject at the beginning of chapter 11 that it has been suggested that another hand, perhaps that of Hippolytus, wrote chapters 11 and 12.[5] Harnack even suggests that both parts of the letter may possibly be his work. But the absence of any ancient attestation for the *Letter* makes any such identification of its author extremely dubious.

Yet another phase of Hippolytus' literary work was as a chronicler. As early as A.D. 222–23 he had written

The Chronicle his *Determination of the Date of Easter*, which is mentioned in the chair list and also by Eusebius (*Church History* vi. 22. 1); the Easter table carved on the side of the chair is taken from it. Aside from that, it is lost, but a similar work in Latin (*De Pascha computus*), written in A.D. 242–43 and wrongly ascribed to Cyprian, may be regarded as a corrected form of it. But now in A.D. 234 he wrote his *Chronicle* (*Chronicon*). In scope the book was a chronicle of world-history from the Creation to A.D. 234, the date of its composition. The Greek original of it is lost, except for some fragments, principally a leaf of a sixth- or seventh-century papyrus book from Oxyrhynchus (*Oxyrhynchus Papyri* vi. 870) and a considerable portion found in a Madrid manuscript. But a good part of it is preserved, sometimes more or less modified, in three different Latin versions, and there is also an Armenian translation. It made use of the "Lit-

[5] Bunsen, Draeseke, Bonwetsch, Lightfoot, Harnack.

tle Chronology" in the *Miscellanies* of Clement of Alexandria (i. 21. 109–36) and also of the *Chronography* of
Julius Africanus, which had recently appeared, A.D.
221. Hippolytus shared the view of Africanus that the
"Last Day" (of a thousand years) would follow the
year of the world 6000 and was careful to prove that
the year he wrote was the year of the world 5738. One
of the book's most important features was the "Diamerismos" or "Division" of the earth among the pos-
terity of Noah (Genesis, chap. 10), which was often
reflected in later writers. The Madrid manuscript
shows that the "Diamerismos" included the "Stadias-
mos" or measurement in stadia of the Great Sea, a kind
of navigation book for the Mediterranean.

Recent research has restored to us still another lost
work of Hippolytus and revealed another side of his

*The
Apostolic
Tradition*

literary activity. In the list of Hippolytus' works on the chair, one line reads:
"The Apostolic Tradition About Gifts"
(*charismata*), which probably covers two
works, one the *Apostolic Tradition*, and the other *About
Gifts*. These have long been reckoned among his lost
writings. But a series of discoveries and researches has
now resulted in the recovery of the *Apostolic Tradition*,
which is identified with the so-called *Egyptian Church
Order*. This work came to be so named because it first
came to modern notice in a Coptic translation, brought
from Egypt and published by Tattam in 1848. But, in
1900, Hauler discovered and published, from a palimpsest at Verona, a Latin form of it much nearer to the
original Greek and strongly suggesting that the work

was in substance not Egyptian at all. The investigations of Schwartz (1910), and others independently carried on by Connolly (1916),[6] showed that the book lying back of these versions or revisions was none other than the long lost *Apostolic Tradition* of Hippolytus, and in this view scholars have generally concurred.[7]

The book tells how bishops, presbyters, and deacons are to be ordained, giving the prayers to be uttered; tells of confessors, widows, virgins, new converts, crafts forbidden to Christians, of baptism, confirmation, church observances, fasts, prayers, etc.—all in a most concise and practical fashion. It is clear that Hippolytus has the distinction of having been the leader in codifying church procedure. The book is a small compact manual, written probably about A.D. 215, in the last part of the episcopate of Zephyrinus, of whom Hippolytus complained that he was ignorant of the rules of the church (*Refutation* ix. 11 [Eng. ix. 6]).

The *Apostolic Tradition* was later re-written and worked into the *Apostolical Constitutions*, viii. 4–32. From these the so-called *Constitutions through Hippolytus* were epitomized. The so-called *Canons of Hippolytus*, preserved in Arabic and Ethiopic, also reflect the *Apostolic Tradition*, much altered.

[6] *The So-called Egyptian Church Order and Derived Documents* (Cambridge, 1916).

[7] So B. S. Easton, *The Apostolic Tradition of Hippolytus* (Cambridge, 1934), and Gregory Dix, *The Treatise on the Apostolic Tradition of St. Hippolytus of Rome* (London, 1937); but not Rudolf Lorentz, *De aegyptische Kerkordening en Hippolytus van Rome* (Leiden, 1929).

Hippolytus is also significant for his testimony to the New Testament as understood at Rome in his day.

His New Testament He gives no list of New Testament books (unless, as some have thought, the Muratorian Fragment is a translation of something from his pen), but a close examination of his writings, or such parts of them as survive, gives us a fairly clear picture. His New Testament was not particularly different from that of his teacher Irenaeus. He accepted the Four Gospels as scripture and acknowledged thirteen letters of Paul, but not Hebrews. His famous Roman contemporary Gaius held the same view of the Pauline collection. Hippolytus also accepted Acts and three Catholic letters—I Peter and I and II John. The Revelation of John completed his New Testament, making a total of twenty-two books.

But Hippolytus knew numerous other Christian writings from the first and second centuries, among them Hebrews, the *Shepherd* of Hermas, the *Revelation of Peter*, and the *Acts of Paul*. He is the first Christian writer to reflect II Peter, and he must have known James and Jude at least slightly, for he once quotes the first verse of James with the words, "As the saying of Jude in his first letter to the Twelve Tribes proves."[8]

With Hippolytus the curtain falls upon Greek Christianity in Rome. He was a Puritan in morals and in discipline, sternly opposing a series of Roman bishops on both practical and doctrinal issues. He worked in a time of conflict with laxity, venality, and heresy within the church and proved himself a stalwart in the

---

[8] Hippolytus (Achelis ed.), p. 231, l. 10.

fight, struggling valiantly to hammer out Christian views of morals, practice, doctrine, and interpretation. Little that he accomplished can be considered final, of course, but he made a substantial contribution to Christian development. Further discoveries will undoubtedly increase our knowledge of him and his times and works, at least four-fifths of which, and perhaps much more, seems at present to have been lost.

CHAPTER XIV

ORIGEN

Origen was the greatest Christian scholar and the most prolific Christian writer of antiquity. Epipha-

*His Volu-
minous
Writings*

nius declared that he wrote six thousand works, doubtless meaning rolls, or scrolls, of ordinary length, about that of Matthew or Acts. Rufinus laughed at this and called Epiphanius a crazy old man (*delirus senex*), but Jerome rather took his side: "Which of us," said Jerome, "can read all that he has written?"

Origen was a native of Alexandria, where he was destined to carry the great tradition of Pantaenus and Clement to its peak. He was born in A.D. 184–85. His father was a Christian teacher and suffered martyrdom in the persecution of Severus, A.D. 202, which had driven Clement from the city. Origen, then sixteen or seventeen, undertook to support his widowed mother and his six brothers and sisters by teaching, and a year later, in 202–3, Demetrius, the bishop, put him at the head of the catechetical school, when he was hardly eighteen years old. For a dozen years he carried on that work with marked success. It is a stern token of the rigorous asceticism then stirring in Egypt that Origen, in this period of his life, and influenced by a literal interpretation of a saying in Matt. 19:12, emasculated himself.

This was his first Alexandrian period. In the course of it he traveled to Rome, visited the church there, and heard Hippolytus preach. He was also summoned to Arabia by the governor there for an interview (*Church History* vi. 19. 15). In A.D. 215 Caracalla's furious attack upon the Alexandrians interrupted Origen's work at the school and drove him from the city.

He took refuge in Palestine and lived for perhaps two years in Caesarea, preaching in the churches at the request of the bishops of Jerusalem and Caesarea. As he was not ordained, this offended his old friend Demetrius, the bishop of Alexandria, and he called Origen back to resume his conduct of the school, probably about A.D. 217. About this time Origen found an able assistant in Heraclas, whose lectures later drew Julius Africanus to settle in Alexandria for a time to hear them (*Church History* vi. 31. 2). It was in this second Alexandrian period, which lasted for thirteen years, that Origen's real work of writing began.

In 230 he traveled to Greece on some church business and, stopping at Caesarea on his way, was ordained as a presbyter by Theoctistus, the bishop there. When Demetrius heard of this, he felt that his authority had been flouted, and, on Origen's return, Demetrius assembled a synod which decreed that Origen should no longer teach or live in Alexandria. Only the bishops of Palestine, Phoenicia, Arabia, and Greece stood by Origen. In this most unhappy way his work in Egypt, which was destined to prove so historic, was ended.

Origen now removed to Caesarea, where he prosecuted his studies and his work of teaching, preaching, and writing. His fame spread over the East. The emperor's mother, Julia Mamaea, invited him to visit Antioch so that she might hear him preach (*Church History* vi. 21. 3, 4). He also revisited Athens and Arabia in these years. The persecution of Maximin, A.D. 235–38, may have driven him to take refuge in Caesarea in Cappadocia and spend two years there, as Palladius says (*Lausiac History* 64), though this is not altogether certain. But in the Decian persecution Origen was imprisoned, and suffered tortures in consequence of which he soon afterward died, probably in Caesarea, but perhaps in Tyre, A.D. 254, at the age of sixty-nine.

About the time of Origen's return to Alexandria, in A.D. 217, or soon after, he made a great friend in Ambrose, a man of means and position whom he had won over from Valentinian views. Ambrose became his friend, patron, and publisher. Eusebius' account of this connection gives us the clearest picture of an ancient writer and his publisher that has come down to us anywhere. It is doubly important not only as showing one early Christian publishing house actually at work but for the light it throws upon the immense literary output credited to Origen by ancient writers.

Eusebius says that Origen "began his commentaries on the divine scriptures being urged thereto by Ambrose, who employed innumerable incentives, not only exhorting him by word, but furnishing abundant means. For he dictated to more than seven amanuenses, who relieved each other at appointed times. And he employed no fewer copyists, besides girls who were

skilled in elegant writing. For all these Ambrose fur-
nished the necessary expense in abundance" (*Church
History* vi. 23. 1, 2). It will be seen that Ambrose not
only expedited the publication of books thought of
and written by Origen but urged further undertakings
upon him; in particular his commentaries on the scriptures. "To the management and support of Ambrose,"
said Harnack, "we owe a great part of the works of
Origen."[1] Origen long refused to have his sermons
taken down stenographically, but after he was sixty
he allowed this to be done. It is clear that all that
ancient methods could do was done to encourage Origen to produce, and to circulate his product. So urgent
did Origen's publisher sometimes become in his demands for new books that Origen once humorously
described him as his taskmaster, or slave-driver (*ergo-
dioktes*).

Origen's writings may be conveniently grouped
under five heads.

Ever since the founding of the Alexandrian Museum
more than four centuries before, Alexandria had been
On Text   the home of textual study, especially of
                Homer, and Origen now turned a schol-
ar's eye upon the *text* of the Greek Old Testament,
which formed so great a part of the Bible of the early
church. He knew it was a translation from the Hebrew, so he got a Hebrew Bible, in his day of course a
mass of rolls, and learned Hebrew. The standard
Greek form of the Old Testament among the churches

[1] A. Harnack, *Geschichte der altchristlichen Litteratur* (3 vols.; Leipzig,
1893–1904), I, 328–29.

was the Septuagint version, but other translations had been made in the second century by Aquila, Theodotion,[2] and the Ebionite Symmachus. Origen sought for still others and found them, one at Nicopolis, near Actium. He also found three more translations of the Psalms, one of them, Eusebius says, in a jar in Jericho.

Origen conceived the magnificent idea of setting out these four versions side by side, with the Hebrew and a Greek transliteration of it in parallel columns, to facilitate their study. This enormous work, which would obviously be at least six times the size of the Old Testament, seems to have been actually copied out but could hardly have been published. This was Origen's celebrated Hexapla, his "sixfold" Old Testament, a work which, judging from the size of the Vatican manuscript, written a century later, must have reached nine thousand pages.[3] It does not seem likely that it was ever recopied, but the original passed into the hands of Origen's admirer Pamphilus and remained for many years in the library that he gathered in Caesarea to enshrine the memory of Origen.

The great Sinaitic manuscript of the Greek Bible, now in the British Museum, has notes in a hand of about A.D. 600, at the end of Esther and of Esdras (Ezra-Nehemiah) which state that the manuscript had been compared with a very ancient one which in turn had been corrected in prison by the martyr Pamphilus with the aid of Origen's own copy of the Hexapla.

---

[2] Theodotion's work was really for the most part a revision of the Septuagint version.

[3] Eusebius *Church History* vi. 16. 1–4; Jerome *On Illustrious Men* 75.

Jerome consulted the Hexapla in the library at Caesarea toward the end of the fourth century. The library, with the Hexapla in it, seems to have existed until the Saracens took Caesarea early in the seventh century (A.D. 638), for in 616–17 Paul of Tella, a Syrian bishop, translated the Septuagint column of it into Syriac, retaining Origen's critical marks; and his translation, about half of which is preserved in an eighth-century manuscript, is now the best window through which we can observe the textual work of Origen.

Origen must have been a man of prodigious energy, for he worked with titanic force in every field of Christian literature. Besides pioneering in the textual study of the scriptures, his work in *interpretation* covered every book of the Old and New Testaments. This ranged all the way from his scholia, or brief notes on difficult or decisive texts, through homilies, prepared or *ex tempore*, to those full-size commentaries which Ambrose prevailed upon him to undertake. His homilies or expository sermons numbered twenty-eight on Numbers, twenty-six on Joshua, thirty-two on Isaiah, forty-five on Jeremiah, twenty-five on Matthew, thirty-nine on Luke, twenty-seven on Acts, etc.; these are only a few of the items given in a long list of the works of Origen found in a letter from Jerome to Paula and Eustochium. Not until he was sixty, it must be remembered, would Origen permit his homilies to be taken down when he delivered them. The list reaches at least 444 for the Old Testament (a few figures for individual psalms

Interpretation

have been lost) and 130 for the New. But, of these, only 21 have survived in the Greek original and only 186 in the Latin translation.

Even more important for interpretation, of course, were his commentaries, which ran to twenty-five books on the Minor Prophets, twenty-five on Matthew, thirty-two on John, fifteen on Romans, fifteen on Galatians; etc. Origen held that each text had an inner, spiritual, mystical sense, in addition to its literal and historical meanings. Like most ancients, pagan, Jewish, or Christian, he made much use of allegory in interpretation; it was, of course, by the use of allegory that the Stoics had succeeded in making Homer the Bible of the Greeks.

In Jerome's list, which is probably far from complete, the commentaries ran to at least 177 books (rolls) for the Old Testament, and 114 for the New, or 291 in all, and, of these, only 16 books are preserved in Greek. It is safe to say that they represent no more than 5 per cent of the total bulk of the commentaries; nineteen-twentieths of them have disappeared. Even in Latin we have less than half the commentary on Matthew, and Rufinus' recast of that on Romans and part of that on the Song of Songs.

It must be added that no small amount of Origen's exegetical work survived piecemeal in the catenas— those collections of valuable observations found in early writers which began to be made very early, and by A.D. 500, in the hands of Procopius of Gaza, were in full swing.[4]

---

[4] H. Jordan, *Geschichte der altchristlichen Literatur* (Leipzig, 1911), p. 413.

On the theological side Origen's principal works
were his two books *On the Resurrection* and his four
Theology   books *On First Principles* (*De principiis*).
The latter is perhaps the greatest of Ori-
gen's works and marks a long step toward the formu-
lation of a Christian theology, even though to the
modern reader Origen seems overinfluenced in some of
his thinking by philosophy and appears more Greek
than Christian. In it he followed the path Clement
had taken before him, and sought to bring Greek philosophy and Christian teaching together. Unfortunately, the original Greek form of it has disappeared,
except for a number of fragments, and we are dependent for our knowledge of it upon a free Latin translation of it published in Rome in A.D. 398–99 by the diligent Rufinus, the friend and then the enemy of Jerome.
It was, in fact, Rufinus' unguarded reference in his preface to Jerome's admiration for Origen that offended Jerome. Jerome himself later made a more faithful translation of the book, of which only a score or so of fragments survive. The book *On the Resurrection* has also
perished, except for some fragments; it called forth a
reply from Methodius of Olympus (†311), which is itself extant only in an Old Slavonic version but adds to
our knowledge of what Origen's book contained. The
book *On the Resurrection* may be regarded as a prelude to
the larger work *On First Principles*. Jerome's list of
Origen's works mentions also two dialogues *On the
Resurrection* now lost.

Like his teacher Clement, Origen left behind him
his *Scrapbooks*, or *Miscellanies* (*Stromateis*), in ten

books, but these, too, have been lost except for a few small fragments.

With Origen's doctrinal works may be grouped two highly practical writings of his, one *On Prayer*, written at the request of Ambrose, and one *On Martyrdom*, addressed to two Christian leaders, urging them not to flinch from it in the persecution of Maximin then just beginning (A.D. 235). Both are fortunately extant in Greek.

In the *apologetic* field Origen's great work was his reply to Celsus. That pagan thinker had directed a

Apologetics   searching attack against Christianity, some two generations earlier, under the name of the *True Discourse*, pointing out with much penetration the faults Judaism had to find with Christian teaching and then the faults the Platonic philosophy had to find with it. It was altogether the ablest attack of the kind made upon Christianity in ancient times. It is generally referred to about A.D. 178, and it has long since disappeared, so that what we really know of it is derived from the quotations Origen makes from it in his reply. No less than three-fourths of Celsus' work are preserved in this way. Origen wrote this, as he did so much of his best work, at the request of Ambrose, who felt that, although almost sixty years had passed since Celsus wrote, his book had never been adequately answered. As a matter of fact, a good many of Celsus' objections to the Christian views and claims of his day were sound and could not be answered, as Origen's effort showed. Origen sometimes resorted to what now seem artificial devices to get around them, and it took all his deep religious conviction and sound religious feeling to outweigh his pagan opponent. It has been well characterized as the peak of early Christian apologetic. The *Against Celsus* was written in A.D. 246–48 and is fortunately preserved in full in Greek.

Origen's other apologetic or polemic works were no more than the taking-down of his disputations with various persons: Bassus, Beryllus of Bostra, a Valentinian named Candidus, and some Jews. These are mentioned by Africanus, Eusebius, Jerome, or Rufinus but are no longer extant.

Origen's *letters* were also numerous and important. A hundred of them were gathered into a collection by

His Letters   Eusebius himself, perhaps in the days when he catalogued the Origen Library at Caesarea for his teacher and patron Pamphilus (*Church History* vi. 36. 3). Jerome's list of Origen's works, probably taken from that of Eusebius, now lost, mentions others. One of the letters, written to Fabianus, bishop of Rome, in defense of his works, grew to the proportions of a treatise, in two books. But, of all these letters, only two have been preserved: the one to Africanus, in defense of Susanna as part of Daniel, and the one to Gregory Thaumaturgus, who had been converted by him and had been one of his pupils. In it Origen urges his pupils to make full use, in advancing the Christian cause, of all that Greek thought had achieved.

The enormous quantity of Origen's writing makes it necessary to group it thus according to the various fields with which it dealt. But there is also a value in viewing his principal works in their chronological order. While Origen's activity as a writer was not notable in the early part of his work at Alexandria, down to 215–16, even in those years he was learning Hebrew and producing his Hexapla. But after his return from Caesarea to the headship of the catechetical school, in 217–18, when he was about thirty-three, his literary activity began to develop fast. It was in 218 that he began his lifelong work upon his commentaries, at the suggestion of Ambrose, who provided the publishing facilities already described. In this second Alexandrian period, 217–30, he produced his four books *On First Principles* and the ten books of *Miscellanies*. After his removal to Caesarea in 232 he wrote his exhortation *On Martyrdom* (235) and his eight books *Against Celsus* (246–48), the masterpiece of early Christian apologetic.

Especial interest attaches to Origen's New Testament. He was fully aware of the differences that ex-

His New Testament isted among Christians as to what books should be included in the New Testament; and, in view of these, he was careful to divide the books which he thought belonged to the New Testament into two classes, the accepted or acknowledged books, which all Christians accepted as scripture, and the disputed books, which some did not accept. As Acknowledged books Origen listed the Four Gospels, fourteen letters of Paul (including Hebrews and the letters to Timothy and Titus), the Acts of the Apostles, I Peter, I John, and the Revelation of

John—twenty-two in all. The Disputed books, which he himself accepted as belonging to the New Testament, were James, II and III John, Jude, II Peter, Barnabas, and the *Shepherd* of Hermas. This gave him eight general epistles and two revelations, John and Hermas. This New Testament of twenty-nine books is precisely that of the Sinaitic manuscript of the fourth century, discovered by Tischendorf in 1859.

While Origen paid little attention to literary finish in his writings, he had great literary as well as doctrinal influence. His bold liberal views were much criticized in aftertimes (Anastasius, bishop of Rome, condemned him in A.D. 400), but no man had more loyal and distinguished followers. His books in Caesarea passed into the hands of his great admirer Pamphilus, who formed about them the most famous Christian library of antiquity, so diligently studied and faithfully catalogued by Eusebius (*Church History* vi. 32. 3). A few years later Pamphilus wrote a *Defense of Origen*, in five books, to which Eusebius added a sixth, probably after Pamphilus' martyrdom in A.D. 309 (*Church History* vi. 23. 4; Photius *Bibliotheca* 118). "What we know of and about Origen," said Harnack, "we owe almost exclusively to Pamphilus and Eusebius."[5] Half a century later, in A.D. 360, Gregory of Nazianzus and Basil the Great made an anthology of what they thought the best passages in Origen, which was called the *Philocalia*, and preserves much that would otherwise have been lost.

It will be seen that two-thirds of Origen's homilies

[5] *Geschichte*, II, 2, p. 26.

are lost, and of his commentaries nineteen-twentieths of the Greek original have disappeared. The work *On the Resurrection* is gone, as is the great one *On First Principles*, except for what is almost a re-writing of it in Latin by Rufinus. The *Miscellanies*, too, in ten books, are gone, as well as the overwhelming bulk of the letters. To this neglect of his works, what seemed the dangerous liberality of his views no doubt contributed. Yet Origen certainly deserved to be called the father of Christian theology and the founder of biblical science.

CHAPTER XV

JULIUS AFRICANUS AND DIONYSIUS
THE GREAT

When the emperor Septimius Severus campaigned
against Osrhoene and the region of Edessa on the

*Julius
Africanus*

Upper Euphrates in A.D. 195, one of his
officers was a young man from Aelia Capitolina, as the Romans called the city that
replaced Jerusalem after the Bar-Cochba War, in A.D.
135. His name was Sextus Julius Africanus. He pene-
trated to Mount Ararat and spent some years at Edessa,
where he enjoyed the friendship of King Abgar II and
went hunting with the Edessene princes. Later in life
we find him settled at Emmaus in Palestine and engaged in literary work. From Emmaus he led a delega-
tion that was sent to the emperor Alexander Severus to
ask that the town be restored, and in consequence it
was rebuilt as Nicopolis. At Rome he designed a beautiful library for the emperor in the Pantheon. He removed to Alexandria for a time to hear the lectures of
Heraclas, who later became the successor of Origen as
head of the catechetical school. Africanus knew Origen and, as late as A.D. 240, exchanged letters with
him. He was a devout believer in the scriptures, but he
was not a presbyter or a bishop but a soldier, at home
in both camps and courts, and a man of letters.

In A.D. 221 he published his *Chronography*, or *Chroni-*

cle, in five books. It traced the course of history from the Creation, making use of the Old Testament and other chronological sources, Greek and Jewish, among them the account of the Jewish kings written by Justus of Tiberias.

The aim of Africanus was to show that human history fell into six days of a thousand years each;[1] that the coming of Christ occurred in the year of the world 5500; that five hundred years later, the final thousand years, the millennium, would begin. Although controlled by this mistaken idea, the main features of this chronology (the so-called Alexandrian era) were widely adopted in the East. The *Chronography* was full of valuable excerpts from earlier chroniclers, but its scattered fragments have not yet been fully assembled. Yet it has been called the root of Christian chronography and proved an important source for Hippolytus, for the *Chronicle* of Eusebius, and later for the *Paschal Chronicle* early in the seventh century, and Georgius Syncellus, late in the eighth.

The other chief work of Africanus was his *Cestoi*, or *Paradoxa*—a sort of notebook of strange pieces of curious information on all sorts of subjects, medical, military, magical, scientific, and literary—the miscellanies accumulated by a traveled and inquiring mind. The book was dedicated to the emperor Alexander Severus, the author's friend and patron.

[1] It was Psalm 90 that said a thousand years were in God's sight like yesterday when it was past; the *Letter of Barnabas* said a day was a thousand years. II Peter says both (3:8). The two statements, while mathematically the same, are rhetorically opposites. On the whole, *Barnabas* seems to have influenced Africanus.

The length of the *Cestoi* was variously given by later writers; Syncellus said it contained nine books, Photius said fourteen, while Suidas gave the number as twenty-four. But a papyrus of two columns of it, written in the middle of the third century (almost in the lifetime of Africanus) and found at Oxyrhynchus, solved the problem.[2] It preserves the end of one book and concludes: "Of Julius Africanus Cestus 18." It is evident that Suidas was right in giving the number at twenty-four. Africanus is discussing a long magical incantation supposed to have been uttered by Odysseus in summoning the shades of the dead, in *Odyssey* 11. He tells just where the manuscripts are in which he has found it—one in Aelia Capitolina, one in Nysa in Caria, and one in the Pantheon library already mentioned. Africanus wondered whether it was Homer himself or the Peisistratidae, the early editors of Homer, who had left the passage out. He recorded the lines as at any rate "a most valuable product of Epic art."

Africanus also wrote some very significant letters. One, addressed to a certain Aristides, about the genealogies of Christ, appealing to the Jewish practice of levirate marriage to reconcile their differences in Matthew and Luke, was used by Origen in his earliest homilies, on Luke. But his most famous letter is that written about A.D. 240 to Origen to show that the story of Susanna cannot have been an original part of the Book of Daniel. Africanus argued that, for one thing, Daniel's play upon words when he asked each

[2] *Oxyrhynchus Papyri* iii. 412.

of the wicked elders under what kind of a tree he had seen Susanna meet her lover was a Greek play and could not possibly be a translation from the Hebrew. This was certainly a point well taken, and Origen in his answer, written from Nicomedia where he was staying, although he said a good deal by way of reproof, was not able to meet it.[3]

Here, as so often, the works of our author have almost entirely perished, but enough remains to show that here was a man, in the Christian church, on friendly terms with kings and emperors, keenly interested in Christian history and prophecy, and bringing a fresh and open mind to literary questions in pagan and Christian literature alike.

Three men named Dionysius were active and influential in the early church: Dionysius, bishop of Cor-

Dionysius of Alexandria

inth (who was contemporary with Soter, bishop of Rome from A.D. 166 to 174); Dionysius, bishop of Rome, A.D. 259–68; and Dionysius the Great, bishop of Alexandria from A.D. 247 to 264, who has been called the most significant of the personal pupils of Origen.

He came of heathen parentage and was at first a pagan, then a Gnostic; a man of position and means, who stood high with the authorities. When Demetrius, bishop of Alexandria, forced Origen to break off his work there and leave the city (A.D. 230), his as-

---

[3] Harnack has argued that the Greek translation of Tertullian's *Apologeticus* used by Eusebius was made by Africanus (*Texte und Untersuchungen*, Vol. VIII, No. 4 [1892]; *Geschichte der altchristlichen Litteratur* [3 vols.; Leipzig, 1893–1904], Part II, Vol. II, 91).

sistant Heraclas took his place at the head of the catechetical school, but a year later, A.D. 231, Heraclas became bishop of Alexandria and turned over the direction of the school to Dionysius. When Heraclas died, sixteen years later, Dionysius became bishop in his place but seems to have retained the headship of the school, not unworthily carrying forward the great tradition established for it by Pantaenus, Clement, and Origen.

Dionysius ably united the practical and intellectual sides of the Christian faith. He was a vigorous churchman of world-wide interests; the problems of Eastern and Western Christianity found him alert and energetic in dealing with them. He corresponded with Rome, Antioch, Laodicea in Phoenicia, Caesarea in Palestine, even Armenia, and concerned himself with questions that arose anywhere in the church, practical, doctrinal, and even critical, and with remarkable sense and skill.

Dionysius had hardly become bishop of Alexandria when a local persecution broke out there, and the following year the Decian persecution began. Like Cyprian in the same situation at Carthage, Dionysius fled before the storm, or rather he permitted himself to be rescued from the soldiers who had arrested him. It seems that a certain Timothy, a member of his household, perhaps his son, came to Dionysius' house on the way to a wedding, and, seeing what was going on, proceeded to the wedding and told the assembled company what was happening. As one man, they arose from the table, rushed to the bishop's house, put the soldiers to flight, and seizing the astounded Dionysius carried him off by force. Indeed, he thought at first that he was being mobbed or kidnaped. He was hustled upon the back of a saddleless animal and hurried off to a place of safety, where he remained with only two attendants until the death of Decius in 251. It reminds one of the seizure of Luther and his removal to the Wartburg by the emissaries of the Great Elector, for his protection.

We owe this story to the attack made afterward upon Dionysius for his flight by a certain Germanus, which Dionysius answered with a full account of what actually happened (Eusebius *Church History* vi. 40 and vii. 11), in his *Letter to Germanus*, written in A.D. 259, in defense of his course in the persecutions of both Decius and Valerian.

Soon after the death of Decius and the return of Dionysius to Alexandria, the persecution of Valerian broke out and occasioned his banishment to obscure places, first in Libya and then in the Mareotis in Egypt. The toleration edict of Gallienus, A.D. 260, made it possible for him to return to Alexandria in 261, but a new series of calamities soon set in. The prefect of Egypt revolted against Gallienus and set himself up as emperor and had to be put down. Famine and pestilence added to the misery of the Alexandrians, and amid such scenes Dionysius died, A.D. 264–65. The new bishop of Antioch, Paul of Samosata, had antagonized the churches by his views on the person of Christ—that he was mere man, though filled with divine power from his birth—and a synod was held in

Antioch to settle the matter. Dionysius had been un-
able to attend but had sent his written opinion to the
gathering. Paul was not only bishop of Antioch but
also viceroy of Zenobia, the famous queen of Palmyra,
who for a time wrested Egypt from the Romans.

Of between fifty and sixty writings of Dionysius,
including letters, only one or two letters have come
His Works   down to us in full; but, thanks to Eusebius, we know something of the scope of
his work and possess some important fragments of it
(*Church History* vi. 40—vii. 28). He wrote an exposition of the beginning of Ecclesiastes (*Church History*
vii. 26. 3), fragments of which are preserved in Procopius of Gaza, and a work *On Nature*, cast in the form
of a letter to his "son" Timothy, refuting the atomistic views of the Epicureans, with which he seems to
have been well acquainted. Eusebius preserves portions of it in his *Preparation for the Gospel* (xiv. 23–27).
There was also a work *On Temptations*, addressed to one
Euphranor (*Church History* vii. 26. 2), but this has
entirely disappeared.

A work *On Promises*, in two books, was called forth
as a reply to a *Refutation of the Allegorists*, which had
been written by Nepos, bishop of Arsinöe, before his
death. Nepos seems to have been a successful hymn
writer; Dionysius says that the brethren still enjoy his
hymns (*Church History* vii. 24. 4). But Nepos held that
the scriptures should be understood "in a more Jewish
manner and that there would be a certain millennium
of bodily luxury upon this earth," and appealed to the
Revelation of John in support of it.

This led Dionysius in his *On Promises* to examine the claims of apostolic authorship made for the Revelation. He compared its style and ideas with those of the Gospel of John and came to the conclusion that they can hardly be from the same hand and that the Revelation must be figuratively understood. This judgment of Dionysius shows a thoroughly sound critical sense on his part and was in part responsible for the doubt with which the Revelation was ever after regarded in the Eastern church. It is characteristic of Dionysius that, while he disagreed with the millennial views of Nepos, he spoke of him in cordial and generous terms:

I confess that in many other respects I approve and love Nepos, for his faith and industry and diligence in the scriptures, and for his extensive psalmody, with which many of the brethren are still delighted, and I hold him in the more reverence because he has gone to rest before us. But the truth should be loved and honored most of all [*Church History* vii. 24. 4].

In 260–61 Dionysius wrote his *Refutation and Apology against Sabellius*, addressing it to Dionysius, bishop of Rome. It was in four books and is lost except for some fragments preserved by Athanasius in his work *On the Opinions of Dionysius* and by Basil in his work *On the Holy Spirit*, both works of the following century, and a considerable quotation in Eusebius (*Preparation for the Gospel* vii. 19). Athanasius came to the defense of Dionysius, who was being, as he thought, wrongfully quoted by the Arians in defense of their views on the relation of the Son to the Father. Dionysius had previously addressed four letters on Sabellianism to correspondents of his and had sent extracts from these to Xystus, bishop of Rome, in the single year of the latter's office, August, 257, to August, 258. On the basis of these, apparently, Dionysius was charged with doctrinal irregularity before Dionysius of Rome, to whom he replied with this *Refutation*. It will be seen that he was in frequent correspondence with the bishops of Rome, writing to Stephen, Xystus, and Dionysius.

The schisms of Nepos and of Sabellius were not the only ones with which Dionysius dealt. In his numerous letters sent in all directions, he discussed the rebaptism of heretics, the treatment of the lapsed, the schism of Novatian (whom he advised to give up his episcopal pretensions in the interests of the peace of the church), and finally the case of Paul of Samosata, the bishop of Antioch, whose views of the person of Christ were disturbing the Eastern church in Dionysius' last days.

Eusebius tells of at least fifty such letters, some of them virtually treatises in the form of letters, which were written by Dionysius between 249 and 264. The works *On the Sabbath*, *On Exercise*, and *On Marriage* were of this kind. It had been the custom of the bishops of Alexandria to determine each year the date at which Easter was to be celebrated and to announce this in a letter sent to all the churches concerned. Dionysius took occasion in these letters to instruct the churches on other questions of immediate importance to them, and a whole series of these letters are mentioned by Eusebius (*Church History* vii. 20–23).

If we could recover the writings of Dionysius, we

should have the portrait of a wise, sincere, and able Christian leader in the trying times of Origen, Cyprian, and Novatian, the fateful middle years of the third century. But, of them all, we have less than ten pages, probably not one-twentieth of what he wrote, and we must list among the lost works of early Christian literature not only the bulk of his letters but, except for a few fragments, his major writings, *On Nature*, *On Trials*, *On Promises*, the *Refutation and Apology*, and his partial *Exposition of Ecclesiastes*.

CHAPTER XVI

CYPRIAN AND NOVATIAN

When Tertullian was at the height of his powers, a boy was growing up in Carthage who was to do *Cyprian of Carthage* a great service to Latin Christianity in North Africa. His name was Cyprian.

Caecilius (earlier called Thascius) Cyprianus was born, probably at Carthage, about A.D. 210, or soon after. His parents were people of position and means, and he received a good education. He was engaged in the teaching of rhetoric and oratory in Carthage when he came in contact with the Christian forces there. His discussion with representatives of the new faith, especially with the presbyter Caecilianus, led to his conversion, about A.D. 246. He entered into the work of the church with ardor and soon became a presbyter. In 248–49, little more than two years after his conversion, he was made bishop of Carthage in response to a popular demand on the part of the church.

The ten years that followed were years of great stress and peril for the Christians of Carthage and of great literary activity for Cyprian. Decius became emperor in A.D. 249 and soon after issued an edict which seems to have aimed at the complete extinction of the Christian movement. It ushered in the first really general persecution of the church. Cyprian saved himself by leaving Carthage, probably warned by news from

Rome of what was in the wind. He was severely criticized for doing so, but afterward defended his course
as taken in the interest of the church as a whole. Persons suspected of Christian beliefs were called upon
to offer heathen sacrifice, before witnesses, and many
complied and were given little papyrus slips recording
that they had offered sacrifice to the gods, made liba-
tions, and tasted the offerings. Many such *libelli*, as
they were called, have been found in Egypt.

The reign of Decius was short; he was killed in battle with the Goths in the Dobrudja in A.D. 251. There
was a temporary lull in the persecution, and Cyprian,
who from his place of concealment had succeeded in
keeping in touch with the church at Carthage by letters and messengers, was able to return.

Important matters soon called for his attention.
Through the months of Cyprian's concealment the
bishop's chair in Rome had been vacant, and now it
was claimed by two rival bishops, Cornelius and Novatian, the latter a man of especial culture and literary
ability. They differed sharply on the treatment of the
lapsed—those persons who had been driven by persecution to leave the church but now wished to return to
it. Cornelius held that, upon establishing the sincerity
of their repentance, they might be readmitted, but
Novatian held they should not be readmitted at all.
Cyprian seems at first to have favored the stricter pol-
icy, but he soon changed and, with characteristic vig-
or, took the side of Cornelius, who succeeded in establishing himself as bishop.

Popular animosity against the Christians was roused

again by the spread of the pestilence which had first
appeared in the reign of Decius, and persecution revived. Cornelius, the new bishop of Rome, was banished and died, and Cyprian himself was threatened.
He made himself useful in organizing aid for those
stricken with the disease. The party of Novatian had
separated from the Roman church to follow his stricter
principles, but now some of them were returning, and
the question arose: Should they again be baptized?
Cyprian maintained that they should, but the new
Roman bishop Stephen (254–57) declared it unnecessary and claimed the right as the successor of St. Peter
to overrule his brother-bishops.

In the time of Cornelius, Cyprian had strongly maintained the unity of the church, which he found in the
unity of the bishops, and while he fully recognized the
historical importance of the Roman church, he boldly
denied the inferences of superior authority which Stephen sought to draw from it. Stephen retorted by excommunicating the African bishops. This controversy
was interrupted by the renewal of the persecution under the new emperor Valerian (A.D. 253–60), whose
first edict, of A.D. 257, banished the higher clergy from
their sees. Stephen died in August of that year, and in
the same month Cyprian was banished to the African
town of Curubis, some forty miles from Carthage.

But the edict proved ineffective. The banished bishops simply organized new churches, in the places of
their banishment, and a year later Valerian issued a
new and much sterner edict. The substance of it is preserved in one of Cyprian's letters (*Epist.* 80): the vari-

ous classes of Christians were threatened with varying degrees of confiscation, degradation, slavery, and even death, but the penalty for the clergy was death. Cyprian learned that he was to be summoned to Utica for trial, or probably condemnation, and made his escape, for, as he wrote his congregation, he wished to suffer in Carthage. When the proconsul next visited Carthage, Cyprian returned and was arrested. The following day, September 14, A.D. 258, he was tried, convicted, and beheaded.

Into these twelve momentous years Cyprian crowded a great deal of writing in the Christian cause. *His Letters* The collection of his letters contains eighty-one pieces, sixty-five of which are from Cyprian's hand. The others are letters to him or to persons near him. There are also twelve more formal literary works of his, the treatises—all, of course, more or less closely related to practical church problems of the day.

The letters written or received by Cyprian during the years of his episcopate mirror the march of events in Rome and Carthage in that decade in the most illuminating and delightful way. We find ourselves right in the midst of the problems and controversies that beset those two great centers of Western Christianity, and we hear the words of their great leaders, Cyprian, Cornelius, Novatian, and a number of others, as well as Firmilian of Caesarea. A wealth of scholarly labor has established in general the years from which these letters come, and the chronological arrangement of them is perhaps the most readily comprehensible.

Letters 5–43[1] belong to the time of Cyprian's concealment, or flight, covering about fifteen months,
from December of A.D. 249 to March of 251. Even the
exact order in which these thirty-nine letters were
written has been pretty generally agreed upon by
scholars. Cyprian was able from his place of concealment to communicate not only with his own diocese
but, through it, with the Roman church, to which he
sent a number of letters in the course of these fifteen
months, and no less than thirteen of his letters to his
own people he collected and instructed them to forward to the Roman church (Nos. 5–7 and 10–19).
This little group may therefore be regarded as the nu-
cleus of the whole collection.

Two important matters appear now and again in
these thirty-nine letters. One was the behavior of Cyprian in going into hiding in the time of persecution.
The Roman clergy wrote to the clergy at Carthage on
this matter, pointing out that a good shepherd gave
his life for his sheep; but on this point Cyprian was
able to satisfy them. They were the more easily satisfied since Cyprian agreed with them about the other
matter—their attitude toward those who had lapsed
in the persecution.

This was a point that divided the churches of both
Carthage and Rome. There was a group in each church
that believed that those who had fallen away from the

---

[1] The numbers are those of Hartel's edition in the Vienna series of Latin
fathers, *Corpus Scriptorum Ecclesiasticorum* (1868–71). The English translation
in the *Ante-Nicene Fathers* (American ed.), Vol. V, follows a different numer-
ation.

faith in persecution should not be readmitted to the church at all. Such people were led in Rome by Novatian, and in Carthage by Felicissimus. Cyprian held such persons should upon proper conditions be readmitted to the church, and this was the view of the majority of the Roman clergy. Felicissimus, however, found so many supporters for his position in the church at Carthage that a schism arose there on the subject, which caused Cyprian, hampered by his absence from the scene, the greatest difficulty.

A second group, of twenty letters, can be referred with confidence to the period from the spring of 251 to the summer of 253. They comprise the letters exchanged between Cyprian and two bishops of Rome, Cornelius and his successor Lucius. About the time the persecution relaxed and Cyprian returned to Carthage, Cornelius was chosen bishop of Rome (March, 251) in the face of the strong opposition of Novatian and his followers, who immediately countered by electing Novatian bishop. The situation was made more acute by the Carthaginian presbyter Novatus, who took the side of Novatian. But Cyprian sided with Cornelius, who came to be the recognized bishop. It was natural for Cyprian to do this, as Cornelius and he were in agreement as to the way the lapsed should be treated.

A third group of letters, Nos. 67–75, come from the time of Stephen, who succeeded Lucius as bishop of Rome in A.D. 254 and continued in that office until 257. The question whether schismatics, like the former followers of Novatian, should be admitted to the church without rebaptism was now up, and on it Cyprian and

Stephen differed sharply, Cyprian holding they should be rebaptized, but Stephen maintaining that, as they had been baptized once, the impartation of the Holy Spirit through the laying-on of hands was enough. In the spring of A.D. 255 a council of African bishops was held in Carthage, and another a year later was attended by seventy-one bishops from Africa and Numidia. On September 1 of that year a third council was held, of bishops of Africa, Numidia, and Mauretania, and voted that returning schismatics should be rebaptized but favored tolerance if an individual bishop thought differently. Firmilian of Caesarea wrote Cyprian to express his agreement with him, but Stephen, as we have seen, went so far as to excommunicate the African bishops who had refused to accept his ruling on the matter.

A fourth group of letters, Nos. 76–81, belongs to the year of Cyprian's banishment, August, 257, to September, 258; No. 81 was written not long before his execution.

There remain only seven letters, 1–4, 62, 63, and 65, which cannot be exactly enough dated to be fitted into this reconstruction of his correspondence. The whole series gives an amazingly clear picture of Christian thought and action in Cyprian's day and of the rapid movement of events, seen for the most part through the eyes of an able, energetic, educated, devoted, and, on the whole, considerate Christian man. For the history of the church in the middle years of the third century they are of the utmost value.

While some of Cyprian's letters run to considerable length, his more massive works were his treatises.

His Treatises

They, too, like his letters, sprang from the practical conditions of church life. Twelve of them which may be regarded as genuine have been preserved, but two of these may be dismissed as little more than compilations. One is addressed to Fortunatus, who had asked Cyprian to collect the scripture passages that were calculated to fortify Christian believers in the midst of persecution. Cyprian grouped them under a series of statements, on the emptiness of idolatry, the supremacy of Christ, etc. It was entitled *To Fortunatus: On Exhortation to Martyrdom*.

The other was addressed to a certain Quirinus, who seems to have asked Cyprian to summarize the scriptures for him book by book. Cyprian laid down a series of statements of Christian truth, following each with a group of the scripture passages teaching it. The first book relates to the relation of the Jews to their scriptures and to the church, the function of the Law, etc. The second deals with the nature and work of Christ, presenting the passages of scripture that throw light upon it. The third book was written in response to a later request of Quirinus and presents the practical teachings of Christianity, supported with the appropriate passages of scripture. The work was called *To Quirinus: Three Books of Testimonies*, to which title was later sometimes added "against the Jews."[2]

[2] Collections of scripture passages bearing on particular points of Christian belief were very early made, according to some scholars. J. Rendel

Of the ten principal treatises, the earliest was that addressed *To Donatus*, a friend of other days, to whom Cyprian explains what drove him to be a Christian and describes the conditions of life in the pagan world in which he had grown up, its violence, brutality, and depravity, in contrast with the peace and satisfaction he had found in the Christian faith. It was evidently written soon after his conversion, probably in A.D. 246.

His second treatise, *On the Dress of Virgins*, was designed to instruct unmarried women in the church who have dedicated themselves to Christ, to dress plainly, avoid jewelry, cosmetics, mixed bathing, boisterous wedding parties, and dyeing their hair, and to tell them how to behave themselves generally. Cyprian was by this time bishop of Carthage, so that the work was probably written in A.D. 249.

In the third treatise, *On the Lapsed*, Cyprian praises the martyrs and calls upon those who had failed to acknowledge Christ in the persecution but had offered sacrifice to idols and saved themselves by accepting a *libellus* or ticket from the authorities, to repent in dust and ashes and give unmistakable evidence of the sincerity of their contrition in the hope that God will forgive them. This treatise, and the next, *On the Unity of the Church*, were probably written before he returned to Carthage from his withdrawal or flight, and when Felicissimus was making trouble at Carthage, that is,

---

Harris believed they appeared as early as the first century and even underlay the Gospel of Matthew, but this seems improbable (see J. Rendel Harris, *Testimonies* [Cambridge, 1916, 1920], Vols. I and II).

early in A.D. 251. The one *On the Lapsed* was sent, probably in the summer of that year along with that *On the Unity of the Church*, to the church at Rome, where a movement was on foot, led by Novatian, to refuse the lapsed readmission to the church on any terms.

The fourth treatise, *On the Unity of the Church*, which Cyprian seems to have brought with him when he returned to Carthage, in A.D. 251, was probably later revised, when Novatian broke away from the Roman church, as a rival bishop to Cornelius, whose views on the lapsed he considered too lax. It was Cyprian's contention in this treatise that the guaranty of the unity of the church was the agreement of the bishops. The greatest danger to the church lay not in persecution but in heretical sects. While the work was primarily conditioned by the spirit in the Carthaginian church precipitated by Felicissimus, it was valid also with some revision for the kindred situation in Rome brought on by Novatian, and so Cyprian sent it in its revised form with the treatise *On the Lapsed* to Rome, probably in the summer of 251.

The fifth treatise, *On the Lord's Prayer*, presents a practical interpretation of the prayer, illustrating it richly from scripture. Cyprian teaches that prayer should be accompanied by acts of charity and discusses the times at which prayer should be offered.

The sixth treatise, *To Demetrianus*, an individual otherwise unknown, who had ascribed the disasters and calamities of the times to the Christians' failure to worship the old gods, puts the blame for these things on the pagans instead, who not only refused to worship the true God but persecuted his people. It was probably written after the death of Decius (who, as we have seen, was killed in battle with the Goths), probably late in A.D. 251 or early in 252.

The seventh, *On the Mortality*, deals with the pestilence then ravaging the country, and indeed the empire, showing that such things were foretold by Christ and that, while death seems to overtake Christians and pagans alike, it means very different things to them.

The eighth, *On Works and Charity*, urges the practice of liberal giving.

The ninth, *On the Advantage of Patience*, was written in the midst of the controversy with Stephen over rebaptizing heretics and seeks to soften its acerbities. It was written early in A.D. 256.

The tenth, *On Jealousy and Envy*, explains the dangers and divisions to which those vices lead and was probably written, like that *On the Advantage of Patience*, in 256, when the struggle with Rome over the rebaptism of heretics was at its height. It shows what a powerful and searching preacher Cyprian must have been.

Much light is thrown upon the work and martyrdom of Cyprian by a short eulogistic *Life* of him written soon after his death, probably as early as 259, by his deacon Pontius. There is also an account of his trial and death written very little later, on the basis of the official report of them. Eusebius gives us some information about him in his *Church History* (vi. 43. 3; vii. 3), and Jerome deals with him in *On Illustrious Men* 67.

The "Life" of Cyprian

The *Life* by Pontius runs through the questions dealt
with in the treatises so accurately that a collection of
them, and probably of the letters, must have lain before the deacon when he wrote. The famous Cheltenham list of the books of scripture, found by Mommsen
in a tenth-century manuscript in the library of Sir
Thomas Phillipps in Cheltenham, England, in 1885
(though composed as early as A.D. 359), includes also a
list of the works of Cyprian—fourteen treatises and
thirty-four or thirty-five letters, concluding with the
Life of Cyprian. The length of each work is given in
stichoi, or lines of sixteen syllables. Only one of the
treatises is missing—the compilation addressed *To
Quirinus*—and only two of the many spurious pieces
that were eventually ascribed to Cyprian have crept into the list—*Against the Jews* and *In Praise of Martyrdom*.

These pseudo-Cyprianic treatises are quite as numerous as the genuine ones, and, for their own sake as well
as for their connection with Cyprian's name, they call
for mention here. The most famous is the one entitled
That Idols Are Not Gods (*Quod idola dii non sint*), a blast
against idolatry, beginning with the sweeping statement that the heathen gods are simply ancient kings
who have been deified, a doctrine reminiscent of Wisd.
14:15-20. This work is of interest for its manifest use
of the *Octavius* of Minucius Felix, in Parts I and II,
chapters 1-9, and of Tertullian's *Apologeticus* in Part
III, chapters 10-15. An effort has been made to show
it to be the work of Novatian, but there is little basis
for this, although it is a work of the latter part of the
third century.

Another famous old Latin treatise that has been

ascribed to Cyprian is that *Against Dice-throwers* (*Ad Aleatores*); Harnack has given strong reasons for assigning it to Victor, bishop of Rome A.D. 189–99, of whom Jerome said that he was the earliest Latin Christian writer.

A third is the chronological work composed early in A.D. 243 to correct Hippolytus' faulty formula for determining the date of Easter (*De Pascha computus*).

A fourth, *To Novatian*, Harnack would assign to the Roman bishop Xystus II, A.D. 257–58, but most scholars despair of identifying its author.

A fifth, *In Praise of Martyrdom*, is in the form of a sermon, and was probably written by Novatian, about the end of 249 or the beginning of 250, before he became a schismatic.

Nine other works have at various times been assigned, though on insufficient grounds, to Cyprian:

On the Trinity (really a work of Novatian)

On Shows (probably also Novatian's)

On the Advantage of Modesty (probably by Novatian)

Against the Jews (probably by Novatian)

On Rebaptism, which Harnack assigns to a Roman Ursinus, in the conflict between Cyprian and Stephen

On Mounts Sinai and Zion

On Repentance

On the Singleness of the Clergy (*De singularitate clericorum*)

To Vigilius the Bishop: On the Unbelief of the Jews

Cyprian's Feast (probably written about A.D. 400 in southern Gaul by another Cyprian, who also composed a poem covering the Hexateuch)

Cyprian's New Testament is clearly reflected in his treatises addressed *To Fortunatus* and *To Quirinus*, which consist so largely of quotations from scripture. It was precisely that of his Roman contemporary Hippolytus (who died ten years before Cyprian's conversion), except that Cyprian makes no use of II John. It contained the Four Gospels, the Acts, thirteen letters of Paul (that is, it did not include Hebrews), I Peter, I John, and the Revelation of John. As compared with the New Testament of Tertullian's later years, Cyprian's differs only in omitting Jude. Western Christianity still clung to the short New Testament, without Hebrews and with only two or three Catholic letters.

His New Testament

Cyprian's great interest in scripture is evidenced by the story about him that after his conversion he read nothing else. Of course, this is not to be taken literally; for one thing, it would conflict with that other story already told in connection with Tertullian, of Jerome's aged acquaintance who in his youth had been told by one of Cyprian's secretaries that Cyprian did not let a day pass without reading something of Tertullian and that he would call for Tertullian's works by saying, "Bring me the Master."

The ablest Christian leader at Rome in Cyprian's day was clearly Novatian. He had received baptism on a sickbed, the so-called clinical baptism, but he became a presbyter of the Roman church and evidently its leading presbyter, for when the see was vacant, after the martyrdom of Fabianus, in A.D. 250, he had charge of the affairs of

Novatian of Rome

the church and wrote two letters in its name to Cyprian, probably in August–September of that year (*Epistles* 30, 36). When Cornelius was elected bishop in 251, however, Novatian refused to acknowledge him as bishop and allowed himself to be chosen rival bishop, by a minority in the church, on the issue of refusing readmission to the church to the lapsed—those who had left the church during the persecution and now wanted to return to it. Cornelius favored readmitting them, but Novatian held they could never return to Christian fellowship. From this doctrine of a "pure" church, which was very much that held by Hippolytus twenty years earlier, Novatian and his followers came to be called Cathari, or Puritans. It must be noted that the schism had nothing to do with the doctrine of the church but only with its discipline. But Novatian and his supporters were excommunicated at a Roman synod, held in October of 251, though the Cathari succeeded in maintaining their separate existence for two and perhaps three centuries thereafter.

Novatian must have left Rome for a time in the persecution under Gallus (A.D. 251–53) or Valerian (253–60), for he seems to have written pastoral letters to his flock from some place of refuge; such as his works *On Shows*, *On Jewish Foods*, and *On the Advantage of Modesty*. The historian Socrates († after 439) says that he suffered martyrdom in Valerian's persecution, A.D. 257 (*Church History* iv. 28), but in 257–58 the treatise *To Novatian* was addressed to him, as Harnack thinks by Xystus II, bishop of Rome, so that we really do not know when or how he died.

Eusebius gives an account of the Novatian affair in *Church History* vi. 43, with some quotations from a letter of Cornelius to Fabius of Antioch about it, and from Dionysius of Alexandria to Novatian, urging him to relinquish his claims and return to the church. Eusebius always calls him Novatus, confusing him with the Carthaginian presbyter of that name. He accepts Cornelius' judgment of him—that he was a designing and self-seeking adventurer.

Novatian was the first considerable Latin writer of the Roman church. Jerome, in his account of him (*On Illustrious Men* 70), gives a list of nine works of his: *On the Passover, On the Sabbath, On Circumcision, On the Priesthood, On Prayer, On Jewish Foods, On Zeal, On Attalus,* and *On the Trinity* and adds that he wrote many others. The work *On the Trinity* Jerome describes as a great volume, "a sort of epitome of the work of Tertullian, which many mistakenly ascribe to Cyprian," but it is among the works of Tertullian that Novatian's book *On the Trinity* has been preserved.

No work of Novatian has come down to us under his own name, and yet some of his writings have survived *His Works* as part of the writings of Tertullian or Cyprian. It would seem that the ancients found so much value in them that they could not resist copying them but could not bring themselves to credit them to the notorious Roman schismatic. In the long list of fourteen pseudo-Cyprianic writings, Harnack is satisfied that no less than five were written by Novatian: *On the Trinity, On Shows, On the Advantage of Modesty, Against the Jews,* and *In Praise of Martyrdom.* There is most doubt about the work *Against the Jews;* most scholars now recognize *On the Trinity* as certainly, and *On Shows, In Praise of Martyrdom,* and *On the Advantage of Modesty,* as probably, his.

Of the works listed by Jerome, only two, *On Jewish Foods* and *On the Trinity,* have survived. These are unquestioned writings of Novatian. *On the Trinity* was far from being "the sort of epitome of the work of Tertullian" that Jerome called it. It was the basis for Novatian's reputation as a theologian and went far to justify it. In the presence of the numerous heresies that had invaded the church, Novatian felt, as Tertullian had felt before him, that Christians should be shown what the true Christian positions were, as established by the Christian scriptures and the tradition of the church. From these had emerged the baptismal confession—the brief, compact statement of what it meant in terms of belief to be a Christian: to believe in God the Father, in Jesus Christ his Son, and in the Holy Spirit. Novatian makes this confession the framework of his discussion, which owes much to Tertullian and something also to Irenaeus. His book is the work of a man trained in Stoic philosophy, skilled in dialectic, possessed of a poetical prose style, and equipped with all the resources of ancient rhetoric.

The work *On Jewish Foods* was written as a sort of pastoral when Novatian was absent from his flock, probably because of persecution, and in response to a request for such a discussion. It deals with the clean and unclean creatures named in Leviticus and arrives at an allegorical explanation of the unclean ones as symbolizing human sins and failings—indulgence, lust, and greed, essentially like that of the *Letter of Barnabas*. In this book Novatian expressly refers to previous works of his on the true *Priesthood* and on the true *Circumcision*.

If we undertake to arrange the works of Novatian in the order in which they were written, they fall into the following sequence.

On the Trinity was written before he became a schismatic in 251, so probably before 250, perhaps as early as 245.

In Praise of Martyrdom was also written before he became a schismatic and probably at the end of 249 or the beginning of 250.

Letters 30 and 36 (among the *Letters of Cyprian*) Novatian wrote probably in August–September, 250.

On the Priesthood and *On Circumcision* were written after Novatian became rival bishop in 251 and before *On Jewish Foods*, which mentions them both.

On Shows, *On Jewish Foods*, and *On the Advantage of Modesty* are pastoral letters written to his people while he was compelled to be away from Rome to avoid arrest in the persecutions under Gallus, 251–53, or Valerian, 253–60.

The works *Against the Jews* and *In Praise of Martyrdom* were already ascribed to Cyprian when what we know as the Cheltenham list of Cyprian's works was first composed, about A.D. 359.

As early as the times of Rufinus (†410) the work *On the Trinity* was credited to Tertullian, as Jerome reports. Both it and the work *On Jewish Foods* passed in

medieval manuscripts (now lost) as writings of Tertullian and were published among his works in the first
printed editions of them in 1545 and 1550. By 1579,
however, both works were recognized as Novatian's
and republished under his name.

Out of twelve or possibly thirteen works of Novatian, therefore, of which we know, aside from the two
letters to Cyprian, we now possess five, or possibly six:
On the Trinity, *On Jewish Foods*, *On Shows*, *On the Advantage of Modesty*, *In Praise of Martyrdom*, and, if it is
genuine, *Against the Jews*. Seven are lost: *On the Passover*, *On the Sabbath*, *On Circumcision*, *On the Priesthood*,
On Prayer, *On Zeal*, and *On Attalus*. The twenty treatises bearing the name of Origen found some years ago
by Batiffol (1900) and later ascribed to Novatian are
now believed to be the work of Gregory of Iliberris
(Elvira) in Spain († after 392).

CHAPTER XVII

THE LATER LATINS

At Sicca, in North Africa, there lived at the close of
the third century a teacher of rhetoric and oratory

Arnobius named Arnobius. He was for a long time
a pagan and a vigorous opponent of
Christianity but was at length converted. Jerome says
that when he asked to be admitted to the church the
local bishop demanded proof of his sincerity, and he
responded by writing a work *Against the Heathen*, in
seven books, and was accepted forthwith. Whatever
may be thought of this quaint story, from Jerome's
Chronicle for the year 2343, or A.D. 327, *Against the
Heathen* does seem to have been rather hastily written
and shows very little acquaintance with the Bible, except the Gospels. Arnobius had read Plato and Cicero,
however, and he also knew Clement's *Address to the
Greeks (the Protrepticus)*. It is not unlikely that he was
an elderly man when he was converted, and that was
why the bishop was doubtful and why later hearers of
his story were so impressed.

Arnobius' book was evidently written when Diocletian's persecution was still in progress, probably in
A.D. 304–10. In fact, it is a defense of Christianity, an
apology. In Books i and ii he presents Christianity,
and in the rest he attacks paganism. Book i takes up
the argument that Christianity had brought disaster

upon the world; but there had always been wars and
famines before Christianity came. In fact, Christianity
gives some hope of remedying such things, for war, at
least, would be done away with, if Christianity prevailed. The gods should not be displeased with the
Christians, for Christianity teaches the fear of God.
He discusses the points brought against Christianity—
that Christ was a man and that he died on a cross, both
of which Arnobius seeks to reconcile with Christ's
divine nature. Book ii maintains that Christ introduced the true religion and develops Arnobius' curious
doctrine of the soul as not necessarily of divine origin
or immortal unless it knows God and throws itself on
his mercy.

Book iii meets the charge that Christians do not
worship the national gods by saying that their worship of God the Creator and Father of all covers the
whole ground. Book iv deals with the absurdities,
trivialities, and indecencies of pagan mythology.
Book v declares that these myths cannot be dismissed
as mere poetic fancies, for the historians, too, have
dealt with them. The mysteries are described and bit-
ingly analyzed. Book vi deals with the temples and
their idols, and Book vii with the futility of material
sacrifice. The work seems to break off rather than to
reach a finished end. The whole forms a bewildering
series of glimpses of ancient mythologies and religious
practices from the pagan world of the third and fourth
centuries.

Arnobius' book seems to have been little read; Lactantius, who is said by Jerome to have been his pupil,

doubtless while Arnobius was still a pagan (*On Illustrious Men* 80), shows no particular acquaintance with it in his works, some of them written a few years later, and its subsequent influence is slight; Jerome is about the only writer who read it and speaks of it, but he does so several times. Only one manuscript of it has ever been found, written early in the ninth century, but many a better work of Christian literature has fared even worse, as we have seen. In the "Gelasian Decree" on books to be received and those not to be received, really a work of the sixth century, Arnobius' work is designated as apocrypha.

It was as the eighth (*octavus*) book of Arnobius' *Against the Heathen*, it will be remembered, that the *Octavius* of Minucius Felix was preserved and has come down to us.

Among those who studied rhetoric under Arnobius at Sicca, in Africa, was Lucius Caecilius Firmianus *Lactantius*   Lactantius. He came of heathen parents and was born not later than A.D. 250. Probably his first work, written before he became a Christian, was his *Symposium*, or *Banquet*, now lost. He was teaching rhetoric at his home in Africa when Diocletian, who was developing Nicomedia in Bithynia as the capital of the eastern section of the empire, summoned him to that city to teach there (*Institutes* v. 2. 2). Lactantius recorded this journey in hexameter verse in his *Journey to Nicomedia*, which is also lost. A third work of his, probably from this early period, and now lost, was his *Grammar*.

Whether he became a Christian before or after he

left Africa is not certain; probably after. But the outbreak of Diocletian's persecution in A.D. 303 interrupted any public work he was doing at Nicomedia
and limited him to writing; he was already at work
upon his principal book, the *Divine Institutes*. But the
intensification of the persecution in 305 forced him
soon after to leave Bithynia. Galerius' edict of toleration in 311 made it possible for him to return, however, and there he seems to have remained until 317,
when the emperor Constantine summoned him to
Trèves, in Gaul, to become the tutor of Constantine's
eldest son Crispus, then about ten years of age. Jerome
says Lactantius was by that time "extremely old" and
that is why his birth must be dated before or about
A.D. 250. There is no record of the date of his death,
but it probably occurred not far from A.D. 325.

Jerome, in *On Illustrious Men* 80, gives a list of twelve
works written by Lactantius: the *Banquet*, the *Journey*,
the *Grammar*, *On the Wrath of God*, the *Divine Institutes*
(in seven books), an *Epitome* of it, *To Asclepiades*, *On
Persecution*, *Letters to Probus* (four books), *Letters to
Severus* (two books), *Letters to Demetrianus* (two
books), and *On God's Workmanship*. Four of these,
which were probably early gathered into a collection,
are still extant: *On God's Workmanship;* the *Institutes;*
the *Epitome*, and *On the Wrath of God*.

Three other works or fragments apparently of Lac-
tantius have come down to us; one is the poem *On the
Phoenix Bird*, another is the remarkable book *On the
Deaths of the Persecutors*, and a third is a short fragment
On the Emotions. The last is probably part of a letter.

The book *On the Deaths of the Persecutors* is probably to be identified with the work that Jerome calls *On Persecution*. Of thirteen works of Lactantius, therefore (aside from the little fragment *On the Emotions*), we possess six—*On God's Workmanship*, the *Institutes*, the *Epitome*, the *Wrath of God*, the *Deaths of the Persecutors*, and the *Phoenix Bird*.

If we seek to relate these books chronologically to the life of Lactantius and the history of the times, the *Banquet*, the *Journey*, and probably the *Grammar* come first and, it is very likely, belong to the time before his conversion. The book *On God's Workmanship* was probably written in Nicomedia in A.D. 304, after the persecution began but before its intensification in 305. It deals in much detail with the constitution of the human frame which some said was inferior to that of the beasts, especially in its liability to disease; Lactantius points out the enormous advantage man has in the possession of mental and spiritual faculties.

In 304 he was already at work upon the *Divine Institutes;* he refers to that undertaking in his book *On God's Workmanship* (15:6; 20:2). Two re-

The Divine Institutes cent philosophical attacks upon Christianity, one by Hierocles, who is said to have instigated Diocletian's persecution, stirred Lactantius to offer a positive presentation of Christianity. This turned out to be his great work. He was busy with it for a number of years, beginning with 304. It was certainly substantially finished by 311, and probably well before that time, though the dedication to Constantine in 1:1 and 7:26, and implied in 2:1, 4:1, and 6:3, presupposes the new edict of toleration issued by Constantine at Milan in A.D. 313, and these touches were probably introduced into a revised edition of the book after that emperor summoned Lactantius to Trèves in 317, though some would say by another hand.[1] Lactantius was therefore writing the *Institutes* at the very time that his old professor Arnobius back in North Africa was writing his work *Against the Heathen*, A.D. 304–10.

The *Institutes* form a book a good deal (almost a third) longer than the New Testament. Some idea of its contents can be gained from the titles of the seven books: (1) "On False Religion": polytheism is false; the best thought of prophets, poets, and philosophers shows that God is one; (2) "On the Origin of Error": polytheism and its causes; (3) "On False Wisdom": the errors of the philosophers; (4) "On True Wisdom and Religion": they are inseparable. The prophets foretold the life and work of Christ; (5) "On Justice," which the Christians seek to bring back to the world; (6) "On True Worship," which consists in serving God and showing justice and mercy to our fellow-men; (7) "On the Happy Life," the right use of this world, the immortality of the soul, and the life to come. Lactantius followed the millennial calculations of

[1] The dualistic additions to the *Institutes* also seem most naturally explained as introduced by Lactantius himself into a revised edition of the work, produced after his removal to Trèves, though why he should then fall a victim to Manichean tendencies is a difficult question; 2:20 and the extended passage at the end of 7:5 are leading examples. These dualistic additions and the occasional apostrophes of Constantine seem clearly by the same hand, which is probably that of Lactantius himself.

Julius Africanus, that Christ was born in the year of
the world 5500 and that, when the sixth "day" of a
thousand years was ended, which would be in about
two hundred years (7:25), the millennium would be
ushered in; to be followed by the release of the devil,
further outbreaks against the church, and the final
resurrection and judgment.

In the years 313 and 314 Lactantius wrote three
books: *On the Wrath of God, On the Deaths of the Persecu-*
Other　　　*tors,* and the *Epitome of the Institutes—*
Writings　　probably in that order. The work *On the*
　　　　　　Wrath of God was dedicated to a certain
Donatus, who had been in prison for six years, A.D.
305–11, and was probably written shortly after the
revision of the *Institutes,* in A.D. 313. The book *On the*
Deaths of the Persecutors, probably to be identified with
what Jerome called *On Persecution,* must have followed
almost at once. This extraordinary work, which seems
both in general and in detail to show the influence of
II Maccabees, tells the fates of the persecuting emperors: Nero, Domitian, Decius, Valerian, and Aurelian are briefly sketched, chapters 1–6, and the bulk of
the book, chapters 7–52, devoted to contemporary persecutors and what became of them—Diocletian, Max-
imian, Galerius, and Maximin. The cruelties perpe-
trated by these emperors against the Christians and
others Lactantius recites unsparingly and relates with
quite understandable if not altogether Christian relish
the dreadful ends which overtook them. Of course, he
sees in the fates of these persecuting emperors the judgment of God for their brutality and violence, not only

against the church but against many others of their subjects, high and low. And while there may well be exaggeration here, there is no doubt that much of what Lactantius says is true.

To this time, probably to 314, belongs also the *Epitome of the Institutes*, written in response to a request from a brother Pentadius. It is a free and bold rehandling of the material of the seven books in a much shorter form but with the inclusion of some new material as well.

Harnack suggests that it was the striking work *On the Deaths of the Persecutors* that led Constantine in 317 to invite Lactantius to Trèves in Gaul to become the tutor of Crispus, the emperor's eldest son. While the authenticity of the book *On the Deaths of the Persecutors* and the poem *On the Phoenix* has been seriously doubted, they are probably both the work of Lactantius, and most modern scholars are disposed to accept them as his. The story of the phoenix, the bird which lives five hundred years and then makes a kind of cocoon and enters it and dies, only to have another phoenix generated by its decay, is as old as Herodotus (ii. 73), and is told also by Pliny the Elder (*Natural History* x. 2) and by Clement of Rome (*To the Corinthians* 25). Just when Lactantius wrote it cannot be determined, but it clearly belongs to his Christian period. It was later imitated by the heathen poet Claudian, about A.D. 400, in a poem of the same name.

Among the lost works of Lactantius are the eight books of his letters: *To Probus* (four books), *To Severus* (two books), and *To Demetrianus* (two books). These were sometimes more like treatises than personal communications; Damasus wrote Jerome that they sometimes ran in length to a thousand lines and complained that they had little to say about doctrine but were about metrical, geographical, and philosophical matters, in which he took little interest. Jerome once speaks (in his commentary on Galatians) of a remark in the eighth book of Lactantius' letters *To Demetrianus*, so that the three groups of letters—of four, two, and two books—probably circulated as a single collection in eight books. Except for a few fragments, they have disappeared.

Lactantius expressed an intention of writing a book *Against All Heresies* (*Institutes* iv. 30. 14) and another *Against the Jews* (*ibid*. vii. 1. 26), but he seems never to have carried out these plans. Though he was not a great theologian or much interested in speculative thought, he had read very widely himself, was much used by Jerome, and was read by Augustine; while the charm of his style and the wealth of his imagination went far to make up for his doctrinal weakness, and he was called the Christian Cicero.

Toward the close of the third century there lived in Poetovio, in Pannonia (the modern Pettau in Styria), a
Victorinus Christian bishop named Victorinus, who suffered martyrdom in 304 in the persecution of Diocletian. He wrote somewhat copiously, Jerome informs us (*On Illustrious Men* 18, 74) producing commentaries on Genesis, Exodus, Leviticus, Isaiah, Ezekiel, Habakkuk, Ecclesiastes, the Song of Songs, Matthew, and the Revelation, but of these only the

commentary on the Revelation has come down to us. Jerome reshaped this work, omitting the highly millennial conclusion, with which he strongly disagreed, and adding sections from his contemporary Tyconius. The Spanish presbyter Beatus, late in the eighth century, made use of Jerome's work in his great commentary on the Revelation.[2]

The commentaries of Victorinus himself owed much to Origen; indeed, Jerome thought he was more expert in Greek than in Latin and spoke slightingly of his Latinity, and Victorinus' modern editor, Haussleiter, finds his style decidedly awkward.

Victorinus also wrote a work *Against All Heresies*, which is mentioned by Jerome but has disappeared, though an effort has been made, notably by Harnack, to identify it with a work of that name that has come down to us appended to Tertullian's *Prescription of Heretics*. About the only objection that can be brought against this attractive idea is that the style seems rather better than Victorinus exhibits in the *Commentary on the Revelation*.

Another small piece from the pen of Victorinus is the fragment *De fabrica mundi* preserved in a single manuscript at Lambeth and published in 1688 by W. Cave. Though it is not mentioned in antiquity, it seems to be a genuine work of Victorinus; the style is like his, and Jerome said he wrote many other things beside the ten he listed.

---

[2] Henry A. Sanders, *Beati in Apocalipsin libri duodecim* (Rome: American Academy, 1930).

CHAPTER XVIII

THE LOST BOOKS OF EARLY CHRISTIAN LITERATURE

With the conversion of Constantine and the adoption of Christianity by the empire, the church entered upon a period of increasingly rigorous definition of both doctrine and discipline. It was a century of great churches, great Bibles, great councils, and great names—Basil, the Gregories, Theodore, Theodoret, Athanasius, Chrysostom, in the East, and in the West, Ambrose, Rufinus, Jerome, and Augustine. It was ushered in by the Council of Nicaea and the figure of Eusebius, and it was a time of great scholars and great theologians; but the pristine radiance of the movement and the literature, the heroic period, which we have been surveying, was gone.

While book production in the first Christian centuries had reached a high degree of proficiency, the necessity of writing every book by hand being largely offset by the abundance of slave labor, the barbarians ended all that sort of thing, and the methods of book-copying in the Middle Ages were quite unequal to preserving either pagan or Christian literature, both of which suffered great losses. The wonder is that so much of either was preserved at all, after the highly efficient ancient methods of publication disappeared with the old Greco-Roman civilization.

It is, of course, a melancholy business, reporting the tragic losses early Christian literature has sustained. But our scientific friends sometimes conclude a subject with a list of problems awaiting solution, and it is reasonable to think that we are more likely to go on finding these lost books if we have a clear idea of what we are to look for. The lost writings found in whole or in part in the last fifty years are a goodly company: the *Revelation of Peter*, the *Apology of Aristides*, Melito's *On the Passion*, the *Epistle of the Apostles*, the *Acts of Paul*, Irenaeus' *Demonstration of the Apostolic Preaching*, the *Odes of Solomon*, the *Apostolic Tradition* of Hippolytus, and numbers of others. And it may help in the identification of others to assemble a list of books which are now little more than names to us but which might, and in some cases certainly would, throw much needed light upon this history.

In the list "no text" is to be understood as meaning "no extended body of text." I have not taken account of scattered fragments.

The Letter of Polycarp to the Philippians; no complete Greek text

The Epistle of the Apostles; no Greek text

The Letter of the Gallican Churches; no complete text

The Shepherd of Hermas; no complete Greek text

The Revelation of Peter; no complete Greek text

The Sibylline Books, Books ix, x, and xv; no text

The Pistis Sophia; no Greek text

The Gospel of the Egyptians; no complete text

The Gospel of the Hebrews; no complete text

The Gospel of Peter; no complete text.

The British Museum Gospel; no complete text
The Gospel of Thomas; no complete text
The Traditions of Matthias; no text
The Secret Sayings of Matthias; no text
The Gospel of Matthias(?); no text
The Gospel of the Ebionites; no text
The Gospel of Basilides; no text
The Gospel of Judas(?); no text
The Gospel of Truth; no text
The Gospel of Philip; no text
The Gospel of Bartholomew(?); no text
The Gospel of Barnabas(?); no text
The Gospel of Apelles(?); no text
The Gospel of Cerinthus(?); no text
The Gospel of Eve(?); no text
The Gospel of Perfection(?); no text
The Acts of Paul; no complete text
The Acts of John; no complete text
The Acts of Peter; no complete text
The Acts of Andrew; no complete text
The Clementine Recognitions; no complete Greek text
The Preaching of Peter; no text
The Apology of Quadratus; no text
Aristo, Dialogue of Jason and Papiscus; no text
The Apology of Aristides; no complete text
Justin, Dialogue with Trypho; no complete text
    Against the Greeks; no text
    Against All Heresies (the Refutation?); no text
    On the Sovereignty of God; no text
    Psaltes; no text
    On the Soul; no text
    Against Marcion; no text
The Letter to Diognetus; no complete text

Tatian, The Diatessaron; no Greek or Syriac text
    Problems; no text
    On Perfection according to the Savior; no Greek text
    On Demons(?); no text
    Chronicle(?); no text
Rhodo, Solutions; no text
    Against the Heresy of Marcion; no text
    On the Six Days' Work of Creation; no text
Marcion, The Contradictions; no text
The Teaching of the Apostles, short form; no Greek text
Papias, Interpretations of Sayings of the Lord; no text
The Odes of Solomon; no Greek text
Hegesippus, Memoirs; no text
Melito, On the Passover; no text
    On the Conduct of Life and the Prophets; no text
    On the Church; no text
    On the Lord's Day; no text
    On the Faith of Man; no text
    On His Creation; no text
    On the Obedience of Faith; no text
    On the Senses; no text
    On the Soul and Body; no text
    On Baptism; no text
    On Truth; no text
    On the Creation and Generation of Christ; no text
    On Prophecy; no text
    On Hospitality; no text
    A Key (to the Scriptures); no text
    On the Devil and the Revelation of John; no text
    The Apology; no text
    Selections from the Old Testament; no text
Theophilus of Antioch, Against the Heresy of Hermogenes;
    no text
    Against Marcion; no text

Catechetical Books; no text
Commentary on Proverbs; no text
On History; no text
A Gospel Harmony(?); no text
Irenaeus, Refutation of Gnosticism; no Greek text
Demonstration of the Apostolic Preaching; no Greek text
On Knowledge; no text
On Schism; no text
On the Ogdoad; no text
On Sovereignty; no text
Against Marcion(?); no text
Clement of Alexandria, The Outlines (of Scripture); no text
On the Passover; no text
On Fasting; no text
On Evil-speaking; no text
On Patience; no text
On Providence; no text
On the Prophet Amos(?); no text
Tertullian, On Baptism; no Greek text
On the Hope of the Faithful; no text
On Paradise; no text
Against the Followers of Apelles; no text
On the Origin of the Soul; no text
On Fate; no text
On Ecstasy; no text
The Garments of Aaron; no text
To a Philosophic Friend; no text
On Flesh and Soul; no text
On Submission of Soul; no text
The Superstition of the World; no text
On Shows; no Greek text
On the Veiling of Virgins; no Greek text

On Clean and Unclean Animals(?); no text
On Circumcision(?); no text
Hippolytus, Refutation of All Heresies; no complete Greek text
On Daniel; no complete Greek text
On the Song of Songs; no Greek text
On the Blessing of Moses; no Greek text
On the Story of David and Goliath; no Greek text
The Six Days of Creation; no text
What Followed the Six Days; no text
The Blessing of Jacob; no text
The Blessing of Balaam; no text
Moses' Song; no text
Elkanah and Hannah; no text
The Witch of Endor; no text
On the Psalms; no text
On Proverbs; no text
On Ecclesiastes; no text
On Isaiah (part); no text
On Ezekiel (part); no text
On Zechariah; no text
On Matthew (part); no text
The Parable of the Talents; no text
The Two Thieves; no text
On the Revelation; no text
Against Marcion; no text
Against Artemon, the Little Labyrinth; no text
Against Thirty-two Heresies; no text
Heads against Gaius(?); no text
In Defense of the Gospel and Revelation of John; no text
On the Resurrection; no text
On the Universe—against the Greeks and Plato; no text

On Good and the Source of Evil; no text
Address to Severina; no text
Determination of the Date of Easter; no text
The Chronicle; no Greek text
The Apostolic Tradition; no Greek text
Gaius, Dialogue with Proclus; no text
Origen, The Hexapla; no text (a Syriac version of the Septuagint column)
> Homilies; 554 out of 574 lost in Greek; 388 not even in the Latin version
> Commentaries; 275 out of 291 lost in Greek; very little preserved in Latin
> On First Principles; no Greek text
> Letters; Eusebius' collection of 100 lost, except for 2
> Miscellanies, ten books; no text
Julius Africanus, Chronography; no text
> Cestoi, or Paradoxa; no text
> Letter to Aristides; no text
Dionysius of Alexandria, On Nature; no text
> On Trials; no text
> On Promises; no text
> The Refutation and Apology; no text
> Exposition of Ecclesiastes (partial); no text
> On Temptations; no text
> Fifty Letters, most of them; no text
Nepos of Arsinoë, Refutation of the Allegorists; no text
Novatian, On the Passover; no text
> On the Sabbath; no text
> On Circumcision; no text
> On the Priesthood; no text
> On Prayer; no text
> On Zeal; no text
> On Attalus; no text

Pamphilus, Defense of Origen; no Greek text; only Book i
in Latin

Lactantius, The Banquet (Symposium); no text

    Journey to Nicomedia; no text

    Grammar; no text

    Letters to Probus, four books; no text

    Letters to Severus, two books; no text

    Letters to Demetrianus, two books; no text

Victorinus, Against All Heresies; no certain text

    Commentaries on Genesis, Exodus, Leviticus, Isaiah,
Ezekiel, Habakkuk, Ecclesiastes, Song of Songs,
Matthew; no text

There were, of course, a host of minor writers whom
I have not enumerated, some of whose writings might
prove of unexpected significance, and the above list is
not complete even for all the authors named. But the
progress of excavation and research will unquestion-
ably bring us in the next half-century not a few of the
books listed above as lost.

SELECT BIBLIOGRAPHY

CHAPTER I. EARLY CHRISTIAN LITERATURE

ALTANER, BERTHOLD. *Patrologie*. Freiburg, 1938.

BARDENHEWER, OTTO. *Patrologie*. 3d ed. Freiburg, 1910.

———. *Geschichte der altchristlichen Literatur*. 5 vols. (Vols. I–II, to Eusebius). 2d ed. Freiburg, 1913–32.

BARING-GOULD, S. *The Lives of the Saints*. 16 vols. Rev. ed. Edinburgh, 1914.

CAMPBELL, J. M. *The Greek Fathers*. London and New York, 1929.

CRUTTWELL, CHARLES T. *A Literary History of Early Christianity*. 2 vols. London, 1893.

DIBELIUS, MARTIN. *A Fresh Approach to the New Testament and Early Christian Literature*. New York, 1936.

FARRAR, FREDERIC W. *Lives of the Fathers*. 2 vols. Edinburgh, 1889.

HARNACK, A. *Geschichte der altchristlichen Litteratur*. 3 vols. Leipzig, 1893–1904.

HENNECKE, EDGAR. *Neutestamentliche Apokryphen*. 2d ed. Tübingen, 1924.

HORT, F. J. A. *Six Lectures on the Ante-Nicene Fathers*. London, 1895.

HOSIUS, CARL, and KRUEGER, GUSTAV. *Geschichte der roemischen Litteratur* (Hadrian to Constantine), ed. MARTIN SCHANZ. 3d rev. ed. Munich, 1922.

JAMES, M. R. *The Apocryphal New Testament, Being the Apocryphal Gospels, Acts, Epistles and Apocalypses, ... Newly Translated*. Oxford, 1924.

JORDAN, HERMANN. *Geschichte der altchristlichen Literatur*. Leipzig, 1911.

KRUEGER, GUSTAV. *History of Early Christian Literature in the First Three Centuries*, trans. CHARLES R. GILLETT. New York, 1897.

———. *Geschichte der altchristlichen Literatur*. 2d ed. Freiburg, 1898.

———. "A Decade of Research in Early Christian Literature," *Harvard Theological Review*, Vol. XXVI (1933).

LAKE, K., and OULTON, J. E. L. *Eusebius: The Ecclesiastical History, with an English Translation*. ("Loeb Library.") 2 vols. London and New York, 1926 and 1932.

LAWLOR, H. J., and OULTON, J. E. L. (trans.). *Eusebius: The Ecclesiastical History and the Martyrs of Palestine*. 2 vols. London, 1927–28.

LEIGH-BENNETT, ERNEST. *Handbook of the Early Christian Fathers*. London, 1920.

McGIFFERT, ARTHUR C. *Eusebius*. ("Select Library of Nicene and Post-Nicene Fathers of the Christian Church: Second Series," Vol. I.) New York, 1890.

PUECH, AIMÉ. *Histoire de la littérature grecque chrétienne depuis les origines jusqu'à la fin du ive siècle*. 3 vols. Paris, 1928–30.

RAUSCHEN, GERHARD. *Grundriss der Patrologie*. 11th ed. Freiburg, 1931.

ROBERTS, ALEX.; ROBERTSON, JAMES; and MENZIES, ALLAN. *The Ante-Nicene Fathers. Translations of the Writings of the Fathers down to A.D. 325*. 9 vols. New York, 1896–99.

SMITH, HAROLD. *Ante-Nicene Exegesis of the Gospels*. 6 vols. London, 1925–29.

STAEHLIN, OTTO. *Die altchristliche Litteratur*. (Von Christ's *Geschichte der griechischen Litteratur*, Part II, 2d half.) Munich, 1924.

STEARNS, W. N. *A Manual of Patrology*. New York, 1899.

SWETE, HENRY B. *Patristic Study*. London, 1902.

THURSTON, HERBERT, and ATTWATER, DONALD. *The Lives of the Saints*, by ALBAN BUTLER (1756–59), revised and enlarged. 12 vols., Jan.–Dec. London and New York, 1925–38. Index vol., *A Dictionary of Saints*, by DONALD ATTWATER. London and New York, 1938.

WILLIAMS, A. LUKYN. *Adversus Judaeos. A Bird's-Eye View of Christian Apologiae until the Renaissance.* Cambridge, 1935.

CHAPTER II. LETTERS

BIHLMEYER, K. *Die apostolischen Vaeter.* A revision of Funk's short text edition. Part I. Tübingen, 1924.

BINDLEY, T. H. *The Epistle of the Gallican Churches, Translated, with Introduction.* London, 1900.

DELEHAYE, H. *Les Passions des martyrs et les genres littéraires.* Brussels, 1921.

FUNK, F. X. *Patres Apostolici.* 2 vols. 2d ed. 1901. Vol. II rev. by F. Diekamp, 1913.

GEBHARDT, HARNACK, and ZAHN. *Patrum Apostolicorum opera.* 3d smaller ed. Leipzig, 1900.

GOODSPEED, EDGAR J. *Index Patristicus.* Leipzig, 1907.

HARNACK, A. *Einfuehrung in die alte Kirchengeschichte: Das Schreiben der roemischen Kirche an die korinthische aus der Zeit Domitians (Erster Clemensbrief).* Leipzig, 1929.

HARRISON, P. N. *Polycarp's Two Epistles to the Philippians.* Cambridge, 1936.

HEMMER, OGER, LAURENT, and LELONG. *Les Pères apostoliques.* 4 vols. Paris, 1907–12.

LAKE, KIRSOPP. *The Apostolic Fathers.* Greek texts and English translation. ("Loeb Library.") 2 vols. London and New York, 1913.

LIGHTFOOT, J. B. *The Apostolic Fathers.* 5 vols. 2d ed. London and New York, 1889, 1890.

HALL, EDWARD H. *Papias and His Contemporaries.* Boston, 1899.

HARNACK, A. *Judentum und Judenchristentum in Justins Dialog mit Trypho.* Leipzig, 1913.

———. *Neue Studien zu Marcion.* Leipzig, 1923.

———. *Das Evangelium vom fremden Gott.* 2d. ed. Leipzig, 1924.

HILL, J. HAMLYN. *The Earliest Life of Christ . . . . Being the Diatessaron of Tatian . . . . Literally Translated.* 2d ed. Edinburgh, 1910.

OTTO, J. S. *Iustini . . . . Opera.* 2 vols. 3d ed. Jena, 1876.

PUECH, AIMÉ. *Les Apologistes grecs du II⁰ siècle de notre ère.* Paris, 1912.

PURVES, GEORGE T. *The Testimony of Justin Martyr to Early Christianity.* New York, 1889.

SCHWARTZ, E. *Tatiani Oratio ad Graecos.* Leipzig, 1888.

WILLIAMS, A. LUKYN. *Justin Martyr: The Dialogue with Trypho. Translation, Introduction and Notes.* London, 1930.

CHAPTER VIII. MANUALS, MEMOIRS, HYMNS AND HOMILIES

BERNARD, J. H. *The Odes of Solomon.* Cambridge, 1912.

BRYENNIUS, P. Διδαχὴ τῶν δώδεκα ἀποστόλων. Constantinople, 1883.

HARNACK, A., and FLEMMING, J. *Ein juedisch-christliches Psalmbuch aus dem ersten Jahrhundert.* Leipzig, 1910.

HARRIS, J. RENDEL. *The Teaching of the Twelve Apostles* (with facsimile of the MS). Baltimore and London, 1887.

———. *The Odes and Psalms of Solomon.* 2d ed. Cambridge, 1911.

HARRIS, J. RENDEL, and MINGANA, A. *The Odes and Psalms of Solomon.* 2 vols. Manchester, 1916, 1920.

SCHLECHT, J. Διδαχὴ τῶν δώδεκα ἀποστόλων. Freiburg, 1900.

CHAPTER IX. THE SUCCESSORS OF JUSTIN

BONNER, CAMPBELL. *Homily on the Passion by Melito Bishop of Sardis*. London, 1940.

GEFFCKEN, J. *Zwei griechische Apologeten*. Leipzig, 1907.

SCHWARTZ, E. *Athenagorae Libellus pro Christianis: Oratio de resurrectione cadaverum*. Leipzig, 1891.

CHAPTER X. IRENAEUS

HARVEY, W. W. *Sancti Irenaei episcopi Lugdunensis Libros quinque Adversus haereses*. 2 vols. Cambridge, 1857.

ROBINSON, J. ARMITAGE. *St. Irenaeus: The Demonstration of the Apostolic Preaching*. London, 1920.

CHAPTER XI. CLEMENT OF ALEXANDRIA

BARNARD, P. M. *The Biblical Text of Clement of Alexandria in the Four Gospels and the Acts of the Apostles*. Cambridge, 1899.

CASEY, R. P. *Excerpta ex Theodoto of Clement of Alexandria*. London, 1934.

HORT, F. J. A., and MAYOR, J. B. *Clement of Alexandria: Miscellanies Book vii*. London, 1902.

KAYE, J. *Some Account of the Writings and Opinions of Clement of Alexandria*. London, 1835. 3d ed. 1898.

PATRICK, J. *Clement of Alexandria*. London, 1914.

STAEHLIN, OTTO. *Clemens Alexandrinus, Werke*. (Prus. Acad. Series.) 4 vols. Leipzig, 1905–36.

TOLLINGTON, R. B. *Clement of Alexandria: A Study in Christian Liberalism*. 2 vols. London, 1914.

CHAPTER XII. TERTULLIAN

BAYLIS, H. J. *Minucius Felix and His Place among the Early Fathers of the Latin Church*. London, 1928.

DeLABRIOLLE, PIERRE. *History and Literature of Christianity from Tertullian to Boethius*. London, 1924.

MAYOR, J. E. B., and SOUTER, ALEX. *Q. Septimi Florentis Tertulliani Apologeticus: Text and Translation.* Cambridge, 1917.

REIFFERSCHEID, A., WISSOWA, G., and KROYMANN, E. *Q. S. Tertulliani Opera.* ("Corp. Script. Eccles. Lat.") 2 vols. Vienna, 1890–1906.

CHAPTER XIII. HIPPOLYTUS

ACHELIS, HANS. *Hippolytstudien.* Leipzig, 1897.

BONWETSCH, ACHELIS, WENDLAND, and BAUER. *Hippolytus, Werke.* (Prus. Acad. Series.) 5 vols. Leipzig, 1897–1929.

DIX, GREGORY. *The Treatise on the Apostolic Tradition of St. Hippolytus of Rome,* Vol. I. London, 1937.

EASTON, B. S. *The Apostolic Tradition of Hippolytus Translated into English.* Cambridge, 1934.

ELFERS, HEINRICH. *Die Kirchenordnung Hippolyts von Rom: Neue Untersuchungen,* . . . . Paderborn, 1938.

HAULER, EDMUND. *Didascaliae Apostolorum Fragmenta Veronensia Latina.* Leipzig, 1900.

LORENTZ, RUDOLF. *De Aegyptische Kerkordening en Hippolytus van Rome.* Leiden, 1929.

CHAPTER XIV. ORIGEN

BUTTERWORTH, G. W. *Origen On First Principles.* London, 1936.

KOETSCHAU, KLOSTERMANN, PREUSCHEN, BAEHRENS, and RAUER. *Origenes Werke.* (Prus. Acad. Series.) 11 vols. Leipzig, 1899–1937.

LEWIS, G. *The Philocalia of Origen.* Edinburgh, 1911.

CHAPTER XV. JULIUS AFRICANUS AND DIONYSIUS THE GREAT

BUREL, J. *Denys d'Alexandrie: sa vie, son temps, ses œuvres.* Paris, 1910.

CONYBEARE, F. C. "Newly Discovered Letters of Dionysius of Alexandria to the Popes Stephen and Xystus," *English Historical Review*, Vol. XXV (1910).

FELTOE, C. L. *The Letters and Other Remains of Dionysius of Alexandria.* 1904.

REICHARDT, W. *Die Briefe des Sextus Julius Africanus an Aristides und Origenes.* Leipzig, 1909.

CHAPTER XVI. CYPRIAN AND NOVATIAN

BENSON, E. W. *Cyprian, His Life, His Times, His Work.* London, 1897.

FAUSSET, W. YORKE. *Novatian's Treatise on the Trinity: De trinitate.* Cambridge, 1909.

HARTEL, G. *Th. C. Cypriani Opera.* ("Corp. Script. Eccles. Lat.") 3 vols. Paris, 1868–71.

MOORE, HERBERT. *The Treatise of Novatian on the Trinity.* Introduction and translation. London and New York, 1919.

CHAPTER XVII. THE LATER LATINS—ARNOBIUS, LACTANTIUS, VICTORINUS

BRANDT, S., and LAUBMANN, G. *L. Caeli Firmiani Lactanti Opera omnia.* ("Corp. Script. Eccles. Lat.") Vienna, 1887.

HAUSSLEITER, J. *Victorini episcopi Petavionensis Opera.* ("Corp. Script. Eccles. Lat.") Vienna, 1916.

REIFFERSCHEID, A. *Arnobii Adversus nationes libri vii.* ("Corp. Script. Eccles. Lat.") Vienna, 1875.

CHRONOLOGY

(*fl.* = flourished; † = died)

309

A.D.

Ca. 170	Dionysius of Corinth
Ca. 170–80	Acts of John
Ca. 167–87	Melito *fl.*
Ca. 177–80	Letter of the Gallican Churches
Ca. 177–80	Athenagoras, Apology
Ca. 180	Hegesippus, Memoirs
Ca. 180	Theophilus, To Autolycus
Ca. 181–89	Irenaeus *fl.*
Ca. 185?	Gospel of the Ebionites
Ca. 190–210	Clement of Alexandria *fl.*
Ca. 190–200	Book of James
Ca. 200	Muratorian Fragment
Ca. 200–220	Acts of Peter
Ca. 200–225	Acts of Thomas
Ca. 160–225?	Tertullian
Ca. 170–236	Hippolytus
Ca. 240	Minucius Felix, Octavius
Ca. 185–254	Origen
Ca. 195–240	Julius Africanus *fl.*
Ca. 210–58	Cyprian
Ca. 247–64	Dionysius the Great *fl.*
Ca. 250–58	Novatian *fl.*
Ca. 250–60	Acts of Andrew
Ca. 250	Pistis Sophia
Ca. 250	Abgar Letters
Ca. 200–300	Letter to Diognetus
Ca. 300	Victorinus *fl.*
Ca. 300	Apostolic Church Ordinances
Ca. 304	Arnobius, Against the Heathen
Ca. 250–325	Lactantius
311	Methodius †
326	Eusebius, Church History

LATER WRITERS AND DOCUMENTS CITED

A.D.

Ca. 325–50	Acts of Archelaus
Ca. 348	Cyril of Jerusalem *fl.*
Ca. 354	Liberian Catalogue
Ca. 360	Gregory of Nazianzus *fl.*
295–373	Athanasius
373	Efrem the Syrian †
379	Basil the Great †
Ca. 380	Tyconius *fl.*
Ca. 380	Apostolic Constitutions, Bk. vii.
Ca. 383	Philastrius *fl.*
After 392	Gregory of Elvira †
394	Gregory of Nyssa †
339–97	Ambrose of Milan
Ca. 400	Anastasius of Rome *fl.*
Ca. 400	Macarius of Magnesia *fl.*
Ca. 400	Euodius *fl.*
Ca. 400	Apostolic Canons
403	Epiphanius of Cyprus †
405	Innocent I *fl.*
354–407	Chrysostom
410	Rufinus †
Ca. 347–419	Jerome
392–428	Theodore *fl.*
Ca. 430	Philip of Side *fl.*
354–430	Augustine
Before 431	Palladius †
After 439	Socrates †
439–50	Sozomen *fl.*
458	Theodoret †
V. century	Evagrius of Gaul

A.D.

Ca. 500	Procopius of Gaza *fl.*
520–65	Philoponus *fl.*
Ca. 570	Stephen Gobarus *fl.*
Ca. 490–583	Cassiodorus
538–94	Gregory of Tours
VI. century	Gelasian Decree
VI. century	Abdias
616	Paul of Tella *fl.*
Late VI. century	Andreas of Caesarea
662	Maximus the Confessor†
675–749	John of Damascus
Ca. 700	Anastasius of Sinai †
VII. century	Paschal Chronicle
VII.–VIII. century	Barlaam and Joasaph Romance
Before 800	List of 60 Canonical Books
VIII. century	Georgius Syncellus
VIII. century	Beatus
840	Agobard †
Ca. 842	Georgius Hamartolus *fl.*
Ca. 850	Stichometry of Nicephorus
Ca. 890	Photius *fl.*
914	Arethas *fl.*
XII. century	Nicetas of Thessalonica
XII. century	Bar-Salibi
Ca. 1250	Robert Grosseteste
Ca. 1320	Nicephorus Callisti *fl.*
1363	Abu'l Barakat †

INDEX